Putin as Celebrity and Cultural Icon

Though in recent months Putin's popularity has frayed at the edges, the dearth of comparably powerful and experienced political leaders in Russia leaves no doubt that he will continue to be a key political figure. During his tenure as Russia's President and subsequently as Prime Minister, Putin transcended politics, to become the country's major cultural icon. This book examines the nature of his iconic status. It explores his public persona as glamorous hero, endowed with vision, wisdom, moral and physical strength—the man uniquely capable of restoring Russia's reputation as a global power. In analysing cultural representations of Putin, the book assesses the role of the media in constructing and disseminating this image and weighs the Russian populace's contribution to the extraordinary acclamation he enjoyed throughout the first decade of the new millennium, challenged only by a tiny minority.

Helena Goscilo is Professor and Chair of the Department of Slavic and East European Languages and Cultures at The Ohio State University in Columbus, Ohio.

BASEES/Routledge Series on Russian and East European Studies

Series editor:
Richard Sakwa, *Department of Politics and International Relations, University of Kent*

This series is published on behalf of BASEES (the British Association for Slavonic and East European Studies). The series comprises original, high-quality, research-level work by both new and established scholars on all aspects of Russian, Soviet, post-Soviet and East European Studies in humanities and social science subjects.

1. **Ukraine's Foreign and Security Policy, 1991–2000**
   Roman Wolczuk

2. **Political Parties in the Russian Regions**
   Derek S. Hutcheson

3. **Local Communities and Post-Communist Transformation**
   Edited by Simon Smith

4. **Repression and Resistance in Communist Europe**
   J.C. Sharman

5. **Political Elites and the New Russia**
   Anton Steen

6. **Dostoevsky and the Idea of Russianness**
   Sarah Hudspith

7. **Performing Russia – Folk Revival and Russian Identity**
   Laura J. Olson

8. **Russian Transformations**
   Edited by Leo McCann

9. **Soviet Music and Society under Lenin and Stalin**
   The baton and sickle
   Edited by Neil Edmunds

10. **State Building in Ukraine**
    The Ukranian parliament, 1990–2003
    Sarah Whitmore

11. **Defending Human Rights in Russia**
    Sergei Kovalyov, Dissident and Human Rights Commissioner, 1969–2003
    Emma Gilligan

12. **Small-Town Russia**
    Postcommunist livelihoods and identities: a portrait of the intelligentsia in Achit, Bednodemyanovsk and Zubtsov, 1999–2000
    Anne White

13. **Russian Society and the Orthodox Church**
    Religion in Russia after Communism
    Zoe Knox

14. **Russian Literary Culture in the Camera Age**
    The word as image
    Stephen Hutchings

15. **Between Stalin and Hitler**
    Class war and race war on the Dvina, 1940–46
    Geoffrey Swain

16. **Literature in Post-Communist Russia and Eastern Europe**
    The Russian, Czech and Slovak fiction of the changes 1988–98
    Rajendra A. Chitnis

17. **The Legacy of Soviet Dissent**
    Dissidents, democratisation and radical nationalism in Russia
    Robert Horvath

18. **Russian and Soviet Film Adaptations of Literature, 1900–2001**
    Screening the word
    Edited by Stephen Hutchings and Anat Vernitski

19. **Russia as a Great Power**
    Dimensions of security under Putin
    Edited by Jakob Hedenskog, Vilhelm Konnander, Bertil Nygren, Ingmar Oldberg and Christer Pursiainen

20. **Katyn and the Soviet Massacre of 1940**
    Truth, justice and memory
    George Sanford

21. **Conscience, Dissent and Reform in Soviet Russia**
    Philip Boobbyer

22. **The Limits of Russian Democratisation**
    Emergency powers and states of emergency
    Alexander N. Domrin

23. **The Dilemmas of DeStalinisation**
    A social and cultural history of reform in the Khrushchev era
    Edited by Polly Jones

24. **News Media and Power in Russia**
Olessia Koltsova

25. **Post-Soviet Civil Society**
Democratization in Russia and the Baltic states
Anders Uhlin

26. **The Collapse of Communist Power in Poland**
Jacqueline Hayden

27. **Television, Democracy and Elections in Russia**
Sarah Oates

28. **Russian Constitutionalism**
Historical and contemporary development
Andrey N. Medushevsky

29. **Late Stalinist Russia**
Society between reconstruction and reinvention
Edited by Juliane Fürst

30. **The Transformation of Urban Space in Post-Soviet Russia**
Konstantin Axenov, Isolde Brade and Evgenij Bondarchuk

31. **Western Intellectuals and the Soviet Union, 1920–40**
From Red Square to the Left Bank
Ludmila Stern

32. **The Germans of the Soviet Union**
Irina Mukhina

33. **Re-Constructing the Post-Soviet Industrial Region**
The Donbas in transition
Edited by Adam Swain

34. **Chechnya – Russia's "War on Terror"**
John Russell

35. **The New Right in the New Europe**
Czech transformation and right-wing politics, 1989–2006
Seán Hanley

36. **Democracy and Myth in Russia and Eastern Europe**
Edited by Alexander Wöll and Harald Wydra

37. **Energy Dependency, Politics and Corruption in the Former Soviet Union**
Russia's power, oligarchs' profits and Ukraine's missing energy policy, 1995–2006
Margarita M. Balmaceda

38. **Peopling the Russian Periphery**
Borderland colonization in Eurasian history
Edited by Nicholas B Breyfogle, Abby Schrader and Willard Sunderland

39. **Russian Legal Culture Before and After Communism**
Criminal justice, politics and the public sphere
Frances Nethercott

40. **Political and Social Thought in Post-Communist Russia**
Axel Kaehne

41. **The Demise of the Soviet Communist Party**
Atsushi Ogushi

42. **Russian Policy towards China and Japan**
The El'tsin and Putin periods
Natasha Kuhrt

43. **Soviet Karelia**
Politics, planning and terror in Stalin's Russia, 1920–1939
Nick Baron

44. **Reinventing Poland**
Economic and political transformation and evolving national identity
Edited by Martin Myant and Terry Cox

45. **The Russian Revolution in Retreat, 1920–24**
Soviet workers and the new Communist elite
Simon Pirani

46. **Democratisation and Gender in Contemporary Russia**
Suvi Salmenniemi

47. **Narrating Post/Communism**
Colonial discourse and Europe's borderline civilization
Nataša Kovačević

48. **Globalization and the State in Central and Eastern Europe**
The politics of foreign direct investment
Jan Drahokoupil

49. **Local Politics and Democratisation in Russia**
Cameron Ross

50. **The Emancipation of the Serfs in Russia**
Peace arbitrators and the development of civil society
Roxanne Easley

51. **Federalism and Local Politics in Russia**
Edited by Cameron Ross and Adrian Campbell

52. **Transitional Justice in Eastern Europe and the former Soviet Union**
Reckoning with the Communist past
Edited by Lavinia Stan

53. **The Post-Soviet Russian Media**
Conflicting signals
Edited by Birgit Beumers, Stephen Hutchings and Natalia Rulyova

54. **Minority Rights in Central and Eastern Europe**
Edited by Bernd Rechel

55. **Television and Culture in Putin's Russia**
Remote control
Stephen Hutchings and Natalia Rulyova

56. **The Making of Modern Lithuania**
Tomas Balkelis

57. **Soviet State and Society Under Nikita Khrushchev**
Melanie Ilic and Jeremy Smith

58. **Communism, Nationalism and Ethnicity in Poland, 1944–1950**
Michael Fleming

59. **Democratic Elections in Poland, 1991–2007**
Frances Millard

60. **Critical Theory in Russia and the West**
Alastair Renfrew and Galin Tihanov

61. **Promoting Democracy and Human Rights in Russia**
European organization and Russia's socialization
Sinikukka Saari

62. **The Myth of the Russian Intelligentsia**
Old intellectuals in the new Russia
Inna Kochetkova

63. **Russia's Federal Relations**
Putin's reforms and management of the regions
Elena A. Chebankova

64. **Constitutional Bargaining in Russia 1990–93**
Information and uncertainty
Edward Morgan-Jones

65. **Building Big Business in Russia**
The impact of informal corporate governance practices
Yuko Adachi

66. **Russia and Islam**
State, society and radicalism
Roland Dannreuther and Luke March

67. **Celebrity and Glamour in Contemporary Russia**
Shocking chic
Edited by Helena Goscilo and Vlad Strukov

68. **The Socialist Alternative to Bolshevik Russia**
The socialist revolutionary party, 1917–1939
Elizabeth White

69. **Learning to Labour in Post-Soviet Russia**
Vocational youth in transition
Charles Walker

70. **Television and Presidential Power in Putin's Russia**
Tina Burrett

71. **Political Theory and Community Building in Post-Soviet Russia**
Edited by Oleg Kharkhordin and Risto Alapuro

72. **Disease, Health Care and Government in Late Imperial Russia**
Life and death on the Volga, 1823–1914
Charlotte E. Henze

73. **Khrushchev in the Kremlin**
Policy and government in the Soviet Union, 1953–1964
Edited by Melanie Ilic and Jeremy Smith

74. **Citizens in the Making in Post-Soviet States**
Olena Nikolayenko

75. **The Decline of Regionalism in Putin's Russia**
Boundary issues
J. Paul Goode

76. **The Communist Youth League and the Transformation of the Soviet Union, 1917–1932**
Matthias Neumann

77. **Putin's United Russia Party**
S. P. Roberts

78. **The European Union and its Eastern Neighbours**
Towards a more ambitious partnership?
Elena Korosteleva

79. **Russia's Identity in International Relations**
Images, perceptions, misperceptions
Edited by Ray Taras

80. **Putin as Celebrity and Cultural Icon**
Edited by Helena Goscilo

81. **Democracy versus Modernization**
A dilemma for Russia and for the world
Edited by Vladislav Inozemtsev and Piotr Dutkiewicz

82. **Putin's Preventative Counter-Revolution**
Post-Soviet authoritarianism and the spectre of Velvet Revolution
Robert Horvath

83. **The Baltic States – From Soviet Union to European Union**
Richard Mole

84 **The EU–Russia Borderland**
New contexts for regional cooperation
Edited by Heikki Eskelinen, Ilkka Liikanen and James W. Scott

85. **The Economic Sources of Social Order Development in Post-Socialist Eastern Europe**
Richard Connolly

86. **East European Diasporas, Migration and Cosmopolitanism**
Edited by Ulrike Ziemer and Sean P. Roberts

Putin as Celebrity and Cultural Icon

Edited by
Helena Goscilo

Routledge
Taylor & Francis Group
LONDON AND NEW YORK

First published 2013
by Routledge
2 Park Square, Milton Park, Abingdon, Oxon OX14 4RN

Simultaneously published in the USA and Canada
by Routledge
711 Third Avenue, New York, NY 10017

Routledge is an imprint of the Taylor & Francis Group, an informa business

British Library Cataloguing in Publication Data
A catalogue record for this book is available from the British Library

Library of Congress Cataloging in Publication Data
Putin as celebrity and cultural icon / ed. Helena Goscilo.
pages; cm.—(BASEES/Routledge series on Russian and East European Studies ; 80)
1. Putin, Vladimir Vladimirovich, 1952– 2. Presidents–Russia (Federation) 3. Putin, Vladimir Vladimirovich, 1952–Public opinion. 4. Russians–Russia (Federation)–Attitudes. 5. Putin, Vladimir Vladimirovich, 1952– In literature. I. Goscilo, Helena, 1945– II. Series: BASEES/Routledge series on Russian and East European Studies ; 80.
DK510.766.P87P88 2012
947.086'2092–dc23
2012004446

ISBN: 978-0-415-52851-1 (hbk)
ISBN: 978-0-203-10804-8 (ebk)

Typeset in Times New Roman
by Book Now Ltd, London

MIX
Paper from responsible sources
FSC® C004839

Printed and bound in Great Britain by the MPG Books Group

For Elizabeth and Saul, without whose four decades of friendship life would be a lesser feast

HG

Contents

Figures

Contributors

Brian James Baer is Professor of Russian and Translation Studies at Kent State University and a member of the Institute for Applied Linguistics. His many publications on post-Soviet culture focus on gender and sexuality. Author of *Other Russias: Homosexuality and the Crisis of Post-Soviet Identity* (Palgrave, 2009), a Choice Outstanding Academic Title in 2011, he recently published the edited volume *Contexts, Subtexts, Pretexts: Literary Translation in Eastern Europe* (Benjamins, 2011) and *No Good without Reward: The Selected Writings of Liubov Krichevskaya* (University of Toronto, 2011); his anthology, *Russian Writers on Translation*, co-edited with Nataliya Olshanskaya, is forthcoming from St. Jerome Publishing. He is the founding editor of the journal *Translation and Interpreting Studies* (TIS) and the general editor of the Kent State Scholarly Monograph Series in Translation Studies, and currently, he is completing a manuscript on translation and multilingualism in modern Russian culture.

Julie A. Cassiday is Professor of Russian in the Department of German and Russian at Williams College. She received her PhD in Slavic Languages and Literatures from Stanford University. She is the author of *The Enemy on Trial: Early Soviet Courts on Stage and Screen* (Northern Illinois University Press, 2000) and has published articles on theatre, theatricality and cinema in Russian and Soviet culture. Her current projects include a monograph on gender and theatricality in early nineteenth-century Russia, an article on the Stalinist detective film and research on Moscow's hosting of the Eurovision Song Contest in 2009.

Michael S. Gorham is Associate Professor of Russian Studies at the University of Florida and Associate Editor of *The Russian Review* and *Russian Language Journal*. His book *Speaking in Soviet Tongues: Language Culture and the Politics of Voice in Revolutionary Russia* (Northern Illinois University Press, 2003) received the Choice Outstanding Academic Book award and the 2004 AATSEEL award for Best Book in Literary and Cultural Studies. His current research on language, politics and national identity from *glasnost* to Twitter has appeared in 12 different peer-review journals and edited volumes. He is also a core member of the international working group The Future of Russian: Language Culture in the Era of New Technology, sponsored by the Norwegian Research Council (http://www.uib.no/rg/future_r).

Helena Goscilo is Professor and Chair of Slavic at The Ohio State University in Columbus. Over the last two decades she has explored Russian/Soviet culture, gender, graphics, art, folklore, film and, secondarily, Polish culture. Her most recent publications include *Reflections and Refractions: The Mirror in Russian Culture*, a guest issue of *20th and 21st Century Literature* (2010/2011), and *Celebrity and Glamour in Contemporary Russia: Shocking Chic* (Routledge, 2011), co-edited with Vlad Strukov. Currently, she is involved in three volumes: the richly illustrated *Baba Yaga: The Wild Witch of the East in Russian Fairy Tales*, with Sibelan Forrester, Martin Skoro and Jack Zipes (University of Mississippi Press, 2012); *Embracing Arms: Cultural Representations of Slavic and Balkan Women in War*, with Yana Hashamova (Central European University Press, 2012); and *Fame in Flight: Russian Aviation*, with Vlad Strukov.

Emily D. Johnson is Associate Professor of Russian Language and Literature at the University of Oklahoma. She received her PhD in Russian Literature from Columbia University. Her book, *How St. Petersburg Learned to Study Itself: The Russian Idea of Kraevedenie* (Penn State University Press, 2006), received both the South Central MLA book prize and the Likhachev Fund's Antsiferov prize for the best work on St. Petersburg by a non-Russian author. Johnson is also the co-editor of *Rites of Place: Public Commemoration and Celebration in Russia and Eastern Europe* (Northwestern University Press, forthcoming). She is currently working on a monograph on Soviet private labour camp correspondence from the Stalin period.

Tatiana Mikhailova, Instructor of Russian Studies at the University of Colorado at Boulder, participated in the Freedom Support Act Professional Development Program at the University of Illinois at Urbana–Champaign (1995). She has published on the representation of femininity in Soviet and post-Soviet culture. Her recent article on the politics of glamour in Oksana Robski's writings appeared in *Celebrity and Glamour in Contemporary Russia: Shocking Chic* (Routledge, 2011).

Andrei Rogatchevski studied at the Moscow State University, the University of Glasgow, Charles University in Prague and the University of West Bohemia in Pilsen. He has taught at the following universities, among others: the University of Helsinki, Masaryk University in Brno, the University of Mainz/Germersheim and the Royal Conservatoire of Scotland. Currently, he is the Russian Programme Director at the University of Glasgow. His publications include *A Biographical and Critical Study of the Russian Writer Eduard Limonov* (Edwin Mellen Press, 2003) and *Filming the Unfilmable: Casper Wrede's One Day in the Life of Ivan Denisovich* (Ibidem-Verlag, 2010).

Lara Ryazanova-Clarke is Senior Lecturer in Russian and Academic Director of the Princess Dashkova Russian Centre at the University of Edinburgh. She works in several fields within Russian language studies: sociolinguistics, discourse analysis, metaphorical studies, language policy, ideology and identity.

Acknowledgements

Our collective thanks to Peter Sowden at Routledge for his speedy efficiency and support, to Richard Sakwa at the University of Kent for his responsiveness, and to the individuals who gave permission to include the visuals in this volume: Blue Noses, John Deering, Sergei Elkin, Aleksei Merinov, Ralph Gibson at Ria Novosti and kind strangers (a thriving Blanche Dubois heritage) who have posted items on Wikimedia Commons for public use that appear in the volume. The generosity of Sasha Shaburov (Blue Noses) and Sergei Elkin would inspire faith in any skeptic requiring evidence of human largesse.

I am grateful to the College of the Arts and Humanities at The Ohio State University for the research funds that underwrote the illustrations in the first and final chapters as well as work on the index, assembled with his customary skill by Alex Trotter. On a more personal note, I am happily indebted to Karen Dawisha, Ludmila Isurin, Tatiana Mikhailova, Serguei Oushakine, Elizabeth Pleeter and Vlad Strukov for their readiness to share information and materials that inform those chapters.

Every effort has been made to acquire rights for the reproduction of copyrighted material. The authors and the publishers would be pleased to hear from any rights holder they have failed to track down and acknowledge appropriately.

Introduction

Inseparable from the milestone Paris Uprising of 1968, which irreversibly transformed intellectual life and modes of thought in Europe and the United States, the late Guy Debord's (1931–1994) incendiary *La société du spectacle* (1967)[1] could easily function as an extended epigraph for our volume on Putin as cultural icon and celebrity. A committed Marxist, Debord deplored capitalist social organization as the source of modern alienation, arguing that the mercantile system deprives humans of autonomy by controlling consumers through media and sundry forms of popular culture. In the book's opening salvo, which generally anticipates Jean Baudrillard's gloomy *Simulacres et Simulation* (1981, trans. 1994),[2] Debord declares the following:

> The whole life of those societies in which modern conditions of production prevail presents itself as an immense accumulation of spectacle. All that once was directly lived has become mere representation.
>
> Images detached from every aspect of life merge into a common stream, and the former unity of life is lost forever. Apprehended in a *partial* way, reality unfolds in a new generality as a pseudo-world apart, solely as an object of contemplation. [. . .]. The spectacle in its generality is a concrete inversion of life, and, as such, the autonomous movement of non-life.
>
> The spectacle appears at once as society itself, as a part of society and as a means of unification. As a part of society, it is that sector where all attention, all consciousness, converges. Being isolated – and precisely for that reason – this sector is the locus of illusion and false consciousness [. . .].
>
> (Thesis 1–3, Debord 1994, 12)

Yet anyone conversant with the Soviet Union – capitalism's most vociferous enemy – would find the above criticism relevant to its long-standing forms and practices.

Public life under Soviet rule required theatrical skills and participation in pompous, hollow rituals divorced from genuine experience and calculated to promulgate the state's chief product – ideology. Unity was illusory and nonlife thrived.[3] Debord's contention that in 1989 "the Russian bureaucracy suddenly, and as one man [*sic*], [. . .] convert[ed] to the *ideology* of democracy – in other words, to the dictatorial freedom of the Market, as tempered by the recognition of the rights of Homo Spectator" (9) is a gross generalization ("as one man"?), likewise symptomatized in the first three Theses quoted above by the iteration of "all," plus the sweeping "whole," "every," "solely," and "forever." Moreover, Debord's apodictic assertions fail to draw sufficient distinctions by taking into account the active role of the consumer in the *creation* of spectacle and the risk-laden refusal of some skeptical citizens – admittedly, a minority, tagged as "dissidents" or "internal émigrés" – to participate in it. As may be said of much contemporary French theory, the strokes are too broad to withstand close scrutiny.

At the same time, it would be foolhardy to deny that during the 2000s, when petrodollars dramatically altered Russians' economic and social status in the world, galvanizing Russians' seeming insatiability for shopping and acquisition, spectacle became the order of the day. It differed from Soviet spectacle chiefly in style and especially scale, owing to globalization and the accelerated expansion, in recent decades, of media through technological innovation. Spectacle above all has accompanied the construction of Vladimir Putin's public persona, to the design and dissemination of which the Kremlin, the state-controlled media, wily entrepreneurs, sycophantic celebrity figures, the citizenry, and Putin himself have contributed. Indeed, "the Putin phenomenon" belongs to the Wagnerian genre of *Gesammtkunstwerk*.

The eight chapters comprising this collection analyze the production of "Putin" as a series of cultural processes, focusing on the myriad features that have revived the phrase frequently invoked in Russia and the West – "cult of personality." Accordingly, Chapter 1 investigates the avalanche of items, ranging from foods to operas and bed linens, which have created a Putin museum that doubles as a temple to the man credited with restoring Russia's international reputation. If Putin's initial dispassion and vacuity facilitated the ascription of contrary convictions to him, with time his combatant nationalism and recuperation of selective Soviet elements and procedures cemented his popularity as a strong leader intent on protecting traditional endemic values and Russia's independence of the West. The universal human desire for a charismatic hero as the head of state, the impulse to participate, however tangentially, in a celebrity's life, and the recognition that "Putin" had become a best-selling brand all encouraged the staggering profusion of cultural genres labeled Putin found in stores, museums, government buildings, in the press, on the streets, the Internet, and television. Putin's transformation into a national icon illustrates a major tenet of celebrification, which stipulates unremitting media attention of any stripe as the prerequisite for achieving celebrity – a principle that Putin quickly assimilated and continues to exploit as prime minister while the 2012 presidential election looms on the horizon, with Putin as the presidentially endorsed United Party candidate, who will appoint Dmitri Medvedev as prime minister, in a predictable musical-chairs quid pro quo.[4]

To what extent the *Blitzkrieg* of Putiniana may be analogized with Stalin's cult of personality is the key question addressed in Chapter 2. Sifting through the pertinent materials, the authors note the glaring dissimilarities between the politicohistorical contexts in which the cults, separated by more than half a century and elaborated within two distinct political regimes, developed. While readily conceding the conspicuous similarities, Julie Cassiday and Emily Johnson legitimately object to a simplistic collapse into sameness of strategies enacted during the peak of Soviet totalitarianism and those flourishing during the post-Soviet adoption of a managed market economy. For all it may superficially resemble earlier Soviet-era leader cults, the Putin phenomenon, they insist, represents the product of distinctly postmodern social and communicative relations. Characterized by rhetorical and philosophical indeterminacy, it offers ordinary Russian citizens a degree of agency without any precedent in the Soviet period.

Resonating with Cassiday and Johnson's major thesis, Chapter 3 targets Putin's repeatedly photographed affection for animals and children, expressed in kisses and caresses that the media tirelessly capture and post on multiple Internet sites. On first glance, such actions may seem to reveal Putin's "softer" side while simultaneously inscribing his reassuring protection of the nation's resources and the vulnerable segment of its population. Yet, Tatiana Mikhailova maintains, these images above all function as postmodern representations of power that rely, not on political arguments, but on the spectacles that manipulate the public imagination. Putin-era visual politics represent the ultimate instance of *Kulturindustrie*, generating a postmodern simulacrum of democracy in which the entertainment provided by politicians offers a surrogate for genuine political life, which is notable for its absence. Mikhailova's chapter most directly embraces the precepts articulated by Debord and shares his debt to Daniel Boorstein's concept of the pseudo-event [*The Image: A Guide to Pseudo-events in America* (1962)] and the Frankfurt School's notion of the cultural industry's self-perpetuation.

Whereas the first three chapters construct their arguments primarily on the evidence of visuals, the following two chapters investigate Putin's discourse. Chapter 4 combs through Putin's many speeches during his first presidential term so as to identify the five high-frequency speech profiles that partly account for Putin's resonance with the public: those of the *technocrat, delovoi* ("doer"), *silovik* ("strong man"), *muzhik* ("good ol' boy"), and *patriot.* According to Michael Gorham, these five rhetorical modes not only explain Putin's popularity but also offer insight into the underpinnings of his political success and suggest the linguistic identities competing for symbolic authority in today's Russia.

Complementing Gorham's broad-based discussion and at various junctures intersecting with it, Chapter 5 confines its purview to a detailed exploration of Putin's tightly orchestrated annual ritual, *Direct Line with the President*. This spectacle, broadcast on radio and television, entails an exchange with carefully selected individuals who call in questions on the "hot line," thrilled at the opportunity to receive Putin's answers. While the 3-hour "event" is advertised as a genuine conversation between citizens and the president/prime minister, in fact it provides Putin the occasion to consolidate his political agenda – the creation of a seamless "identity narrative" that relies on specific linguistic features to produce meanings central to national identity. According to Lara Ryazanova-Clarke's analysis, the presenters, the public, and Putin join in affirming a united Russia's power and prestige indissolubly wedded to Putin's presidential image of embodied authority as military commander, competent technocrat, and cult figure.

Favoring a broad temporal purview, Chapter 6 surveys fiction and other verbal genres devoted to Putin that have appeared in print from 2000 to 2011. This sizable body of works represents a comprehensive range of political perspectives across a wide geographical span, including Latvia, Ukraine, and the United States. Whenever possible, Andrei Rogatchevski juxtaposes the fictional images of Putin with information gleaned from journalistic reports, interviews, and memoirs. Why, he asks, has Putin figured so frequently as a fictional character, and what, if anything, can be learned from these, often fanciful, representations that cannot be learned otherwise – both about Putin himself and about the Russian public discourse on Putin? Without indulging in unfounded speculation, the chapter attempts to respond to these questions, to which the rest of the volume also offers possible answers.

In this regard, Chapter 7 posits an original thesis, one that, perhaps unexpectedly, points toward the East. According to Brian Baer, self-fashioning is the modal link between Putin and Boris Akunin's astonishingly popular fictional detective hero, Erast Fandorin. Both men construct and present their selfhood through the manipulation of social standards, norms, and products. Often contrasted in terms of their politics, the Russian president/prime minister and Akunin's famous protagonist in fact employ kindred modes of self-fashioning. In particular, through the selective adoption of Eastern values and customs, Putin and Fandorin create a new post-Soviet Russian identity – that of the professional – which nevertheless is thoroughly embedded in traditional Russian cultural scripts.

In the volume's final chapter, Helena Goscilo contends that Putin's carefully calibrated public persona as president (2000–2008) and prime minister (2008–) embraces the concept of energetic virility traditionally inseparable from the perception of decisive, effective leadership. In Putin's case, that image synthetically models itself on the strategies of the Machiavellian prince and Hollywood action heroes. In the years following the impotent, volatile 1990s, collective and individual desire constituted a key motivator not only in the construction of Putin as the embodiment of disciplined hyper-masculinity, but also in the gendering of his image-building constituency. Macho, physically potent, and fearless "Putin" functions as an unattainable ideal for men and triggers a correspondingly prescribed "feminine" response from women, who in diverse, often startling, cultural forms avow love and reverence for the politician as Superman. This dynamic of president-as-hero – an image Putin assiduously cultivates – and population-as-fan-club illustrates the complexity of subject–object relations. Likewise manifested in Putin's interactions with children and animals, these relations never impinge on the impermeability of Putin's touted machismo, thereby reflecting the paradoxical nature of post-Soviet sociopolitical and cultural practices.

Given the contributors' reasoned belief that media play a decisive part in shaping Putin's public persona, the various chapters in the volume inevitably overlap. Certain specific features, such as Putin's increasing divestment (of clothes, not power), serve as occasions for analyses that occasionally lead to divergent conclusions. What links all the chapters is the conviction that Putin's cultural persona feeds into his political image, and that the media are a key factor in the formation and fatiguing propagation of that comics-cum-Hollywood-action-film image. In short, however unwittingly, popular culture and new technology have presided over the channels that render inevitable Putin's reprisal of the presidency in the upcoming elections.

Notes

1 Translated by Donald Nicholson-Smith as *The Society of the Spectacle,* New York: Zone Books, 1992.
2 One has merely to replace "sign" with "spectacle" to locate Debord in Baudrillard. The debt of both to the Frankfurt School is blatant and partly accounts for the sweeping nature of their pronouncements.
3 As much is acknowledged in the popular term for the Brezhnev era, *zastoi* (stagnation).
4 For a conceptual framework and commentary on the phenomenon of celebrity in today's Russia, see the Introduction to Helena Goscilo and Vlad Strukov, eds. *Celebrity and Glamour in Contemporary Russia: Shocking Chic* (London: Routledge, 2011). 1–26. Despite Putin's and Medvedev's coy disclaimers, only naïve observers doubted that Medvedev would concede his United-Party-backed candidacy in the presidential elections, supporting Putin in the expectation of reclaiming his earlier position of (first deputy) prime minister.

1 Russia's ultimate celebrity

VVP as VIP *objet d'art*

Helena Goscilo

Putin is the biggest celebrity in Russia today.

(Dmitrii Vrubel 2004)[1]

He's good, he's strong, he's decent, he's ours and he's president now.

(Vladimir Ivchenko 2001)[2]

He is the only president I know with black belt and PhD in economics. [. . .] Go VVP!

(Don, blogger 2002)[3]

I want a husband who'd be like Vladimir Vladimirovich.

(Yulya Pipilova, 18, member of the 1,500-strong VVP Fan Club in Moscow 2007)[4]

A man for all seasons, and possibly for all time[5]

In 2007, Vladimir Putin topped *Kommersant*'s annual list of Russia's elite for the seventh consecutive year, garnering 82 percent of votes among the 1,600 Russians polled (Alekseev 2007). That rating startled no one, for no Russian or Soviet head of state since Stalin has inspired the widespread hero worship that irradiated Putin's presidency and continues to thrive today, causing western pundits to speculate that, regardless of President Dmitrii Medvedev's de jure post, self-designated Prime Minister Putin remains the country's de facto leader.[6] Revered at home as the savior not only of Russia's economy, but also of its national pride and international status, Putin as president enjoyed such extraordinary popular support, with approval ratings of 70–80 percent, that the impending expiration of his second, final term reportedly plunged some members of his constituency into melancholy at his departure, anxiety regarding the nation's future, and naïve concern about his professional options in the years to come.

Indeed, a controversial, sycophantic letter signed by four *éminences grises* of contemporary culture presumptuously claiming to speak for the entire culture establishment[7] beseeched Putin to seek a third term, in flagrant violation of the constitution, ". . . blagodaria Vashim usiliiam byla dostignuta sotsial'naia stabil'nost' i progress, neobychaino povysilsia avtoritet nashei Rodiny vo vsem mire" [. . . thanks to your efforts, social stability and progress have been achieved; the authority of our Motherland in the whole world has increased extraordinarily] (Pis'mo 2007). The content of this highly publicized document,[8] which evokes the visually memorable sequence in Sergei Eisenstein's *Ivan Groznyi* [Ivan the Terrible] (part 1, 1944) of multitudes supplicating Ivan to return as ruler, coincides almost verbatim with the views espoused in an interview by the spokespeople for Nashi – a nationalistic youth group cum Putin fan club established in 2005, most probably funded by the Kremlin and impervious to any developments in twenty-first century Russia that counter its simplistic convictions: "Putin [. . .] has brought stability and the opportunity for modernization and development of the country" (quoted in Myers 2007). Such a convergence of opinion harbored by old and young generations about Putin's accomplishments characterized *vox populi* throughout his presidency, which systematically ignored, discredited, or quelled the few dissenting voices virtually drowning in the sea of hosannas. As a media celebrity, Putin has no equals, and his celebrity status, unlike that of most personalities in the limelight, is ascribed (Yeltsin's chosen successor), achieved (Russia's perceived rescuer from international ignominy and financial disaster), and attributed (the hero relentlessly championed via Kremlin-controlled media) according to Chris Rojek's taxonomy (Rojek 2001: 17–20).

Adulation of Putin during his presidency assumed not only ideological, but also sundry identificatory, romantic, and creative forms – all reported and disseminated in the media.[9] Doting admirers in Siberia named a kebab house and bar after him (Bar Putin), selling "vertical power" kebabs and "when Vova was little" milkshakes (White and McAllister 2003: 388), while a Siberian native adopted his surname, maintaining, "Putin is the angel who educated me spiritually" (quoted in Toomey 2003). Since 2002, the main street in the Ingush village of Olgety, and since 2008, the main street in Grozny, capital of Chechnya, have borne his name (Volonikhin 2002; Let's learn judo with Vladimir Putin 2008), as have lollipops, a vodka (Putinka), an ice cream, carpets, toys, and other products. Botanist Nikolai Egorov in Cheliabinsk even attempted to christen a frost-resistant tomato after Putin until the Kremlin curbed his horticultural exuberance (Bransten 2002; MacKinnon 2002; Toomey 2003). Rumors linked Putin romantically (and fancifully) with the Australian actress Peta Wilson (Putin's Last Love 2003) and the controversial Russian police lieutenant Oksana Fedorova, Miss Universe in 2002, while in the city of Iaroslavl one of numerous moonstruck women publicly professing "mad" love for him had to be locked up in the city's psychiatric ward owing to the uncontrollable nature of her passion.[10] The tabloid *Moskovskii korrespondent* alleged that Putin had secretly divorced his wife in early 2008 so as to marry the then 24-year-old former gymnast and Olympic medalist Alina Kabaeva (a deputy in the State Duma) – a provocative item that predictably led to the paper's closure ("Russia: Putin romance rumors keep public riveted" 2008). Though such items are standard fare for film and television stars, pop music icons, and sports heroes, political leaders rarely inspire such impassioned involvement in what is popularly called their love life. Even Putin's KGB/FSB past,[11] which distressed those familiar with the organization's activities, seemed to cast a haze of romantic mystery around him by analogy with Stirlitz, James Bond, and the actors who have portrayed them.[12] Such a perspective endowed a reportedly mediocre functionary treading water in Germany, who moved on to occupy his country's chief executive position, with the glamorous aura of an international spy.

Romantic and erotic fantasies woven around Putin likewise proliferated when upscale confectioner Konfael created a 12" by 19" chocolate portrait of him, weighing over 3 pounds and priced at approximately $700. Considered a work of art by Konfael personnel, this "limited edition" of the edible president (only two were manufactured) went on sale in 2003. Asked what they would do if they owned such an anomalous piece of confectionary, men claimed that they probably would hang it in their offices, whereas young women wished to kiss it, while their middle-aged counterparts dreamed of eating a chocolate Putin ear (BBC Monitoring 2003b). In a no less fantastic scenario, presumably as a therapeutic outlet for what she diagnosed as a widely shared sexual fixation on Putin, one female fan contributed to *Komsomol'skaia pravda*, a needlework pattern in cross-stitch based on a widely disseminated photograph of a bare-chested Putin, sporting sunglasses and rain hat, fishing. In light of these and similar strategies for attaining virtual intimacy with Putin, it seems reasonable to conclude that the young blogger rhapsodically proclaiming her adoration of him as a "sex symbol, a real Man" [seks symbol, nastoiashchii muzhik] ("Tainstvennaia pop-gruppa poet osanny Putinu" 2002) summed up sentiments rampant among the female segment of the Russian population, irrespective of age or class (Figure 1.1). For countless women, Putin appears as a glamorous, elite sexual icon, whose image and name dominate the country's landscape yet who remains elusive owing not only to the astronomical cost of high-end purchasable products imprinted with his visage, but also to the seductive remoteness of any national leader.

Eroticism played bedfellow to a mythology of ethics, for the Kremlin deployed the media for its indefatigable campaign of projecting Putin as a paragon of civic-minded commitment, intent not on consolidating personal power and accruing a sizable fortune, but on restoring Russia's glory and its citizens' economic and psychological health. According to Steve LeVine, Vladislav Surkov, Putin's chief of domestic policy, masterminded "the transformation of the president's visage into a savior-of-Russia icon, gargantuan and granite-faced, gazing from billboards, television screens, and newspapers throughout Moscow" (LeVine 2008: 34). Yet these modes of putinating the capital were only the tip of the iceberg, for Putin's formidable virtual omnipresence during his presidency was not wholly engineered by the Kremlin.[13] His face adorned *znachki* [pins], coins, cakes, countless T-shirts, salt shakers, posters, postcards, playing cards (Figure 1.2), notebooks, and calendars throughout the country, while his portraits in oil, Swarovski crystal, amber and semi-precious stones (Figure 1.3), copper, mosaics, and charcoal, as well as busts and full-figure sculptures, became a booming business.

Figure 1.1 Showcasing Putin's virility (presidential pecs), religiosity (Orthodox cross), and skill at reeling in Big Fish (rod at crotch level) while on vacation in Tuva, Siberia, 2007.

Source: Courtesy of the Presidential Press and Information Office, www.kremlin.ru, on Wikimedia Commons.

A muse for men as well as a far from obscure object of desire for women, Putin inspired a spy thriller by the Latvian author Alexander Olbik *Prezident* [The President] (see Chapter 6 by Andrei Rogatchevski), a headline-making pop song by the female duo called *Poiushchie vmeste* [Singing Together] (Leeds 2002; "Singing together" 2002),[14] and an opera by the Saratov composer Vitalii Okorokov titled *Monika v Kremle* [Monica in the Kremlin], which features Monica Lewinsky's aspirations to non-political congress with him. Like Peter the Great before him, Putin also metamorphosed into a bronze monument: a bronze statue of him on horseback materialized in a Novgorod prison; in 2001, the St. Petersburg sculptor Aleksandr Palmin created a bronze bust of Putin as a tribute to his idol (Traynor 2001); and 3 years later a huge bronze tribute to the martial-arts president in judo garb, executed by Zurab Tsereteli, was installed in the middle of a showroom at the Zurab Tsereteli Art Gallery (Figure 1.4). For several years, Putin's portraits covered a sizable part of one wall in the centrally located Moscow bookstore Biblio-Globus, across from Lubianka; in 2001, a Moscow gallery mounted an exhibition of presidential portraits titled *Nash Putin* [Our Putin]

Figure 1.2 VVP as the ace of hearts, having played his cards right.

Source: Photo by Helena Goscilo.

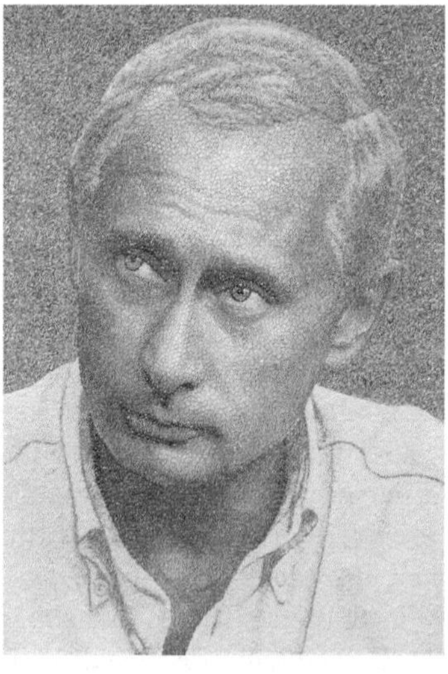

Figure 1.3 An earnest, idealized Putin in amber and pebble pieces, exhibited by Yantarny Dom Company in St. Petersburg at the seventeenth Junmex International Jewelry Forum, 2009.

Source: Photo by Aleksei Danichev, courtesy of RIA Novosti.

Figure 1.4 Russia's premier celebrity in bronze at the Zurab Tsereteli Art Gallery in Moscow, December 2004, photographed October 2005.

Source: Photo by Sergei Piatakov. Courtesy of RIA Novosti.

(Traynor 2001); and a best-selling loose-leaf calendar for 2002 captured a different expression on his face for each of the 12 months (skeptical in January, downcast in December), with a cover featuring Putin as "a genius of judo" in the lotus position (Sidlin 2001).[15] His deadpan visage stared impassively at shoppers from watches sold to the tune of chimes and $56 at a kiosk inside the Federation Council Building in Moscow (Goldman 2008),[16] and a volume titled *Putinki: kratkii sbornik izrechenii prezidenta (Pervyi srok)* [Putinisms: A Short Collection of the President's Sayings (First Term)] (2004), wittily illustrated by Aleksei Merinov, comprised extracts from his inimitable words of wisdom uttered during the first 4 years "on the job," while a fan-club site enabled visitors to download songs mixing techno music with Putin's distinctive speech patterns ("The Putin cult 2007"; see Chapter 4 by Michael Gorham).[17] As Putin's second term began, increasing numbers succumbed to the epidemic, which showed little sign of abating when that term expired in March 2008. Dissent represented a minority stance while hero worship was in full flower (Figure 1.5).

In its comprehensiveness, the official and populist campaign to instill Putin-love in the populace left no social category unscathed. Accordingly, in October 2000, as the academic year in primary schools started, children in St. Petersburg received a booklet with snapshots from the president's childhood (Traynor 2001), and in 2008, a large, luxury photo album of the adult Putin went on sale

Figure 1.5 "Vladimir Vladimirovich – you're God! You emanate radiance!" A court jester awed by Putin as His Omnipotence, illustrating the divine light of kings and, it seems, at least one Russian president. Aleksei Merinov's illustration in *Putinki* (Moscow 2004), 68.

Source: Courtesy of Aleksei Merinov.

in several major bookstores. As dictated by the protocols of canonization, even the locations Putin visited became enshrined. Upon learning that approximately 6 years earlier Putin in his capacity as city official had planted a maple tree by St. Petersburg's Canadian consulate, a local businessman promptly affixed a brass plaque to the tree, with the solemn words, "Planted by V Putin 7 October 1995" (Traynor 2001). The village of Izborsk outside St. Petersburg, where the presidential motorcade made an unscheduled stop in August 2000, subsequently began peddling a walking tour marking the places "where Putin bought a cucumber," "where Putin took off his jacket and tried water from a spring," and "where Putin touched a tree and made a wish" (Traynor 2001). Similarly, Magnitogorsk's city museum exhibited the overalls Putin had worn during his visit (White and McAllister 2003: 388). Though no witnesses have sighted miracles in these venues, the best-known model for such an "itinerary," *mutatis mutandis*, is Christ's Stations of the Cross, with, however, a drastically different *terminus ad quem*. Given the narrative of salvation into which many Russians conscripted Putin's achievements, and their view of VVP as the incarnation of the New Word – Russia's unique path in a global framework – the perceived mapping of Russia's transformation requires few adjustments to conform to the Christological scenario.[18]

On the basis of celebrity conventions, one might expect this hagiographic cultural production to be occasioned by a glitzy, internationally fêted pop celebrity such as Elton John or by a Hollywood superhero along the hypertrophied lines of Arnold Schwarzenegger, but not by a short, balding, nondescript, middle-aged erstwhile KGB agent dubbed Vova Putin by the Cheliabinsk tomato pioneer. Normally reserved for media stars, the paroxysms of swooning adoration targeting Russia's political leader throughout the 2000s bred the neologism Putin-mania and revived the ominously freighted term "cult of personality," designating a phenomenon fostered by and inseparable from Stalin, but one allegedly disavowed by VVP, who reputedly tried to check the epidemic impulse to mythologize him. Less than a year into his first term, he publicly declared:

> I understand that when somebody does such things, he or she is probably guided by the best of intentions, and that he or she thinks well of me. I would like to thank them, but ask them not to do this. [But] I cannot actively stop this.
>
> (Cited in Traynor 2001)

Whether sincere or not,[19] Putin's explicit discouragement failed to subdue what created the impression of being a genuine, if frequently market-driven, love affair between the Russian population and the man it voted into office for a second time in 2004.[20] Why market-driven? Because "Putin" sells – sufficiently so for one Russian journalist, at least, to have called him "a trademark symbol of popular culture and language" (Shchuplov 2002). Fully aware of what an effective sales pitch entails, by 2003 Putin himself acutely observed, "Moe izobrazhenie i imia v sovremennykh usloviiakh iavliaiutsia raskruchennym brendom, kotorym pol'zuiutsia vse komu ne len'" [In contemporary conditions my image and name are a widely marketed brand used by anyone who feels like it] (*Putinki* 2004: 71). Thus the political propaganda of pro-Putinists, the stratagems of profiteering entrepreneurs, and the seemingly insatiable human need to create heroes dovetailed during a period when Putin's statist ideology ensured that lucrative mega-businesses, such as Yukos and Sibneft, reverted to the state (Aron 2006)[21] and Russia's booming oil industry dramatically improved average Russians' buying power and sense of security. The Putin brand was a talisman, a symbol of the Good Life under VVP, and a sign of solidarity with his ambitious vision for the nation as a global power.

The processes set in motion were circular: the human penchant for hero worship and collective enthusiasm fueled Putin's popularity, which in turn intensified that enthusiasm, resulting in a yet greater popularity that whipped up more enthusiasm, etc.. This perpetual escalation not only catapulted Putin to iconic status, but united the population in the common cause of celebrification. If, as Rojek and other theorists of celebrity culture contend, fans of celebrities find affirmation in belonging to a group devoted to the adulation of a glamorous persona, Putin as Russia's symbol bonded Russians through their support of a United Russia – precisely the party he headed, however distanced he appears from it in 2011, when the withdrawal of support by many previous faithfuls has diminished the party's standing.[22]

Cult or calculation?

Throughout the 2000s, those eager to court Putin's favor and express their veneration recognized few restraints in wooing the president. In addition to the luxurious Konstantin Palace just outside St. Petersburg renovated for his use and the $1 billion ski-slope in Sochi masterminded for his sporting self, the extravagant gifts marking his fiftieth birthday in October 2002 staggered the wildest imagination. They did so not only because of Russia's publicized economic hardships before the petrodollars rolled in, but also because of one gift's symbolic implications. Sixty jewelers in the Ural mountains spent 6 months producing the item, insured for $10 million, which consists of an exact replica of the Cap of Monomakh [*Shapka Monomakha*],[23] the ancient ceremonial gold crown, encrusted with jewels and lined with sable, used at the coronation of Russian tsars, including Ivan the Terrible and Putin's much-admired Peter the Great. A symbol of Russian autocracy and "the succession of power from the Byzantine emperors to the Russian monarchs" (Walsh 2002c), the crown figured in newspaper caricatures of Boris Yeltsin, dubbed "Tsar Boris" for his excesses – a detail apparently forgotten or overlooked by VVP's devotees, who surely must have realized his determination to dissociate himself from his predecessor. Ever the opportunist, then Moscow Mayor Luzhkov joined the ingratiatory birthday well-wishers by proposing to restore the statue of Feliks Dzerzhinskii, founder of the Cheka, on Lubianka Square, presumably to please the ex-KGB president (Abdullaev 2002), who, according to various estimates, during his years in office filled 25–50 percent of the top positions in Russia's governmental structures with his former KGB colleagues.[24]

In their own way, more evocative of the Stalin cult were the $500 carpets with Putin's face emblazoned on them, produced in Turkmenistan, and a Kostroma textile manufacturer's undertaking of what the pertinent linen mill's chief weaver called "very responsible and labor-consuming work": the profitable business of manufacturing tapestries with Putin's portrait, based on a photograph that showed what the head of the mill's art department trustfully described, *à la* George Bush, as "his open look [. . . which] convey[s] the openness of his soul"[25] ("Russian textile mill making Putin tapestries" 2003). The allegedly high demand for the tapestries persuaded the manufacturer to follow up with bedspreads, towels, and rugs likewise bearing the Putin image – thereby enabling enthusiasts to sleep, shower, and socialize, however indirectly, with their icon. In short, not unlike Stalin, "*Putin* [*vezde/vsegda*] *s nami*" [Putin is (everywhere/always) with us]. The frequently iterated comparison between the two inspired one tongue-in-cheek "artist," Avi Abrams,[26] to revise Vasilii Efanov's painting *Nezabyvaemoe* [An Unforgettable Meeting] (1936–7) along anachronistic lines, replacing a female delegate at the Kremlin with Putin, thus altering the significance of the momentous handshake from what under Stalin represented achievement of the ultimate goal (contact with The Leader) to a union of kindred spirits. An issue of the Russian *Newsweek* (February 13–19, 2006) similarly remastered for its cover Aleksandr Gerasimov's painting *Stalin i Voroshilov v Kremle* [Stalin and Voroshilov in the Kremlin] (1938) by substituting Putin as Stalin's stroll-mate, both men symbolically joined under one umbrella. The Kremlin's determination to control the portrayal of history, its withdrawal of various archives declassified during the 1990s, and its promotion of a study guide for high-school teachers that characterizes Stalin as "one of the most successful leaders of the USSR" (Levy 2008b) rightly or wrongly strengthen the perceived parallel between the two authoritarian rulers.

What interests me here, however, is not Putin's policies or politics, but a concrete aspect of his remarkable visual celebrification: sundry images reproducing him in genres ranging from "aestheticized" photographs and paintings to carpets, bedding, busts, toys, balloons, graphics, and performances – whether in an idolatrous, satirical, or ambiguous vein. The tradition of depicting deified leaders in twentieth century Russia charted an uneven course. Inaugurated under Lenin, it culminated with Stalin, relentlessly mythologized on canvas and posters by Brodskii, Gerasimov, Nalbandian, Klutsis, Deni, and a host of less memorable artists. As mere mortals, Khrushchev, Andropov, Chernenko, Gorbachev, and Yeltsin were largely bypassed in that respect, and Brezhnev, despite his famous Honecker kiss, similarly inspired few painters during his lifetime and virtually none later, with the notable, ironic exception of Dmitrii Prigov in his *Bestiary* series (1985) and prisoners who tattooed leaders' faces on their bodies as sui generis bullet-proof vests, in the apparently correct assumption that no one would dare shoot at an image of the country's leader.

That for some observers the obsession with pictorially immortalizing Putin implied a parallel with Stalin[27] explains why wary commentators resorted to the red-button, historically fraught label of "cult of personality" (see Chapter 2 by Cassiday *et al.*) (Figure 1.6). Disclaimers voiced by Putin or leaked to the press by members of his entourage insisted on the Russian president's distaste for the diffusion of Putiniana throughout the country – a disavowal that repeatedly made news, adding modesty to the virtues constituting his public profile – and thus far no mammoth statue of him looms over the Volga-Don Canal.[28] The sheer volume and diversity of his iconographic dissemination, nonetheless, eerily recalls the artistic production of the Stalinist era, sparking exaggerated fears of political regression to fatally jollier times ["zhit' stalo luchshe, zhit' stalo veselee . . ."] – fears buttressed by the reinstatement of several Soviet practices and the Kremlin's virtually complete control of the media. Moreover, the Internet facilitates broad access to those images, just as YouTube enables those outside Russia to sample clips featuring Putin as the protagonist of imaginary narratives, such as the ironic mini-video, now no longer available, showing VVP as a cool, daring, Stetsoned cowboy riding the range, with music from Sergio Leone's *Man with No Name* series, starring Clint Eastwood as the fearless gunslinger even more inscrutable and macho than Putin. The visual analogy projected Putin as the strong, silent man of action engaged in manly pursuits – and the numerous shots of him on

Figure 1.6 "Mirror, mirror . . . " – an ironic, admirably pithy version of the Putin-as-Stalin-legatee perspective. Caricature by John Deering, cartoonist at the *Arkansas Democratic Gazette*.

Source: Courtesy of John Deering.

horseback, in helicopters, and in judo poses only consolidated that glamorous image of intrepid (self-)mastery conventionalized by Hollywood and advertisements in print and on television.[29] Putin's celebrity status, in short, rests on his mediated image of an intelligent, reserved, sober patriot of indomitable will and physical prowess, one wholly dedicated to Russia and Russians.

Especially during his first term, Putin undeniably exuded and cultivated an aura of recessiveness or modesty – of a reluctance to attract particular attention. His media-hyped kiss planted on a small boy's stomach on Red Square (2006) aside, for much of his presidency he lacked dramatic flourishes, favored a brisk and occasionally opaque manner of interaction, and operated by steady, even plodding, accretion and scrupulous concern for details, often behind the scenes. His famed abstinence from alcohol and his physical appearance – not his pale basilisk gaze and uncanny resemblance to Dobby, but his compact, athletic slightness – suggest the discipline and control constantly touted as his signature traits (Figure 1.7).[30] His verbal tic of preceding official statements by a promise of laconism matches his physical shortness. Admired for his sporting skills (judo, skiing, swimming, horseback riding) and his dependability, in contrast to his predecessor's fabled expansiveness, self-indulgence, thoughtless off-the-cuff

Figure 1.7 " . . . but how do you manage to be everywhere, Vladimir Vladimirovich?" Putin as the Dobby-double, here, there, and everywhere. Aleksei Merinov's irreverent illustration in *Putinki* (Moscow 2004) 70.

Source: Courtesy of Aleksei Merinov.

statements, and paraded emotionality, he sooner has impressed by an *absence* of qualities, as the song "A Man Like Putin" unwittingly attests,

> Moi paren' snova vlip v durnye dela, podralsia, naglotalsia kakoi-to muti.
> On tak menia dostal–ia ego prognala, i ia khochu teper' takogo, kak Putin!
> [Pripev:] Takogo, kak Putin–polnogo sil, takogo kak Putin–chtoby *ne pil*,
> Takogo, kak Putin–chtob *ne obizhal*, takogo, kak Putin–chtob *ne ubezhal*.[31]
> (Singing Together 2002)

Consonant with Putin's widespread reputation of ideal masculinity (see Chapter 8), by contrasting him with the presumed "average male," the lyrics reveal contemporary's Russia's ongoing crisis in gender identity, especially men's disorientation and instability as vestiges of the blighted 1990s.

Media and celebrification

That not all Russians sang hosannas to VVP as a model of indomitable probity is clear from one blogger's vehement counter-version of the song's lyrics. Slyly interpolating some of Putin's less euphemistic vocabulary (see Chapter 4), it symptomizes the oppositional view, which enjoys appreciably narrower circulation:

takogo kak putin nuzhno dushit'
takogo kak putin nuzhno ubit'.
takogo kak putin nuzhno mochit'.
takogo kak putin nuzhno udavit'
takogo kak putin nuzhno zastrelit'
Takogo kak putin nuzhno ebat',
takogo kak putin nuzhno strelyat',
takogo kak putin nuzhno vzorvat',
takogo kak putin nuzhno zakopat'

(bucovin 68)

Such an irreverent attitude toward Russia's major contemporary icon, however, represented a minority attitude and could not be articulated on television or in the press, but only on the Internet, which to this day remains the sole channel of communication relatively free of the Kremlin's control. As one commentator notes, Russians impatient with "the absence of criticism and debate on television" increasingly have turned to the Internet, which the Russian (unlike the Chinese) government does not censor (Kovalyova 2009). For instance, a television contest in December 2008 intended to identify Russia's greatest historical figures inspired a web site (www.badnameofrussia.ru) asking visitors to vote for public figures who are "the disgrace of Russia" [*pozor Rossii*]. By December 3, 2008, Putin reportedly topped the list with 18,155 votes – more than twice the number cast for the second most "disgraceful" figure, Boris Yeltsin.[32] Astonishingly frank comments by bloggers explain the reasons for their disgust with the former president and now prime minister.[33] More recently, the Ekaterinburg group Rabfak posted a clip on ura.ru in which free-style as well as loosely choreographed dancing accompanies the group's satirical song "Our Loony Bin Is Voting for Putin" [*Nash durdom golosuet za Putina*]. In imaging Russia as an insane asylum, Rabfak revives the master trope of Andrei Konchalovskii's film *House of Fools* [*Dom durakov* 2002].[34] Probably a response to the huge billboard in the capital announcing "Moscow is voting for Putin" [Moskva golosuet za Putina], the song, according to the group's front man, Aleksandr Semenov, has no oppositional intent: "[W]e aren't battling anyone. We simply photograph [*sic*] reality and laugh at what's funny." Such a disingenuous disclaimer from a group famous for such sardonic videos as "A new song about Stalin" and "A new song about the police" can only compound the irony of the current performance, which has taken the Internet by storm. Though clearly many Russians' celebrity hero, Putin is more controversial than suggested in other, more traditional forms of communication and media.

Yet, paradoxically, the Putin cult has benefited immeasurably from the Internet and other technologies, which have documented his high-profile, media-conscious international and domestic activities. In fact, Putin is the first and thus far only Russian head of state to realize the enormous potential of technology to promote a painstakingly elaborated self-image through its dissemination around the world.[35] International access to Russian state-controlled television channels and to YouTube makes available to millions of viewers in the west (and beyond) the "immediacy" of Putin as Russia's revered "icon in action," in scenarios that repeatedly confirm his status as an omnipotent, charismatic star. Moreover, items posted on his web site and the tradition he established while president, of annually spending several hours in telephone dialogue with Russian citizens, who call in to pose questions, seek aid or advice, and complain about their problems (see Chapter 5 by Lara Ryazanova-Clarke), create the impression of a demotic leader invested in the everyday life of "his subjects" – all, of course, captured on camera. As prime minister, Putin has maintained this annual ritual, the continuity reinforcing the general conviction that he remains the chief power in the Kremlin, reinforced by Dmitrii Medvedev's public endorsement in October 2011 of Putin as the United Party's candidate in the March 2012 presidential election. That announcement surprised only the naïve and credulous.

In recent years, photographers have accompanied not only Putin's visits to war zones, factories, schools, museums, and cultural events, but also his vacations in Siberia, where a bare-chested Putin fishing, riding, and climbing trees became immortalized as a sexual commodity when snapshots of his leisurely self flooded the Internet (Figure 1.8). Putin's increased sexualization in recent years via discarded shirts, rumors of liaisons with women less than half his age, and reports of his decisive action in the midst of allegedly dangerous situations have dramatically magnified his image as the post-Soviet exemplar of seductive, reassuring virility (see Chapter 8). Reassurance also derives from Putin's projection of a dispassionate, authoritative self-confidence in his recorded confrontations with foreign heads of state and journalists, as well as Russia's incompetent regional managers and defanged oligarchs, such as Oleg Derepaska, whom he recently humiliated in public for deviousness and lack of professional responsibility (2009) – to the delight of Russian television viewers and YouTube aficionados.

Putin's acquired sophistication in public relations may be measured by the contrast between his dilatory reaction to the *Kursk* disaster in 2000 and his handling of the blast at the Saiano-Sushenskaia hydroelectric plant in Siberia in 2009: his prompt personal visit to the latter site, his expressed concern for victims of the tragedy, and above all the video conference he organized to discuss the emergency reinforced his populist image, prompting bloggers to vent their anger not at the Kremlin, but at local authorities. In doing so, they imitated Putin's strategy of faulting regional administrators for problems that reflect national inadequacies. If retrograde in his attachment to sundry Soviet-era institutions and values, Putin could hardly be more "modern" in his exploitation of technology. What other world leader in the 2000s matched his celebrification engineered through cyberfication?

Lack as luster?

If, as one western commentator observed, during the early 2000s "Putin's popularity [. . . was] the result of anti-politics [. . .], non-engagement" (Lavelle 2003) – after

Figure 1.8 Posing and exposing the 'charismatic' chest on a holiday in Tuva, 2007.

Source: Courtesy of the Presidential Press and Information Office, www.kremlin.ru, on Wikimedia Commons.

the 2004 election, he grew markedly less laconic and more imperial. Indeed, by the second half of the 2000s, Putin's star status and his resultant self-confidence made him less passive and decidedly more authoritarian in front of the cameras. Tellingly, a former KGB master once described Putin as a "nonentity" (Toomey 2003), while the journalist Steve LeVine (2008: 64) noted the "complicity of his inaction" in questions of crime. Lack, in short, was (and perhaps remains) Putin's strong suit, his outstanding features comprising a stylistic anodyne impassiveness and above all a certain "emptiness"; even his contradictory pronouncements ("managed democracy," a strong [i.e., imperialist and controlling] yet humanistic Russia) erase one another. Several years ago Georgii Satarov, a political analyst and former aide to Yeltsin, maintained, "Lack of a position is part of the political style and strategy for Putin."[36] Pollster Iurii Levada nicely summed up the dynamic when he characterized Putin as a "mirror in which everyone, communist or democrat, sees what he wants to see and what he hopes for" (White and McAllister 2003: 385). Indeed, Putin's ability to seem everything to everyone raises the question of what precisely he endorses or represents. Veterans are reassured by his announced regret for the loss of the Soviet Union and his adherence to several familiar Soviet principles; representatives of the Church applaud his seeming commitment to Russian Orthodoxy; the intelligentsia and *Kulturarbeiter* appreciate his ideological and financial support of film, art, and literature as central to Russia's cultural standing in the world, publicly displayed in ritualistic ceremonies during which Putin presents awards, congratulates successful figures, and even takes part in staged events; women thrill to his physical vigor and athleticism as well as his publicized speeches on International Women's Day; children reportedly find his regular visits to schools exciting; his telephone marathons with the public assure the "man on the street" that they can get a fair hearing and help from "the man in charge"; even animals (ranging from goats to fish), with whom Putin frequently has been photographed – feeding, stroking, or kissing them – must feel safeguarded by the apparently protective affection of the nation's leader (see Chapter 3 by Tatiana Mikhailova). In other words, Putin "gives the public what it wants" – a stratagem guaranteed to gain popularity. Yet, apart from his iterated passion for a strong Russia and his hostility toward the United States (and, more recently, the United Kingdom), one would be hard put to define Putin's profoundly held beliefs.

The tidal wave of cultural objects and gestures designed to immortalize Putin attest the rich potential of his vacuity, which allowed not only for the ascription of multiple traits and the projection of myriad desires onto his persona, but also for his transformation into an art object depicted from diverse perspectives – in such genres as the official portrait, graphics, photo collage, logo, greeting card, cartoon, handicrafts, sculpture, and Internet caricatures. Moreover, the register of these visuals spans the gamut from solemnity and pomp to irony, playfulness, and satire. If, as Michel Foucault contends, we should create ourselves as a work of art (Foucault 1984: 351), others perform that task for Putin ("svita igraet korolia" [literally, the entourage plays the king]) and by constantly maintaining the spotlight on his activities, statements, and mere presence at various functions, fortify his celebrity status as the nation's White Knight.

Visualizing VVP

Aiding in the creation of the Putin myth, folklore genres include a sketch of his frowning, almost chinless face by St. Petersburger Gavriil Lubnin, accompanied by the sort of school verses that traditionally treat Russia's famous (for instance, Lev Tolstoy) in a familiar, informal mode, such as the pseudo-naïve rhyming *chastushka* quatrain, "Krasivyi muzhik Volodia/Svityi iz krepkikh zhil/Ezdit v Moskve i khodit/A ran'she v Pitere zhil" [The handsome guy Volodia/ Formed from strong sinews/Rides and walks round Moscow/But earlier lived in Piter].[37] Another folk genre, Russian stacking or nesting dolls (matryoshki), which for almost a century functioned as portable national ideology primarily targeting tourists with a weakness for souvenirs, has "embodied" virtually all Russian and Soviet heads of state, as well as its cultural luminaries, and in this regard Putin was no exception. Nor were the VVP matryoshki exceptional. One of them merely featured a facsimile of his face atop the national colors, with "Rossiia" splashed across them below the two-headed eagle of the Russian empire that replaced the hammer and sickle after the demise of the Soviet Union. Banal and sketchily executed, during the early 2000s these matryoshki symbolically equating Putin with Russia nonetheless sold for 500 rubles/$17 on the Old Arbat.[38] That equation of country and its symbol partly explains the new century's Putinmania, for a glamorous, strong leader implies Russia's recovered identity as a world power with its sui generis allure.

Equally conventional though more revealing is the portrait in oil of *Vladimir Putin, President of the Russian Federation* (2000) by Nikas Safronov (b. April 8, 1956), a "society painter" who shares Zurab Tsereteli's penchant for courting famous subjects in the world of international politics and entertainment.[39] Numerous copies of the portrait, with the original (costing 38,400 rubles/$1,280) exhibited at the art salon on Petrovka, overran offices and Moscow's largest bookstores. Unlike another, lesser known portrait of Putin that Safronov painted the same year, this one captured a formally attired, solemn-faced Putin in a classic ruler pose, elevated above the background of his dominion, visible from a window behind him: the Kremlin and the Moscow River, winding into the distance alongside the vast expanses that merge with the sky ("infinite Russia"). The preponderance of various shades of blue – in iconography, a color associated with tranquility – infuses the portrait with calm reassurance, which Russians in fact attributed to their leader. In other words, the portrait consolidates the image of Putin as confident and capable ruler of a huge realm.

If this rendition simultaneously conveys the salient features of self-restraint and power associated with the president, Safronov's many other portraits of Putin sooner showcase the artist's fawning flights of fancy. Following the current fashion for recasting a sitter as a notable figure from the past,[40] Safronov variously reincarnated VVP as Napoleon on a rearing steed, with uplifted hand pointing, presumably, to the field of battle; as merchant (links with capitalism), cardinal (religious orthodoxy), youthful prince (imperial but romantic leader), and the sixteenth century monarch Francis I, generous benefactor of the arts (Fleishman 2007a). Finally, Safronov's Cubist Putin implies the latter's modern/ist credentials as reformer, patron of culture, and so forth. As any visitor to Moscow can verify, portraits of Putin invade any and all spaces (Figure 1.9).

Analogies with historical rulers of empires likewise clearly operated in several sculptures of Putin, less obviously in that by St. Petersburg's Aleksandr Palmin, who declared that his bronze 10-inch Putin was not a memorial, but "a tribute" to "a historic figure" (Traynor 2001), than in a bust costing 22,032 rubles/$734 at the Salon on Varvarka gallery, modeled on ancient sculptures of Roman emperors – moreover, in ancient ceremonial garb. And when not incarnating state power, VVP appeared in the "uniform" of a judo master, as in Tsereteli's huge bronze statue (2004) and in a doctored photograph, hawked on the Old Arbat for 150 rubles/$5, of a stern Putin in a clinch with a faceless opponent – presumably alluding to VVP's readiness to "take anyone on." The 2008 DVD *Let's Learn Judo with Vladimir Putin*, as well as his "heroic" rescue of a television crew from

Figure 1.9 The face that launched a thousand sighs and schemes. A pen, a pencil, or a president – numerous official portraits as part of essential "Office Supplies" displayed in a Moscow bookstore, June 5, 2006.

Source: Courtesy of Vladimir Menkov on Wikimedia Commons.

an escaped Siberian tiger (Faulconbridge 2008), has "enhanced his macho image" (Walker 2008), emphasized by the camouflage and desert boots Putin sported in the taiga while performing his publicized "rescue" (Faulconbridge 2008).

More ambiguous, though a Kremlin best-seller, was the 2001 calendar by Dmitrii Vrubel and Viktoriia Timofeeva *Dvenadtsat' nastroenii prezidenta* [The President's Twelve Moods], which bordered on caricature, made no effort to idealize Putin's face, and even captured a pouty, sullen VVP with huge, protruding lips. Similarly, the couple's *Putin i chernyi kvadrat* [Putin and Black Square] (2002) depicted Putin in a deliberately crude light evoking a huckster or thug in an ill-fitting suit beneath one of the most enigmatic paintings by arguably the foremost representative of the Russian avant-garde.[41] And an unusual caricature on sale for 500 rubles/$17 on the Old Arbat condensed a fascinating complex of ominous references: Putin's lower body and ears are those of a dragon or serpent, *à la* Russian fairy-tale illustrations and iconography depicting the enemy in World War I and II; the truncated middle part of his body evokes typical folkloric images of Koshchei Bessmertnyi, who repeatedly seizes defenseless women and incarcerates them; on his head Putin wears the historical *Shapka Monomakha* that was recreated for his fiftieth birthday. While the woman gripped in his right fist probably alludes to Putin's masculinist reign and stranglehold on the country, the newspaper crumpled in his left suggests the media censorship characterizing his years in office (Figure 1.10). This far from flattering depiction challenges the homogenizing idealization of canonical Putin portraits.

Figure 1.10 An impudent caricature of Putin's wriggly power, sold on the Old Arbat in the early 2000s.

Source: Photo by Helena Goscilo.

Equally irreverent images focused on Putin's omnipotent ubiquity, satirizing the perceived conviction that "everything is Putin" and "Putin is our all." Thus in the series of witty caricatures titled *Putin Birthday Greetings* issued by polit.ru on October 7, 2004, which include VVP as Superman and medieval despot, one "greeting" features comprehensive putination in a domestic setting: Putin sits at a table reading the book *Putin*, while his dog Connie/Koni, the king and queen on the chessboard, the cactus, and the goldfish in a bowl all have VVP's face (Elkin repet., Figure 1.11). Though realized in another medium, the same concept animates another series: the four photographs collected under the rubric *Rebiata s nashego dvora* [Kids from our Block] (2004) by the subversive, hilariously parodic duo of Viacheslav Mizin and Aleksandr Shaburov, known as Sinie Nosy [Blue Noses] (Figure 1.12). A typical Soviet group photograph of youths united solely by living on the same street is transformed into a series of casually dressed, close-knit male bodies, each topped by Putin's face. Exposing the political edge of the visuals, the subtitle reads "Bezlikie rossiianie v maskakh prezidenta RF Putina, kotoromu oni investirovali svoe doverie" [Common[42] Russians in masks of President Putin, whom they have invested with their trust] (Sinie Nosy 2006: 160–161). Likewise criticizing unthinking glorification of Putin and other cultural icons, a kitschy, colorful,

Figure 1.11 Sergei Elkin's marvelously sardonic take on Putin's voracious omnipresence.

Source: Courtesy of Sergei Elkin.

highly controversial "montage" titled *Gori-gori moia svecha*,[43] produced by Blue Noses the same year, bears the subtitle "Tri glavnykh polozhitel'nykh geroia rossiiskoi gosudarstvennoi mifologii – poet Pushkin, Iisus Khristos i prezident RF Putin – ne daiut pogasnut' sveche russkoi dukhovnosti"[44] (*Sinie Nosy* 2006: 16–17) and depicts a haloed Christ holding a lit candle, flanked by a T-shirted Pushkin with a cigarette lighter and Putin in a bright red T-shirt warming his hand at the candle's flame (Figure 1.13).[45] Indeed, VVP's sacred status, like Pushkin's and Christ's, is protected by the powers that be in Russia, and those criticizing him, religion, and specifically Russian culture do so at their own considerable risk.

The painter Aleksandr Shednov, known as Shurik, learned as much when he attempted to beam a portrait of Putin onto the main administrative building in his home town of Voronezh on June 12, 2009 – Russian Independence Day. Charged with inappropriate behavior after his arrest and interrogation by the FSB, Shednov acknowledged that the portrait constituted a protest against Putin's return to the Kremlin for a third presidential term. Posted on the Internet, the image consists of Putin's face superimposed on the body of a woman with long, dark hair, in a tight, low-cut dress, huge hoop earrings in her ears, her coquettish pose matching the coyness of the words in the upper left corner supposedly spoken by him or her: ". . . oi, nu ia dazhe ne znaiu . . . tretii prezidentskii? . . . nu eto uzh slishkom, khotia Bog liubit 'Troitsy'" (Stewart 2009).[46] Shednov's aesthetic in this instance coincided with that of Blue Noses.

Figure 1.12 All are Putin, having submitted to the cult and united in shared idolatry, as envisioned by the Blue Noses duo in the series *Rebiata s nashego dvora* [Kids from Our Block], 2004.

Source: Courtesy of Aleksandr Shaburov of Blue Noses.

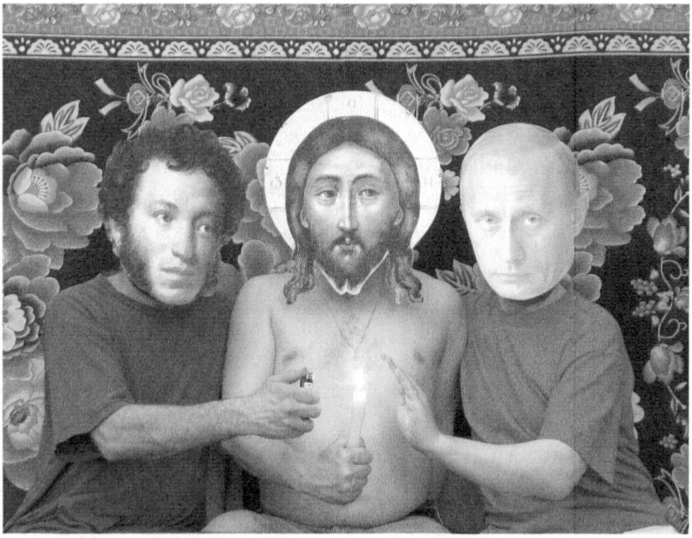

Figure 1.13 The sacred trinity of contemporary Russian culture, in a multi-media work by the irrepressible Blue Noses, titled *Gori-gori, moia svecha* [Keep on Burning, My Life-Candle], 2004.

Source: Courtesy of Aleksandr Shaburov of Blue Noses.

Like most works by Blue Noses, those portraying Putin ironize dogma and cultural conventions; their incendiary potential accounts for protests by conservative groups and for the artists' consequent reputation as hooligans. Reactions to Blue Noses' polemical depictions of VVP peaked in 2006, when Russian customs officials at Sheremet'evo Airport confiscated, among other items, their series of photographs titled *Maski-shou* [Mask show] (2000) being exported for a gallery exhibit in London. Collating images of Bin Laden, Bush, and Putin in underwear cavorting on a couch, the works elicited outrage at their "derogatory manner" of portraying "heads of state." The widely reported incident paralleled the scandal around Vladimir Sorokin's novel *Goluboe salo* [Blue lard][47] and leaves no doubts that Russian airport officials, though hardly affronted by the trivialization of Bin Laden and Bush, were outraged by a less than respectful concept of their Leader.

Similarly, the incisive, tongue-in-cheek images by Sergei Elkin, an inspired cartoonist associated with polit.ru, epigrammatically debunk the specifics of Putin's self-presentation, exposing Putin's promotional stratagems and situating him in a political Imaginary or Wonderland. In their entirety, Elkin's wide-ranging Putin-cartoons create a satirical, illustrated map of Putin's career and aspirations, as well as the populace's perceptions of, and responses to, that unfolding melodrama. Only the Internet allows for such an "anti-genuflectional" stance, accessible at ellustrator.livejournal.com.

In January 2009, Putin turned the tables on his "representers" by assuming the role of artist and submitting his (doctored) painting to a charity auction of art works by celebrities in his home town. Now in its third year, the auction featured as its theme a story by Nikolai Gogol intended to mark the bicentennial of the writer's birth, and required that each painting represent each letter of the Russian alphabet. Putin's simple watercolor of a window with red-patterned curtains, titled *Uzor* [Pattern], "will go for the most," predicted Nadezhda Anfalova, chief artist at the auction, "The buyers look at the name" (O'Flynn 2009). Indeed, at the auction in the Grand Hotel Europe that followed the exhibit, the painting, allegedly executed in 20 minutes and "filled in" by a professional artist, sold for the equivalent of $1.15 million, making it "the most expensive painting sold in Russia" ("Russian Prime Minister Vladimir Putin's sketch sells for $1.15 million at auction" 2009). Natal'ia Kurnikova, owner of Moscow's Our Artists art gallery, admitted that she purchased it for its uniqueness, "This picture shows an interesting side of a prominent personality. Maybe it will be the first and the last picture of its kind" (Titova 2009). Clearly, the glamorous Putin brand still sells and rules.

The most striking aspect of the Putiniana generated during the 2000s, however, is neither its obsequiousness nor its iconoclasm – or even its ludic nature, but the sheer wealth and diversity of Putin images, many of them as "managed" as the "democracy" during his presidency. Proliferating at an accelerated rate as the decade wore on, these museum holdings of Putiniana catapulted him from the realm of history to that of myth. Mining his reputation for unique charisma, as high-powered self-nominated prime minister he has continued to build on his mythological status through media performances, spotlighted participation in photo-op events, and high-profile meetings ("high" being singularly appropriate for the chief advocate of the "power vertical"). In May 2011, sundry postings on YouTube captured Putin's debut as the Russian Fats Domino of the post-Soviet era as, at a charity event in St. Petersburg attended by several Hollywood stars, Putin crooned the popular Fats Domino hit *Blueberry Hill* in heavily accented English after picking out the notes on the piano. The performance evoked a storm of applause.

Where can Putin as adulated leader, savior of the nation, sportsman, martial arts expert, charity supporter, painter, and singer go from here? One obvious answer is – to the 2012 presidential election as its most popular "star" candidate. His formation of the new All-Russia People's Front, "with 400,000 members and massive resources" (Roth 2011), suggests preliminary preparation for the 'obvious' as the career move of choice. With recent defections from the United Russia party and a drop in its approval rating to 53 percent in April 2011 and 51 percent in November,[48] his attempt to create a broad coalition of supporters through the Front has led journalists, political analysts, and scholars such as sociologist Ol'ga Khrystanovska to speculate about the initiative as a "signal of returning" – or, more precisely, a bid to reprise his former post (Meyer and Arkhipov 2011). Shurik, in other words, was prescient in discerning a third (term). It seems highly unlikely that any other candidate would present a threat to Putin's re-election, for Putin's own rating currently holds steady at 61 percent, which doubtless is why the newly constituted Front, according to his press secretary, Dmitrii Peskov, will operate "above the party" and "will be based around Putin, who came up with the idea" (Meyer and Arkhipov). Putin, in other words, looms as the top presidential candidate of two parties, in the spirit of excess that characterizes celebrity. The perceived need for this safety net, nonetheless, suggests that not even the Putin brand and the mythology inseparable from it suffice to guarantee the future.

Notes

1 Cited in Osipovich (2004).

2 Cited in Traynor (2001). Ivchenko is a sculptor in St. Petersburg.

3 The epigraph is from the blog appended to "Tainstvennaia . . . ."

4 Simon Osborne, "We love Putin: Meet the Russian president's teenage fan club." *The Independent* (July 21, 2007).

5 My gratitude to Serguei Oushakine for generously sharing numerous Putin visuals with me over the years. A short, preliminary version of this chapter appeared in Russian as "VVP kak *objet d'art*," *Neprikosnovennyi zapas* [62] 6 (2008). [Online]. Available at: http://magazines.russ.ru/nz/2008/6/go8-pr.html (accessed December 27, 2009) and a more recent version in Helena Goscilo and Vlad Strukov, eds. *Celebrity and Glamour in Contemporary Russia: Shocking Chic*, London: Routledge, 2011. 29–55.

6 BBC correspondent Steven Eke (2008) has speculated that Putin's appointment of two former Kremlin aides "suggests he wants to strengthen his powers at the expense of the new presidency." Putin's live 3-hour question-and-answer session on December 4, 2008, which continued the tradition of his call-in show as president, suggested that he

is "the man Russians should look to in tough times," particularly since Medvedev has not orchestrated such exchanges with the public. Asked during the show what he loved most, Putin, predictably, answered, "Russia" (Isachenkov 2008b).

7 Sculptor Zurab Tsereteli and artist Takhir Salakhov, as, respectively, President and Vice President of the Russian Academy of Art, and Nikita Mikhalkov as President of the Russian Cultural Foundation, trailed by Albert Charkin, Rector of the Repin St. Petersburg State Academic Institute of Art, Sculpture, and Architecture. The institute falls under the authority of the Academy of Fine Arts, headed by Zurab Tsereteli.

8 The letter, published in *Rossiiskaia Gazeta*, prompted an instant disclaimer from those it purported to represent; 775 cultural "workers," led by Marietta Chudakova, sent their own appeal to Putin, criticizing the foursome's letter, "Takoe obrashchenie brosaet ten' ne tol'ko na tekh, kto ego podpisal, no i na Vas kak prezidenta, za gody pravleniia kotorogo vosstanovilis', k sozhaleniiu, mnogie proiavleniia stol' kharakternogo dlia sovetskikh vremen kul'ta liubogo kremlevskogo vlastitelia" [Such an appeal casts a shadow not only on those who signed it, but also on you as President, in the course of whose rule, unfortunately, have appeared many signs of the cult of any and all Kremlin rulers so characteristic of Soviet times] (Chudakova *et al.* 2007).

9 Stephen White and Ian McAllister cover some of the same terrain and rely on many of the same sources, but only up to 2003 (White and McAllister 2003).

10 Bransten (2002), citing a report in *Pravda*.

11 Under Putin, the FSB has enjoyed enormous power, unhindered in its coercive, intimidating, and obstructionist activities, such as raiding offices of media and businesses, threatening voters, denying access to security archives, and so forth. See the series of articles in *The New York Times* punningly titled "Kremlin Rules" by Clifford J. Levy (Levy 2008a, 2008b).

12 In fact, in 2003 Putin presented Viacheslav Tikhonov, who played the cool-headed Soviet double agent (Stirlitz) operating in Nazi Germany during World War II in the TV series *Semnadtsat' mgnovenii vesny* [Seventeen Moments of Spring] (1973) with the Order of Service to the State, third degree, commending the actor for having shaped an entire generation of Soviet youth. The recent parody of *Semnadtsat' . . .* by Marius Balthans/Weisberg, titled *Gitler Kaput!* (2008), reportedly prompted Communists in St. Petersburg to request that the Ministry of Culture prevent the film from opening in theaters, but without success (Barry 2008).

13 The extent to which the Kremlin orchestrated the Putin cult is impossible to determine.

14 According to several sources, rumors – a mainstay of Moscow life and journalism – indicate that the song was generated by Kremlin propaganda, for no stores carried the record, radio stations were ignorant of its provenance, and a promoter of Singing Together (a faceless duo until the song caught on) is a press secretary at the Russian Supreme Court (The Putin Cult 2007).

15 Printed in 1,000 copies, the calendar apparently became the most sought-after Christmas gift in the Kremlin that year. The husband-and-wife team of Dmitrii Vrubel' and Viktoriia Timofeeva used photographs to produce Putin's face, varying in mood according to the month. The President's office reportedly bought the original of the calendar's cover (Owen 2001) and an exhibition titled *Putin's Twelve Moods* was arranged in downtown Moscow (Sidlin 2001). Capitalizing on his widely advertised reputation as a martial arts expert, in 2008 Putin released an instructional judo DVD, *Let's Learn Judo with Vladimir Putin*, which indubitably bolstered his public persona of intrepid "fighter" endowed with rigor and self-control. See http://www.guardian.co.uk/world/2008/oct/07/russia1 (accessed August 23, 2009).

16 *Ot pervogo litsa* [First Person] (2000), Putin's quasi-(auto)biography in interviews, also came out in a sizable run; a biography (2003) printed in 200,000 copies by the Lanrusinvest holding company was distributed by the publishers for free to the Russian public (BBC Monitoring; NTV). Among the ever-increasing Russian volumes devoted to VVP are Roi Medvedev's *Vladimir Putin: Chetyre goda v Kremle* [Vladimir Putin: Four Years in the Kremlin] and the collection titled *Chetyre goda s Putinym* [Four Years with Putin], both issued by Vremia publishers in 2004. See also the irreverent three-volume collection of reports by the Kremlin correspondent Andrei Kolesnikov, *Ia Putina videl!* [I've Seen Putin!], *Uvidet's Putina i umeret'* [See Putin and Die], and *Menia Putin videl!* [Putin's Seen Me!] (Moscow: EKSMO 2005), the first and last titles unambiguously evoking the syrupy socialist realist painting by Dmitrii Mochal'skii, *Oni videli Stalina* [They've Seen Stalin 1949] of schoolchildren and adults beatified through having laid eyes on the post-war, hence deified Stalin.

17 The site, with its URL signaling Putin's Soviet-era allegiances, still exists, its owner now Prime Minister instead of President. It contains photos of a physically active Putin (occasionally topless), a family photo album, and two shots of his Labrador, Koni, who figured in ads for his second presidential campaign.

18 This scenario recalls the public image of Stalin, whom propaganda portrayed as tirelessly working in the Kremlin, even at night, on behalf of the people of the USSR. See, for example, the poster by V. Govorkov's *O kazhdom iz nas zabotitsia Stalin v Kremle* [Stalin in the Kremlin Is Concerned about Each of Us] (1940). Aleksandr Solzhenitsyn ridicules this image in the eighteenth chapter of *V kruge pervom* [The First Circle].

19 Astute enough to realize that popularity increases power, Putin reportedly monitored his public image on television on a daily basis and was adept at using the media, especially television, to foster his persona of a self-confident and reliable national leader. Manifestly, he was far from indifferent to Russians' perception of him.

20 In a highly critical item on Putin, Albats referred to that presidential election as a contest "between those who love Putin more than life and those who love him not quite that much" (Albats 2003).

21 According to Marshall Goldman, "Russian state control over energy assets rose from 10 percent in 2000 to 50 percent in 2007" (Goldman 2008).

22 Defectors from the United Party include its former glamorous pinup, the ballerina Anastasiia Volochkova. See "Vladimir Putin's poster girl, Anastasia Volochkova, dances out of party," (2011) *Bucharest Herald*, 5 February. Available at: http://www.bucharestherald.ro/worldnews/43-worldnews/19527-vladimir-putins-poster-girl-anastasia-volochkova-dances-out-of-party (accessed Feb 15, 2011). Also see Helena Goscilo and Vlad Strukov's, "Russian celebrities at home and abroad: united under Putin, March 2011," (2011) *Celebrity Studies* 2, 2 (July): 190–194.

23 For the historical and symbolic significance of the crown, see Kollmann (2008).

24 The estimated percentage differs, depending on the source: for example, Glasser cites 25 percent; Kasparov, 50 percent. According to Ol'ga Kryshtanovskaia, Russia's premier specialist in scholarly study of the elite, during Putin's tenure, military officers and the FSB (formerly KGB) leadership have accumulated substantial wealth, including shares of ownership in Russia's biggest companies (reported in LeVine 2008: 5). Yet it would be simplistic to make automatic assumptions about the reasons behind Putin's choices in personnel, for, as Lilia Shevtsova contends, he "chose his team, not on the basis of professional allegiances or ideological or political affiliation, but simply because these were the people he knew" (2007: 44).

25 The words uncannily recall George Bush's gushing confession of having looked into Putin's eyes and recognized his inner worth.

26 Avi Abrams is the founder and editor of Dark Roasted Blend, a site teeming with irreverent images and much more.

27 Other developments under Putin susceptible to such an interpretation include the rise of the FSB, the elimination of a free/alternate media, Putin's iterated emphasis on the need for a strong, nationalistic Russia, the reprisal of the Soviet national anthem and classes devoted to military strategy at schools, and the policy introduced several years ago of paying neighbors to spy and report on one another.

28 In fact, it is surprising that Tsereteli has not followed the example of Evgenii Vutetich, whose colossal monument of Stalin was completed in 1952.

29 Available at: http://www.youtube.com/watch?v=ZIPCAl55JCc (accessed October 13, 2008). The numerous Putin videos on YouTube include "Putin 'the legend,'" "Terminator 2 (Putin)," and a rich assortment of often hilarious parodies.

30 The perceived resemblance between Putin and the elf from the film *Harry Potter and the Chamber of Secrets* triggered an impassioned protest from Putin's staunch defenders, who felt offended by what they denounced as a vulgar attempt to trivialize a "world leader." In fact, a Moscow law firm reportedly planned to sue the makers of the film. See Karush (2003) and Smith (2003), who reported that in a BBC poll more than 7,000 stated that Dobby looked like Putin and the sly illustration by Aleksei Merinov in *Putinki* (2004: 70).

31 Emphasis added. For a translation of the entire song, see Leeds (2002). "My guy got into some bad deal again, got into a fight, snorted some junk. / I've had it with him, I kicked him out, and now I want someone like Putin! [Refrain:] Someone like Putin, who's really strong, someone like Putin, who *won't* drink, / Someone like Putin, who *won't* do me wrong, someone like Putin, who *won't* run off."

32 See http://www.badnameofrussia.ru (accessed January 17, 2009).

33 See http://www.badnameofrussia.ru/Putin-Vladimir.html#comments (accessed Jan 17, 2009). What motivated those who established the web site (congratulated for their "daring" [smelost'] by several bloggers) and whether the numbers genuinely reflect visitors' responses is uncertain, but there can be no doubt that such a phenomenon could not appear in print, on television, or on the radio.

34 "Davaite otpravim pesniu 'Nash durdom golosuet za Putina' na Evrovidenie,'" (2011) *ura.ru*, 20 October. Available at: http://www.ura.ru/articles/1036257210.html (accessed October 31, 2011).

35 A firm advocate of new technology, Medvedev uses the Internet extensively, but not for self-promotion.

36 Ol'ga Kryshtanovskaia noted, in the dispassionate tone that is her trademark, "Putin is accused of lacking an ideology, but ordinary citizens themselves do not have any." Quoting a politician who claimed "Putin is neither red nor blue [. . .]. He is colorless," she contended, "That is what so many Russians like about the president" (Kryshtanovskaia 2003).

37 The verses about Tolstoy run as follows, "Graf Lev Nikolaevich Tolstoi, / Pisatel' dvorianskogo klassa, / Khodil po derevne bosoi, / Ne kushal ni rybu ni miasa. / Zhena ego, Sofia Tolstaia, / Naprotiv, liubila poest'. / Ona ne khodila bosaia, / Khranila dborianskuiu chest'. / I plakal velikii pisatel' / I kushal varenyi oves, / I roman ego *Voskresenie* / Chitat' nevozmozhno bez slez. / Ego inuiu knigu pro Annu / Ty na noch' ee ne chitai. / Ot zhizni takoi, ot paskudnoi/Popala ona pod tramvai," etc. My thanks to Nadezhda Azhgikhina and the group of women journalists who recited these verses for me many years ago.

38 Conversion into dollars of all prices in rubles reflect the exchange rates at the time of the relevant works' appearance on the market.

39 Safronov's flattering portraits include those of Yuri Luzhkov, Alla Pugacheva, and Nikita Mikhalkov (who on Safronov's web site lauds the artist's Talent [*sic*]), many foreign heads of state, as well as George Clooney, Clint Eastwood, Mick Jagger, Sophia Loren, and Madonna.

40 See the various photo exhibits of Vladislav Mamyshev, known as Vlad Monroe, and the *Private Collection* of Ekateriana Rozhdestvenskaia, as well as the Polish Michał Pasich's *Pejzaż z portretami* [Landscape with Portraits] (Kraków: The Czartoryski Museum, Conspero Foundation, 2006) and the American Eve Sussman's *89 Seconds at Alcatraz* (2004), inspired by Diego Velázquez' *Las Meniñas*.

41 White and McAllister report that Putin had been called "a dark horse," "an unidentified object," and "a Malevich black square" (2003: 386).

42 *Bezlikie* would be bettered translated as "faceless" or "anonymous."

43 Translated as *The Candle of Our Life* (Blue Noses/Sinie Nosy 2006: 16), the title literally means *Go On Burning, My Life-Candle*.

44 The three main positive heroes of Russian state mythology – the poet Pushkin, Jesus Christ, and President Putin – will never let the candle of the Russian spirit go out (English text edited for accuracy and idiomatic usage).

45 Part of the first Russian Biennale, this work was included in a criminal complaint against Marat Guelmen, the gallery owner who regularly exhibits their works, as well as that of their "mentor," Oleg Kulik, who is perceived by some as the "ultimate agent provocateur" (FitzGerald 2006a, 2006b).

46 Oh, well, I don't know . . . a third presidential term? . . . well, that's a bit much, though God does love the "Trinity"/three's lucky.

47 The gallerist Marat Guelman, a former political consultant for both Yeltsin and Putin, has been attacked verbally and physically for exhibiting what may be interpreted as contemporary anti-religious and anti-establishment art.

48 The first rating nonetheless still topped Medvedev's, which had dropped to 46Percent. Those polled numbered 3,000 (Meyer and Arkhipov). The more recent rating of 51Percent was reported by the independent Levada polling center, which also listed Putin's popularity at 61Percent (Barry 2011).

Bibliography

Abdullaev, N. (2002) "Notes from Moscow: the Bronze Chekist," Transitions Online. Available at: http://www.tol.cz/look/TOLnew/tolprint.tpl?IdLanguage=1&;IdPublication=4&NrI ssue=38&NrSection=17&NrArticle=7395&ST1=body&ST_T1=letter&ST_AS1=1 &ST_max=1 (accessed April 26, 2005).

Albats, Y. (2003) "The West's favorite 'democrat,'" *Washington Post*, September 24.

Alekseev, A. (2007) "VIP-parad 2007," *Kommersant*, No. 241(3817), December 28. Available at: http://www.kommersant.ru/doc.aspx?DocsID=840552 (accessed May 5, 2008).

Arkhangelsky, A. (2007) "The artists' petition," *Russia Profile*, October 29. Available at: http://www.russiaprofile.org/page.php?pageid=Politics&;articleid=al (accessed October 30, 2007).

Aron, L. (2006) "What does Putin want?" *Commentary*, December.

Barry, E. (2008) "A spoof stars a bumbling spy, but many Russian moviegoers aren't laughing," *The New York Times*, September 21. Available at: http://www.nytimes.

com/2008/09/22/world/europe/22spies.html?n=Top?Reference/Times Topics/People/P/... (accessed October 26, 2008).

Barry, E. (2011) "Satirizing Putin with boldly poetic flair." *The New York Times*, November 18. Available at: http:www.nytimes.com/2011/11/19/world/Europe/mocking-Vladimir-putin-with-poetic-flair-in-russia.html?_r=1@emc=eta1 (accessed November 20, 2011).

BBC Monitoring. (2003a) "Russia's Putin 'no longer in control' of Yukos affair – pundit," Ekho Moskvy News Agency, October 3.

BBC Monitoring. (2003b) "Russian firm to distribute Putin's biography free at home and abroad," *NTV*, Moscow, October 7.

BBC Monitoring. (2003c). "Chocolate Putin goes on sale in Moscow shops," November 16.

Birch, D. (2002) "Putin's popularity reaches high note," *Baltimore Sun*, September 3.

Birch, D. (2003) "A return of the people's palace," *Baltimore Sun*, May 11.

Bransten, J. (2002) "From pop songs to vegetables, is a Putin personality cult emerging?" RFE/RL, Prague, September 9.

Blue Noses/Sinie Nosy. (2006) Moscow, Berlin, Milan: M. Guelman Gallery, Galerie Volker Diehl, TomasoRenoldiBracco ContemporaryArtVision bnd.

Chudakova, M. *et al.* (2007) "Otkrytoe pis'mo deiatelei kul'tury Vladimiru Putinu," Ekho Moskvy, October 26. Available at: http://echo.msk.ru/doc/622.html (accessed October 31, 2007).

Davaite (2011) "Davaite otpravim pesniu 'Nash durdom golosuet za Putina' na Evrovidenie'" *ura.ru*, October 20. Available at: http://www.ura.ru/articles/1036257210.html (accessed October 31, 2011).

Eke, S. (2008) "Putin keeps powerful Kremlin aides," *BBC News*, May 13. Available at: http://newsvote.bbc.co.uk/mpapps/pagetools/print/news.bbc.co.uk/2/hi/europe/7397809.stm (accessed November 17, 2008).

Faulconbridge, G. (2008) "Putin saves TV film crew from Siberian tiger: reports. Former KGB spy is shown striding through forest in camouflage, desert boots," *Canada.com*, September 1. Available at: http://www.canada.com/components/print.aspx?id=ce32d329-325e-44f0-9d54-fc288dfeb42@sponsor= (accessed November 19, 2008).

FitzGerald, N. (2006a) "The pranksters of the Russian art scene," *International Herald Tribune*, October 25. Available at: http://www.iht.com/articles/2006/10/23/features/bluenose.php (accessed September 1, 2008).

FitzGerald, N. (2006b) "Moscow artists strike a rich portrait vein." *International Herald Tribune*, November 27. Available at: http://www.iht.com/bin/print.php?id=3684183 (accessed March 13, 2007).

Fleishman, J. (2007a) "Painter has visions of Russian, Hollywood royalty," *Los Angeles Times*, March 31.

Fleishman, J. (2007b) "Creative expressions," *Columbia Missourian*, April 21. Available at: http://www.columbiamissourian.com/stories/2007/04/21/creative-expressions/print/ (accessed January 12, 2008).

Foucault, M. (1984) *The Foucault Reader*, ed. P. Rabinow, New York: Pantheon Books.

Frolov, V. (2008) "Undermining Medvedev: western leaders still ponder who directs Russia's foreign policy," *Russia Profile*, August 5. Available at: http://www.russiaprofile.org/page.php?pageid=International&;articlei (accessed August 14, 2008).

Glasser, S. (2003) "KGB veterans bring tradecraft to elected office," *Washington Post*, September 24.

Gokhman, M. (2002) "President ubiquitous," *Moscow News*, February 12–18.

Goldman, M. (2008) "Petrostate: Putin, power, and the new Russia," Kennan Institute Meeting Report, XXVI, 2. Washington, DC: Kennan Institute, Woodrow Wilson Center.

Isachenkov, V. (2008a) "Putin's wife writes revealing book," *Moscow AP*, September 5.
Isachenkov, V. (2008b) "Putin hosts live Q&A broadcast in Russia," *Moscow AP*, December 4.
Jack, A. (2002) "The Empire strikes back: Putin cult reaches new levels," *Financial Times*, October 12.
Karush, S. (2003) "Moviegoers agree: house elf from *Harry Potter* looks like Putin," *Moscow AP*, January 31.
Kasparov, G. (2003) "KGB state," *Wall Street Journal*, September 18.
Kollmann N.S. (2008) "The cap of Monomakh," in V.A. Kivelson and J. Neuberger, eds. *Picturing Russia: Explorations in Visual Culture*, New Haven and London: Yale University Press. 38–41.
Kots, A. (2007) "Nikita Mikhalkov – Viktoru Erofeevu: Kto tebe skazal, chto ia ratuiu za kul't lichnosti?" *Komsomol'skaia pravda*, October 27. Available at: http://www.kp.ru/daily/23992/77033/print (accessed October 31, 2007).
Kovalyova, A. (2009) "Will Internet kill the television star?" *Russia Profile*, May 28. Available at: http://www.russiaprofile.org/page.php?pageid=Culture+%26+Living&;articleid=a1243532864&print=yes (accessed June 10, 2009).
Kryshtanovskaia, O. (2003) "Mirror of the nation: what the latest polls reveal about President Putin," *Vedomosti*, September 30.
Latynina, Y. (2003) "St. Pete's criminal-business-political elite," *Moscow Times*, June 4 .
Lavelle, P. (2003) "Putin's popularity and anti-politics," *Pravda.ru*, September 4. Available at: http://english.pravda.ru/mailbox/22/99/391/10831_Putin.html (accessed December 12, 2009).
Leeds, L. (2002) "Pop song 'Just Like Putin,'" September 19. Available at: http://www.lLeeds@post.com (accessed September 25, 2002).
Let's Learn, (2008) "Let's learn judo with Vladimir Putin." *The Independent*, October 8. Available at: http://www.independent.co.uk/news/world/europe/lets-learn-judo-with-vladimir-putin-954578.html (accessed May 2, 2011).
LeVine, S. (2008) *Putin's Labyrinth: Spies, Murder, and the Dark Heart of the New Russia*, New York: Random House.
Levy, C.J. (2008a) "Kremlin rules: it isn't magic: Putin opponents vanish from TV," *The New York Times*, June 3. Available at: http://www.nytimes.com/2008/06/03/world/europe/03russia.html?ei= (accessed June 3, 2008).
Levy, C.J. (2008b) "Kremlin rules: nationalism of Putin's era veils sins of Stalin's," *The New York Times*, November 27. Available at: http://www.nytimes.com/2008/11/27/world/europe/27archives.html?_r=1&;emc=et a1&pag (accessed November 27, 2008).
MacKinnon, M. (2002) "A 'personality cult' bedevils wary Putin," *The Globe and Mail*, September 27.
Meyer, H. and I. Arkhipov. (2011) "Putin sets stage for 2012 comeback as leader of Popular Front." *Bloomberg Businessweek*, June 28. Available at: http://www.businessweek.com/news/2011-05=08/putin-sets-stage-for-2012-comeback-as-leader-of-popular-front.html (accessed June 28, 2011).
Myers, S.L. (2007) "Youth groups created by Kremlin serve Putin's cause," *The New York Times*, July 8.
"Nikas Safronov," (2008) *peoples.ru*. Available at: http://www.peoples.ru/art/painter/safronov/index.html (accessed May 3, 2008).
O'Flynn, K. (2002) "Picking the perfect present for Putin," *The Moscow Times*, October 7.
O'Flynn, K. (2009) "Putin, the artist?" *The St. Petersburg Times*, January 16. Available at: http://www.sptimes.ru/index.php?action_id=100&;story_id=28028 (accessed January 16, 2009).

Osipovich, A. (2004) "Looks like celebrity," *The Moscow Times*, March 12. Available at: http://context.themoscowtimes.com/print.php?aid=131187 (accessed February 12, 2005).

Owen, R. (2001) "President becomes a calendar pin-up," *The Times*, December 5.

"Pis'mo Rossiiskoi akademii khudozhestv Vladimiru Putinu," (2007) *Rossiiskaia gazeta*, October 16. Available at: http://www.rg.ru/2007/10/16/pismo.html (accessed October 31, 2007).

Poiushchie, undated"'Poiushchie vmeste': nash udel–bytovukha," (Undated) *Ezhenedel'nik Sobesednik*. Available at: http://www.sobsednik.ru/weekly/147/issue/4032.phtml (accessed April 3, 2007).

Putinki: Kratkii sbornik izrechenii prezidenta (pervyi srok), (2004) Moscow: OOO "Ekho Buk" Illustrations by Aleksei Merinov.

"Putin's last love: foreign actress makes sensational confession," (2003) July 31. Available at: http://www.pravda.ru (accessed August 4, 2003).

Reut, A. (2002) "Putin on a cake, on a carpet, in a book," *Gazeta*, October 7. Available at: http://www.gzt.ru/print.gzt?rubric=english&;id=18050000000002986 (accessed August 7, 2004).

Rojek, C. (2001) *Celebrity*, London: Reaktion Books.

Roth, A. (2011) "Summoned to the Front," *Russia Profile*, June 29. Available at http://russiaprofile.org/politics/39737.html (accessed June 29, 2011).

Rozhin, A. (ed.) (2000) *Contemporary Russian Artists*, [ed. of English text, G. Tchemakova]. Moscow: Mikhail Afanasyev & Helen Lavrinenko. 10–19.

"Russia: Putin romance rumors keep public riveted," (2008) *Radio Free Europe/Radio Liberty*, April 18. Available at: http://www/rferl.org/featuresarticleprint/2008/04/1493ebc1-179c-4e7 (accessed June 16, 2008).

"Russian Prime Minister Vladimir Putin's sketch sells for $1.15 million at auction," (2009) *artdaily.org*, February 21. Available at: http://www.artdaily.org/section/news/index.asp?int_sec=2&;int_new=28492&b=ka zimir (accessed February 21, 2009).

"Russian textile mill making Putin tapestries," (2003) *TVS (Moscow)*, reported by BBC Monitoring, June 8.

Shevtsova, L. (2007) *Russia Lost in Transition: The Yeltsin and Putin Legacies*. Washington, DC: Carnegie Endowment for International Peace.

Shchuplov, A. (2002) "Put a sock in it. Vladimir Vladimirovich Putin has become a folk art hero," *Rossiiskaia gazeta*, October 11.

Sidlin, M. (2001) "Decorate a room with Putin's portrait," *Nezavisimaia gazeta*, December 4.

"Singing together: they want one like Putin," (2002) December 12. Available at: http://www.pravda.ru (accessed January 4, 2003).

Smith, L. (2003) "Spell of trouble for Dobby," *The Evening Standard*, January 28. Available at: http://www.thisislondon.com/news/articles/3113851?source=Event (accessed January 28, 2003).

Stewart, W. (2009) "The portrait of Vladimir Putin as a woman which got artists arrested by secret service," *The Daily Mail*, June 17. Available at: http://www.dailymail.co.uk/news/worldnews/article-1193430/Artist-arrested-secret-service-portraying-Vladimir-Putin-woman.html (accessed November 11, 2009).

"Tainstvennaia pop-gruppa poet osanny Putinu," (2002) translation from *Daily Telegraph*, August 28. Available at: http://Cremlin.ru/comments/00068.html (accessed January 4, 2003).

"The Putin cult: political techno, fan clubs, and the Internet," (2007) *Perspectives on the New Russia*, July 7. Available at: http://putinwatcher.blogspot.com/2007/07/punti-cult-political-techno-fan-clubs.html (accessed July 12, 2008).

Titova, I. (2009) "Novice painter Putin fetches $1.1 million for first work," *The St. Petersburg Times*, January 20. Available at: http://www.sptimes.ru/index.php?action_id=2&;story_ie=28042 (accessed November 1, 2009).

Toomey, C. (2003) "A president's private passions: revealing portraits of Vladimir Putin," *The Sunday Times*, April 6.

Traynor, I. (2001) "Russia starts to make a legend," *MSNBC.com*, March 11.

Volonikhin, I. (2002) "Russian TV shows Ingush village that named its main street after Putin," *TVS (Moscow)*, reported by BBC Monitoring, October 10.

Walker, S. (2008) "Let's learn judo with Vladimir Putin," *The Independent*, October 8. Available at: http://license.copyright.net/user/viewFreeUse.act?fuid=MjAxMDA0Mg%3D%3d (accessed November 2, 2008).

Walsh, N.P. (2002a) "Putin turns 007 in a new thriller novel," *The Observer*, July14.

Walsh, N.P. (2002b) "Monica's back – and this time she's stalking the Kremlin," *The Guardian*, September 18.

Walsh, N.P. (2002c) "Birthday gift for Putin casts autocratic shadow," *The Observer*, October 6.

Walsh, N.P. (2004) "Putin angry at history book slur," *The Guardian*, January 15.

White, G.L. (2003) "The secret of Putin's success," *The Wall Street Journal*, December 5.

White, S. and McAllister, I. (2003) "Putin and his supporters," *Europe-Asia Studies*, 55, May 3: 383–399.

Wines, M. (2003) "Putin, Dobby and the axis of weirdness," *The New York Times*, February 2.

2 A personality cult for the postmodern age

Reading Vladimir Putin's public persona

Julie A. Cassiday and Emily D. Johnson

Vladimir Putin has distinguished himself from leaders of the Russian state of the past 25 years in a number of noteworthy ways. Since Boris Yeltsin's resignation elevated him to the post of acting president on December 31, 1999, Putin has dramatically reshaped Russia's political culture, economy, and social institutions. The first strong national leader to emerge out of the chaos of the immediate post-Soviet period, he has inspired expressions of adulation whose likes Russia has not seen since the Stalin era. Soon after his victory in the presidential elections of March 2000, portraits of Putin appeared for sale in Russian bookstores, and serious Russian artists, such as Timur Kozyrev, Andrei Logvin, and Dmitrii Vrubel began to use the president's face in their work. For example, in a 2002 painting titled *Black Square*, Vrubel' juxtaposes Kazimir Malevich's landmark 1915 canvas with the president's penetrating gaze (Figure 2.1). Other tributes to Putin include a 2001 calendar depicting *The President's Twelve Moods* by Vrubel' and Viktoriia Timofeeva, and a 2004 book titled *Fairytales About Our President*, which renders Putin and his exploits as a series of *lubki* (Kravtsova and Matveev 2002; Miachin *et al.* 2004).[1] In a way that cannot help but remind students of Soviet history and earlier cults of personality, Putin's likeness and biography also quickly found their way into the Russian school curriculum and the lives of Russia's children. Putin's portrait appeared on the walls of primary schools, and textbook authors drafted chapters detailing the new President's life story. In 2006, as part of the contest "Children Draw Putin," which culminated in an exhibition of the winning pictures in Moscow, Russian children themselves had the chance to join the ranks of those propagating the President's image (Konradova 2006). By summer 2007, as journalist Susan Glasser noted, Putin's image was everywhere in Russia: one bookstore in Moscow boasted 28 different versions of the president's likeness (Glasser 2003: A3).[2]

Putin's canonization coincided with staggeringly high approval ratings. Public opinion polls conducted during his first term in office indicate that his approval rating between 2000 and 2004 remained consistently between 70 and 80 percent (White and McAllister 2003: 386; Sil and Chen 2004: 350). After his two terms in office ended in May 2008, a stunning 86 percent of Russians polled expressed approval of Putin.[3] In late 2007, a movement to make Putin Russia's "national leader" received extensive press coverage. An April 2008 poll found that 35 percent

Figure 2.1 Dmitrii Vrubel' and Viktoriia Timofeeva, *Black Square* (2002).

Source: © 2012 Artists Rights Society (ARS), New York/VG Bild-Kunst, Bonn.

of those asked viewed the idea of such a "national leader" either "somewhat positively" or "completely positively," while 27 percent of those questioned thought Putin would remain Russia's real leader even after stepping down from the presidency (Whitmore 2007).[4] The 2008 election, which installed Putin's hand-picked successor, Dmitrii Medvedev, as president of the Russian Federation and moved Putin to the post of prime minister, in many respects realized this vision. Instead of replacing Putin, Medvedev emerged as his satellite: national news broadcasts gave the two leaders essentially equal coverage, and portraits often depicted Putin and Medvedev side by side (Mareu 2008).[5] Putin's announcement in September 2011 that he would run for president again in 2012, preempting his successor, made Medvedev's subsidiary status in the tandem entirely self-evident. Although, since 2009, polls have shown a gradual decline in Putin's popularity in the wake of the global economic crisis and increasingly widespread concerns about the erosion of democracy in Russia, he still outpolls other Russian political figures, including Medvedev, by a significant margin (Osborn 2009; Tsvetkova 2011).[6]

During the past decade, the Kremlin has systematically expanded its control of the country's mass media, and especially of television, to propagate a public image of Putin as a strong, successful leader. As *The New York Times'* Clifford

Levy reported, Putin's political opponents, who only a few years earlier regularly appeared on television, vanished as the campaign preceding the 2008 elections gained momentum. One political analyst critical of Putin found himself digitally erased from a talk show, while actors who "cracked a few mild jokes about Mr. Putin and Mr. Medvedev at Russia's equivalent of the Academy Awards [. . .] were expunged from the telecast" (Levy 2008). Such strong-arm measures have led many commentators to label the current Russian government as either wholly authoritarian or as a "hybrid regime," which allows quasi-oppositional parties and movements to exist but at the same time, through a variety of repressive measures, limits their ability to alter the status quo (Colton and Hale 2009; March 2009). These terms successfully evoke many of the most obvious limitations of the current Russian political system. Yet, by focusing attention on instances in which the Putin regime seems to have reverted to Soviet-style strategies for maintaining social control, they also encourage an exaggerated view of the role that repressive measures and censorship have played in Russia since Yeltsin relinquished power.[7] Restrictions on the press and carefully orchestrated efforts to undercut potential rivals may have helped to maintain Putin's high approval numbers and positive image throughout the 2000s, but, in and of themselves, they do not explain his initial popularity or, for that matter, the startling profusion of grotesquely varied verbal and visual homage that Putin's person has inspired.

A virtual unknown when he first came to power in 1999, Putin soon enjoyed such widespread adoration that, by early 2000 – that is, before he had even won his first election – journalists had begun talking about his "cult of personality."[8] This clearly tendentious phrase draws a broad comparison between the Soviet era and contemporary Russia, suggesting that Putin's popularity serves ends similar to those of Soviet leader cults, particularly the cult of Stalin. Such a parallel might seem to make sense in light of the fact that even as Putin's approval ratings soared, polls showed widespread dissatisfaction with the government he headed (Sil and Chen 2004: 350–351). As scholars have shown, Soviet-style leader cults arose under conditions of economic crisis, social discord, weak support for official ideology, and widespread cynicism about the state's ability to fulfill its promises (Rees 2004: 4). These cults sought to transform a once vanguard movement into a governing regime by reinforcing "symbolic or affective attachment" to the country's leaders at a time when the state could not achieve legitimacy through its policies or accomplishments (Rees 2004: 4). Much like the Stalin cult that preceded it, a Putin cult would seem to offer "psychological and emotional reassurance, a focus of stability and unity, in a world of uncertainties," justifying a regime whose claims to increasing stability and democracy are contradicted by many of its actions (Rees 2004: 13).

However, such sweeping comparisons between cults of personality past and present break down as soon as we move beyond the state controlled media and examine the full range of Putin images and paraphernalia that have flooded Russia since 2000. The image of Putin projected on Russian television news programming – the great, all-knowing leader capable of correcting the route of a planned pipeline in front of a room of embarrassed oil executives, much as Stalin tirelessly edited battle plans in Soviet propaganda – contrasts sharply and exists in constant dialogue with the weirdly varied stream of Putin-associated objects, images, and narratives in forums over which the Russian state exerts less perfect control, such as the Internet, the capitalist marketplace, and the public square (Kramer 2009). Unlike the party-controlled personality cults of the Soviet past, which were both monolithic and static, Putin mania is inherently polysemantic, highly mobile, and easily individualized. Defined by the two most important cultural practices of the post-Soviet era – nostalgia and consumption – it offers Russians, many of whom felt deprived of both cultural and individual identity during the chaotic 1990s, the opportunity to articulate new modes of subjectivity that although they seem to pay homage to a vanished past, also reflect contemporary social, political, and communicative reality.

"There's already a cult . . . But there's no personality . . ."

Putin's rapid rise from obscurity to the Russian presidency meant that he was virtually unencumbered by a public image when he first entered the media limelight in 1999. Although key biographical facts, such as his work in the KGB or early political career in St. Petersburg under mayor Anatolii Sobchak, were available and perhaps should have influenced the public's and media's perceptions of Putin, he was repeatedly described during his first term as having "a nebulous, all-embracing image" (White and McAllister 2003: 385). Pollster Iurii Levada, for instance, described the new president as "a mirror in which everyone, Communist or democrat, sees what he wants to see and what he hopes for" (quoted in White and McAllister 2003: 385). In other words, Putin initially resembled a *tabula rasa*, on which politicians, journalists, and citizens alike could inscribe the qualities deemed lacking in past rulers of the Russian state.[9]

Yet, by 2004, when Putin won the landslide victory that led to his second term in office, his image had acquired several identifiable traits. The president's attributes in both visual and textual media typically include his sobriety, intelligence, competence, vigorous physical and psychological health, and, above all, manliness.[10] Putin's prowess in the judo ring, his boldness on the alpine skiing slope, and his unequivocally masculine physique recur constantly in representations of the Russian president. The Kremlin itself has cultivated this manly image in human interest stories released about Putin. In August 2007, the Kremlin's official website featured a photograph of Putin fishing – topless – during a trip to the Republic of Tuva (Figure 2.2). Comparable images are extremely rare. Prior to this instance, photographs showing a country's leading political figure naked from the waist up had appeared in the media on only two occasions: in 1937, Italy's fascist government published a photo of a shirtless Mussolini (Figure 2.3); in 1966, the Chinese press released pictures showing Mao swimming in the Yangtze River as part of a campaign to show that the Chairman remained vigorous and capable of leading China.[11] The Kremlin's decision to distribute the topless Putin photograph spawned a media sensation, inspiring the newspaper *Komsomol'skaia pravda* to publish a comparable image alongside exercises

Figure 2.2 Mussolini as skier at Terminillo in 1937.

Source: Used by permission of the Mary Evans Picture Library.

promising to give readers abdominal muscles like Putin's (associated Press 2007; Danilova 2007). Similarly, in September 2008, Russian television was flooded with images of Putin, "striding through the forest in camouflage and desert boots," immediately after rescuing a television crew from a Siberian tiger by shooting the endangered animal with a tranquilizer gun.[12] The following October, an instructional book with accompanying DVD titled *Let's Learn Judo with Vladimir Putin* appeared for sale throughout Russia (Schwirtz 2008; Putin *et al.* 2009).

If the Kremlin has championed the image of Putin as sportsman, others have taken the President's manly characteristics in a bolder direction. For example, Aleksandr Ol'bik's (2002) adventure novel *President* portrays Putin as the ultimate commander-in-chief, willing not only to give military orders, but also to carry them out himself if need be (see Chapter 6 by Andrei Rogatchevski). The brief synopsis on the inside cover describes the book's plot:

> It's the hot summer of 2001 [. . .]
> Events develop swiftly and completely unexpectedly.
> The President decides to head out for Chechnia with a *spetsnaz* squad to destroy the rebels' lair [. . .] He does this and is the only one left alive.
>
> (Ol'bik 2002: 4)

Figure 2.3 A topless Putin fishing on the upper Enisei river in the Republic of Tuva in 2007.

Source: The Kremlin's website at http://archive.kremlin.ru/events/photos/2007/08/140910.shtml.

President paints Putin as a Russian Rambo whose physical prowess, like that of Sylvester Stallone's famous character, primarily finds expression on the battlefield rather than in the bedroom. As the following joke illustrates, other less circumspect authors have chosen to emphasize the erotic potential of Putin's manliness:

A political riddle.
Yeltsin's isn't growing,
Ziuganov's is holding up,
Zhirinovsky's is falling,
Iavlinsky's is wavering,
Luzhkov's is in rigor,

Fedorov's is immobile,
Gorbachev's is really small,
Brintsalov doesn't have one at all,
And Putin's is rising.
What is it? APPROVAL RATING!

(Pereviazkin 2001: 7)[13]

In contrast to Yeltsin and the flabby, flaccid leaders of the late Soviet era, Putin has a political identity and public image characterized by masculine sexual potency, a point driven home in the girl group Singing Together's 2002 pop song, "Someone like Putin" (see Chapter 1 by Helena Goscilo). Although "Someone like Putin" may not have made it to the top of the charts, it did make it into several thousand Chinese-manufactured stuffed bunnies, which were reputedly "selling like hot cakes in the Urals city of Yekaterinburg" in early 2004 (AFP 2004). In short, the initially blank slate of Putin's personality was inscribed in the course of his 8 years in office with a highly sanitized version of Russian machismo: the President's image lays claim to sexual, political, and physical prowess, but repudiates vices traditionally associated with masculinity in Russian culture, including drunkenness, smoking, and inconsiderateness.

As a result, Putin's popularity among Russian women has been particularly high, with incidents of Putin hysteria reported occasionally in the media. One article about the President's female fans describes a woman who "has a picture of Putin on her desk at work and carries a keychain with his image in her pocket at all times" and goes on to note, "Rumor has it that most women get stuck to their TV sets when Mr. Putin is on and that they often tell their husbands 'to be more like Putin.'"[14] Other reports have identified Russian women who regard Putin as a son or, as in the case of the elderly Vera Putina from the Republic of Georgia, actually claim to be the President's biological mother (Smits 2003).[15] In 2010, a group of coeds from Moscow State University went one step further: they expressed their affection for Putin by posing in lingerie and high heels for a calendar commemorating his fifty-eighth birthday (Figure 2.4) (Rodina 2010). At the other end of the political spectrum, members of a Ukrainian feminist organization declared their opposition to Russian imperialism in strikingly sexual terms by baring their chests to protest an October 2010 visit by Putin to Kyiv (Figure 2.5) (Motyl 2010). As these incidents show, Putin's carefully crafted manly persona elicits passionate, sexualized reactions from both women who love him and from those who despise him.

If Putin portraits and key chains satisfy fans' appetite for portable versions of the president's public image, the made-for-DVD movie *This Kiss is off the Record* appealed to their voyeuristic impulses by offering a glimpse of Liudmila and Vladimir Putin's private life (Zhulina 2008). Although the film replaces the president's actual surname with his KGB pseudonym, Platov, it depicts key moments in the Putin's married life, creating the impression that Russia's political future depends on the marital stability of its first couple (Kishkovsky 2008).[16] The film's

Figure 2.4 Miss February from the calendar "Vladimir Vladimirovich, my vas liubim! Happy Birthday, Mr. Putin! Kalendar' na 2011-i god" (Moscow: Fakultet, 2011).

Source: Used by permission of Vladimir Tabak.

Figure 2.5 Members of the Ukrainian organization Femen protesting Putin's visit to Kyiv in October 2010.

Source: Used by permission of Sergei Svetlitskii.

producers claim to have adapted the American genre of behind-the-scenes political biography for Russian viewers; however, *This Kiss is off the Record* looks more like a Russian "chick flick" designed to feed the fantasies of Putin's female admirers. Putin himself seems boundlessly confident in his own masculine charisma and ability to play the part of the heartthrob and perhaps, for this very reason, manages to pull off public appearances that could only end in embarrassment for a less self-assured politician. For instance, at a 2011 fundraiser in St. Petersburg, Putin charmed an audience of high-profile Hollywood celebrities when he appeared on stage with a jazz band and a couple of girl back-up singers to croon a cover version the American pop standard "Blueberry Hill," a song made famous by Fats Domino, Elvis Presley, and Ricky Nelson. Neither Putin's thickly accented English nor his obviously limited facility as a piano player made the slightest impression on anyone: Goldie Hawn, Kurt Russell, Kevin Costner, and Sharon Stone all smiled with delight, and, clapping, sang along (Morgan 2010).

Luckily, the Putin craze incorporates humor as well as straight, sycophantic displays. Since Putin first assumed the post of president, he has inspired a significant number of jokes. A short printed collection appeared as early as 2001, and several websites chronicle the ever-growing corpus of such material (Pereviazkin 2001).[17] Interestingly, even Putin humor is rarely unambiguously derogatory. Unlike earlier jokes about Khrushchev, Brezhnev, and Yeltsin, which generally mock the Party leaders' idiocy, incompetence, and/or drunkenness, Putin *anekdoty* often emphasize their subject's "positive qualities," such as his bravery, boldness, or ingenuity, if only in a backhanded way.[18] One popular meta-joke that combines two earlier humorous traditions – comic stories about the fearless spy Shtirlitz and those devoted to the precocious adolescent Vovochka – illustrates this trend:

> Yet one more reason why Putin is our president.
> In his personality two favorite characters from the world of jokes are merged – Shtirlitz and Vovochka.
>
> (Pereviazkin 2001: 16)[19]

In addition to demonstrating the fundamentally flattering tone of most Putin jokes, this anecdote again hints at the nebulousness of Putin's personality. Even after being invested with sobriety, strength, and sex appeal, Putin's image has the curious ability to absorb multiple personae. A parodic Putin fan club website, putinfans.narod.ru, takes this sponge-like quality to its absurd extreme. In addition to suggesting that St. Petersburg be renamed St. Putinsburg, putinfans.narod.ru proposes replacing the head of Vladimir Il'ich with that of Vladimir Vladimirovich on all the country's remaining Lenin monuments, declaring Putin tsar' of Russia, making *Putinoslavie* the country's official religion and cloning Putin to improve the planet's genetic stock until "[t]he year 2025, [when] the ideal society will be created, where 99.9% of the population will be Putins."[20] Not only does Putin seem to be a Russian everyman, but everyone also has the potential to become a Putin.

Appropriately, given the nebulousness of Putin's public image, in many literary works in which the Russian leader theoretically figures, he himself plays a secondary role: as a physical presence, he is accorded what amounts to a cameo. Works about Putin often focus on the strivings and travails of presidential observers or admirers; the reader glimpses the center of power only briefly, and then from such a limited perspective that the President's nature, actions, and accomplishments remain largely unknowable. For example, in *Connie's Stories*, the infamous English-language children's primer describing life from the perspective of the presidential dog, the identity of the black Labrador's eternally busy owner becomes clear only on the last page (Borisova 2004). In Viktor Teterin's 2005 satiric play, *Putin.doc*, with the exception of a final scene, the President also remains an off-stage presence, whose will is made manifest only in letters paraphrased by one of the two central characters, dueling little-men bureaucrats who compete to show who loves the great leader more (Teterin 2005).[21]

Perhaps, because there is so little real Putin-content in the overwhelming majority of Putin products, the image and name of the Russian leader were employed with startling freedom in Russia during the 2000s, appearing even on consumer goods that seem too prosaic to accord with the grandeur of presidential office and in visual contexts that might reasonably be deemed feminizing. For instance, in 2004, a St. Petersburg company named Prosperiti began marketing dental flossers in packets with the President's portrait emblazoned on the front, as well as a version of "the same product available under the portrait of Koni, [....] accompanied by the slogan 'Our Koni Is a Mother Hero'" (Lipman 2004). In 2007, a Putin t-shirt went on sale for some $600 in the boutique of Moscow fashion designer Denis Simachev, featuring a portrait of the smiling president surrounded by an appealingly girly floral garland (Singer 2007). Putin himself has contributed to this type of gender-bending Putiniana: in early 2009, he gave "his people a glimpse of his sensitive side" by providing a pastel drawing based on Nikolai Gogol's story "The Night Before Christmas" [*Noch' pered rozhdestvom*] to a charity auction, where it sold for well over $1 million (R37,000,000), the most, journalists covering the event trumpeted, ever paid for a painting in Russia (Blomfield 2009; Harding 2009). In spite of Putin's oversized signature across the top of the canvas, at least one professional artist questioned the painting's provenance, stating, "It looks as if it was painted by a sentimental woman. It is too sweet; you can feel it in the brushwork and the palette. The core theme is feminine too" (quoted in Blomfield 2009). Such incongruous examples of Putiniana call to mind the caption of a 2004 political cartoon by Aleksei Merinov, "There's already a cult . . . But there's no personality . . ." (Merinov 2004: 116). If even the clichéd, sanitized masculinity that characterizes representations of Russia's second president can at times disappear, then what exactly holds together Putin's persona?

Cults of personality past and present

The phrase "cult of personality" (*kul't lichnosti*) carries heavy negative connotations. Strongly associated with the famous secret speech in which Nikita

Khrushchev denounced the excesses of Stalinism at the Twentieth Congress of the Communist Party of the Soviet Union in 1956 and with the de-Stalinization campaigns of the 1950s and 1960s, it damns any cultural phenomenon to which it is applied by associating it with some of the most notorious human rights abuses of the last century. Its use in both Russian and Western media to describe expressions of affection for Putin suggests that current cultural trends represent little more than a resurgence of old totalitarian patterns of social organization, and that today's Putin mania mirrors the cult of Stalin in both its structure and social function.[22] However, by many measures, the Putin phenomenon differs markedly from its Soviet-era precursors, including, most importantly, the veneration of Stalin as a great leader.

Stalin's cult was "a deliberately constructed and managed mechanism," premised on "the closure of the public sphere" and designed to elicit not only enthusiasm, but also fear from the country's populace (Rees 2004: 4). Although, as scholars such as Sarah Davies and Benno Ennker have noted, initiative from below, including uncoached toadying, certainly played a role in the development of this cultural structure, even unsolicited contributions to the cult were so carefully regulated, edited, and packaged before they were allowed to circulate on the larger cultural stage that they no longer qualified as spontaneous (Davies 2004: 29–30; Ennker 2004: 95–96). Soviet publications sifted through the reader letters they received and selected choice examples for publication; gifts sent in to party leaders by groups of ordinary Soviet citizens got media attention only if the powers-that-be deemed them deserving of such consideration; displays judged clumsy or seemingly in conflict with the leader's carefully managed official image were quickly quashed. As the work of Evgeny Dobrenko, Jochen Hellbeck, and Thomas Lahusen has demonstrated, a surprisingly large portion of the Soviet populace, representing all sectors of society, internalized the constraints of Stalinist subjectivity, which penetrated all levels of public and private life (Hellbeck 2006; Lahusen 1997; Dobrenko 1997, 2001). Consequently, the Stalin cult appeared monolithic in structure and tone and functioned as a single monologic speech act, even though multiple speakers participated in its creation.

In the post-Stalin era, as measures of social control grew less pronounced, Soviet citizens began to speak about their political leaders with greater freedom. Political jokes no longer regularly led to labor camp sentences; in popular humor, the great official cults were sometimes savagely satirized. For example, a series of jokes popular throughout the 1970s and 1980s lists products supposedly produced for the 100th anniversary of Lenin's birth in 1970: a three-person bed, marketed under the name "Lenin is with us" (*Lenin s nami*), the bath soap "Through Lenin sites" (*po Leninskim mestam*), the body powder "Ashes of Il'ich" (*prakh Il'icha*), and the cotton batting "Lenin days" (*Leninskie dni*).[23] As Alexei Yurchak notes in his study of late Soviet discourse, unofficial and official speech existed in this period in separate social spheres: most Soviet citizens navigated between the two, choosing which rules to follow based on the context in which they found themselves. They could masterfully wield officialese at Komsomol meetings and yet, in other situations, tell jokes about the system or organize dances featuring the officially suspect music of Western rock bands (Yurchak 2006: 220, 273–275). In making these shifts, Yurchak explains, individuals did not perceive themselves as hypocrites or as secret oppositionists: they saw authoritative discourse as somehow separate from normal everyday life, as not requiring interpretation at the level of constative meanings as either true or false (Yurchak 2006: 287–288). In essence, they distinguished between the rigid rules and demands of the Soviet order and a social order constituted outside its control.

The Putin phenomenon differs from both the Stalin cult and the great leader cults of the late Soviet era in several respects. Most importantly, it does not appear to exist primarily as a result of official coercion. Although, under Putin, the Russian state has progressively restricted freedom of the press, rights of assembly, and the prerogatives of nongovernmental organizations, it does not yet possess the kind of control over the lives of individual citizens that typified late Soviet society, let alone the high Stalin era. As the digital deletion of the President's critics from television broadcasts suggests, Putin's public relations machine has revived some practices associated with Soviet-era cults of personality, but so far the Kremlin has little power to compel participation in a Putin cult or to control the way in which ordinary citizens use the President's words and likeness. For the most part, people attend pro-Putin rallies and buy Putin portraits because they see some profit in it for themselves or because they want to, not because such actions represent a prerequisite for college enrollment or avoiding punitive assignments at work. In addition, the Putin craze is not monolithic: it incorporates heterogeneous material, including texts, images, and consumer objects that might reasonably be deemed satiric in their intent, such as Putin portraits in chocolate and the calendar featuring the 12 moods of the President. Consequently, Putin mania sometimes reads as a paradoxical fusion of the authoritative discourse that surrounded the person of the great leader in the late Soviet period and its satiric reflection, the send-ups of cultic ritual that flourished in popular humor. If we accept Yurchak's argument that following Stalin's death, Soviet culture underwent a profound transformation whereby "the replication of fixed and normalized forms of [authoritative] discourse became an end in itself, and the constative meanings of these discursive forms became increasingly unimportant," then we can see the Putin phenomenon as a continuation of this "performative shift" rather than as a reversion to earlier Stalinist cultural patterns, as the resurgence of the phrase "cult of personality" usually implies (Yurchak 2006: 26).

Putin mania defies any clear distinction between official and unofficial speech, bringing these realms together in a sometimes baffling amalgam. Styles of discourse that remained largely segregated from each other until the very end of the Soviet period have merged to give rise to a single conversation that is invariably hard to read. Folded into a larger public dialogue on political leadership, the satiric impulses that drove Soviet citizens to repeat jokes about great socialist leaders and their ritual veneration have muted considerably: even the weirdest expressions of enthusiasm for Russia's second president, objects that, like the flossers mentioned earlier, resemble the punch line of the old jokes about the consumer goods produced in connection with the Lenin jubilee, have lost the bite of an external critique. At the same time, such absurdist elements make it difficult to take the Putin phenomenon completely seriously: it is hard to see a singing bunny as an example of sincere leader worship or, for that matter, as a harbinger of totalitarianism. The irreverence of much of the Putiniana that circulates in Russia makes the possibility of a new leader cult less frightening.

The Putin phenomenon also accords ordinary Russian citizens a far greater degree of creative agency than did earlier Soviet leader cults. Enthusiastic amateurs, independent artisans, and small-scale producers churn out new Putin texts and artifacts on a daily basis. Although many may aim to please the powers-that-be and some may even see their work highlighted some day on a government-controlled news broadcast or website, the overwhelming majority operate outside any obvious system of state control. Moreover, because so many Putin objects and texts are ambiguous in tone, consumers, as well as creators of cultic images and paraphernalia, play a role that is arguably creative: each individual must decide how to understand and engage with the Putin craze as a whole and with specific examples of Putiniana. Russians nod approvingly or laugh when they hear rock anthems praising Putin's leadership ability; they buy official portraits to hang in a traditional place of honor in their offices or to display in surroundings that suggest a satiric attitude toward Russia's favorite political demiurge. Individual creators and consumers partake of Putiniana with relative freedom in part because of the mechanisms employed in its dissemination. The capitalist marketplace and the Internet, two forums through which Putin images and artifacts frequently find audiences, are notoriously resistant to central control, unlike parade grounds, government-sponsored creative unions, official funerals, and state museums. Modern methods of communication, private enterprise, and the emergence of a true consumer culture have made the kind of monolithic leader cult that existed in the Soviet Union unsustainable in contemporary Russia.[24]

Putin and nostalgia

The adaptability of the President's image suggests that the Putin phenomenon is about something other than the actual politician Vladimir Putin. The Putin cult, if indeed we can call it such, flourishes in contemporary Russia not because of what it purports to depict – the strong, national leader whom many Russians, beginning in the early 1990s, seem to have felt they needed – but rather because of the forms of communication and the symbolic practices it enables. While the Kremlin might indeed be striving to replicate certain features of Soviet-era personality cults in the state controlled media, the Putiniana proliferating in other spheres of post-Soviet culture appears neither to replicate nor to aim to reproduce earlier leader cults. Rather, the Putin phenomenon constitutes part of a larger cultural trend of stylized expressions of nostalgia for the Soviet past that have flourished in Russia since the Soviet Union's demise.

Scholars generally understand post-Soviet nostalgia as something more than a simple longing for the return of the Soviet past (Boym 2001; Ivanova 1997;

Nadkarni and Shevchenko 2004; Oushakine 2007; Sabonis-Chafee 1999). Nostalgia "emphasizes the irretrievability of the past as the very condition of desire," since it "is never longing for a specific past as much as it is longing for longing itself, made all the safer by the fact that the object of that desire is deemed irrevocably lost" (Nadkarni and Shevchenko 2004: 491). As Maya Nadkarni and Olga Shevchenko demonstrate, post-socialist nostalgia encompasses a wide variety of ambiguous practices, each of which may

> signify a number of different things: a discomfort with the new expressed in a wistful longing for the old sociality; or, on the contrary, skillfulness at consuming the past with "proper" ironic distance by spinning nostalgic images in the new capitalist ways; or even the spirit of *stiob* – sarcastic political humor under the previous regime.
>
> (Nadkarni and Shevchenko 2004: 505)

The sole feature uniting the myriad forms of nostalgia in post-Soviet Russia appears to be its cause, namely, the acute dislocation that has characterized Russians' lives since the collapse of the Soviet Union. Borrowing from Pierre Bourdieu, Nadkarni, and Shevchenko label this disorientation a "*hysteresis of habitus*," the unsettling lack of fit between one's internalized dispositions and the new "rules of the game," while Serguei Oushakine describes the problem as one of "post-Soviet aphasia," a "regression to symbolic forms of the previous historical period that has been caused by society's disintegrated ability to find proper verbal signifiers for the signified of the new socio-political regime" (Nadkarni and Shevchenko 2004: 509; Oushakine 2000a: 994). Both explanations shed light on the polysemy of contemporary Putin mania, as well as on its recycling of the vocabulary, images, and practices of Soviet cults of personality.

Like the portraits featuring contemporary Russian celebrities posed and costumed to mimic the subjects of famous paintings, discussed by Oushakine in a 2007 article, the Putin phenomenon can be read as a nostalgic practice that exploits the forms of a familiar symbolic structure without necessarily conveying either the content or the context of the original (Oushakine 2007: 481). Oushakine suggests that this kind of nostalgic stylization represents a response to "The fragmentation of the relatively homogenized field of Soviet cultural production," which left Russians without "an effective symbolic framework" for integrating "the Soviet and post-Soviet parts of [their] biography" (Oushakine 2007: 481–482). Without the signs or language to express their experiences as post-Soviet citizens, Russians turned the familiar forms of earlier Soviet leader cults into "sites of complex strategies of formal recycling" (Oushakine 2007: 457).

Oushakine's understanding of post-Soviet aphasia, a concept central to his analysis of nostalgic retrofitting, leads him to deduce that the process of transition that characterized the 1990s has been institutionalized in contemporary Russia. By combining anthropologist Victor Turner's notion of a liminal phase with psychoanalyst Donald Winnicott's concept of a transitional object, Oushakine concludes that post-Soviet aphasia has culminated in "the active parasitic re-use of the symbolic vocabulary" of the Soviet era, making it "the object of a *permanent* attachment" (Oushakine 2000a:

1009, 1010). This provocative claim suggests that Soviet discourse, in essence, has become a post-Soviet fetish and that Russia's civil society currently finds itself in a state of arrested development. Our examination of Putin mania leads us to a less gloomy conclusion. If we accept Oushakine's premise that nations pass through life stages roughly equivalent to those experienced by individuals, we can understand both the Putin cult and the earlier personality cults it recalls in terms borrowed from Jacques Lacan's theory of psychosexual development.

As the most vivid example of a cult of personality, the Stalin cult indeed arrested the Soviet Union's cultural development in what Lacan would call the mirror stage (Lacan 2006: 75–81). Much like the individual infant, whose ego is first constituted "through jubilant identification with its reflection, experienced as a powerful gestalt promising mastery, unity, and substantive stature," Soviet society located its all-powerful, collective ego in the image of Stalin, the "father of all peoples," "great architect of communism," and "gardener of human happiness" (Muller and Richardson 1982: 6). In effect captivated in a dyadic relationship with the omnipotent image of Stalin, Soviet society failed to develop a symbolic register that would permit critique of the cult itself and, more importantly, the formation and expression of individual desire. In other words, Soviet cults of personality locked the country in an imaginary realm dominated by the leader's image, which not only constituted national identity through a collective act of *méconnaisance*, but also defined a highly circumscribed subjectivity for the country's citizens. As Lilya Kaganovsky demonstrates in her study of Socialist Realist texts, the castrated and feminized Stalinist subject was little more than an inverted mirror image of Stalin's hypermasculinity (Kaganovsky 2008).

The collapse of the Soviet Union in 1991 stripped the country's inhabitants of their identity as Soviet citizens and, by negating key territorial, linguistic, and cultural boundaries, forced them to remap the limits of their collective self. In this new world, familiar frameworks seemed valuable even if removed from their original context and stripped of their old significance, because of their ability to elicit a flash of (mis)recognition from disparate individuals and, through shared perception, to facilitate the emergence of a new collective self. Putin, as Levada suggests, does indeed function as a mirror: he provides the kind of idealized representation of a Russian collective self that might be expected to inspire a new post-Soviet *méconnaisance* and the restructuring of the country's imaginary order.[25] However, the inherent polysemy of Putiniana, as well as the broader debate over its significance, signals Russia's acquisition of a symbolic register that facilitates critique of the structures borrowed from earlier personality cults and promotes the formation of individual identity and desire. As incongruous, bizarre, and even naïve as much Putiniana may be, its proliferation and diversity throughout the 2000s suggest that Russia has indeed changed in fundamental, irreversible ways since the collapse of the Soviet state.

Putin and consumption

Our interpretation of the Putin craze highlights the polysemy of Putiniana and its ability to articulate individual desire, both of which call attention to the proliferation of Putin-associated consumer goods in contemporary Russia. More media icon than demigod, Putin circulates through Russian pop culture, the consumer marketplace, and, to some extent, even the realm of high art as a kind of fashionable brand.[26] Just as fans around the globe can outfit themselves and furnish their houses and their minds with products associated with their favorite celebrity or cartoon character, Russians can wallpaper their lives with Putin memorabilia. As such, Putin mania represents part of a larger cultural trend: consumption, many scholars have argued, serves as the most important means by which Russian citizens today express individual agency, construct identity, and grapple with political change (Humphrey 2002; Shevchenko 2002a, 2002b). Buying a $600 Putin t-shirt or $1 million Putin canvas gives shoppers an opportunity to express personal preference, as well as to own, wear, display, remake, and perhaps even deface and discard tangible representations of political power (Oushakine 2000b: 102; Shevchenko 2002b: 162).

New technology has played a key role in propagating Putiniana and in helping to define the contours of the Putin craze. In a world in which cultural content and designs can be instantly replicated and developed in new directions by any individual with serviceable computer skills, protecting the ownership of one's ideas, managing one's public image and, for that matter, controlling the meaning and uses of the work that one produces have all become increasingly difficult. More than ever, it is clear that the creators of both objects and texts enjoy no special ability to define the meaning and application of what they make: as Michel de Certeau noted 30 years ago, the reception and utilization of cultural material involve transformative processes so potentially profound that they constitute a kind of "secondary production" (de Certeau 1984: xiii). Reliant on techniques such as sampling, creative reuse, and citation for much of its effect, postmodern culture encourages both creators and consumers to look at the world of art and even the objects marketed by major retailers with fresh eyes and to deploy them in inventive ways.

Creative reuse plays an important role in Putin mania, taking a number of different forms. Many of the most striking examples of Putiniana employ stock footage of the President's generally stiff public appearances or use audio culled from the speeches that he characteristically delivers in a low monotone. Spliced together with other incongruous sounds and images, the President's words and gestures acquire new and unexpected meanings. For instance, a musical number entitled "Putin Raps" [*Putin repuet*] features the president speaking before the Duma to the refrain of his own voice saying, "Who could be president? Who can? Me!"[27] Similarly, campaign material that might have appeared innocuous at a pre-election political rally, can, in another context, look positively grotesque. Sold in a metro station kiosk in the capital or displayed in the office of a Moscow NGO to sarcastic jeers, a bright blue balloon printed with a smiling Putin face may appear either ridiculous or threatening, depending on one's point of view on the current political situation.

Objects such as Putin portraits in chocolate, Putin t-shirts, and Putin balloons have no fixed meaning in and of themselves. Whether or not a particular object

Figure 2.6 Putin at the potter's wheel in the tourist village of Verkhnie Mandrogi in 2001.

Source: The Kremlin's website at http://archive.kremlin.ru/events/detail/2001/08/141906.shtml.

holds "cultic" significance depends, in large measure, on the context in which the consumer sees and buys it, not on the producer's intent. Individual examples of Putiniana are so full of potentially conflicting significance that their meaning remains indeterminate. When Russians buy a postcard of Putin struggling to master a lump of clay at a pottery wheel (Figure 2.6), do they regard it with reverence or amusement? Does it show an elected official being a good sport at a routine public event, or does it mockingly cast Putin as a leader of Soviet-style pretension, intent on reshaping the nation and/or human nature? And how should we read the popular photographs of Putin out for a stroll with a jacket carelessly draped over one shoulder or the romantic, fuzzy-edged Putin posters that show the leader with a Byronic scarf about his neck *à la* Pushkin? Are they sold with an eye to their potential ironic appeal? If so, why do they so often appear in tediously reverent biographies of Putin and on the office walls of Russian bureaucrats? In the context of the Putin craze, all meaning is relative. The contemporary cult accords a surprisingly active and even playful role to ordinary citizens: each individual determines for himself what the presidential brand denotes.

Some of the most vivid examples of the outsize role that individual producers and consumers play in the contemporary cult of personality come from the field of journalism. Reporters such as Andrei Kolesnikov, a member of the Kremlin pool of journalists and author of some ten books devoted to Putin, have used the act of reporting on the Putin presidency to establish their own celebrity. The titles of two of Kolesnikov's earliest Putin books – *I Saw Putin!* [Ia Putina videl! 2004]

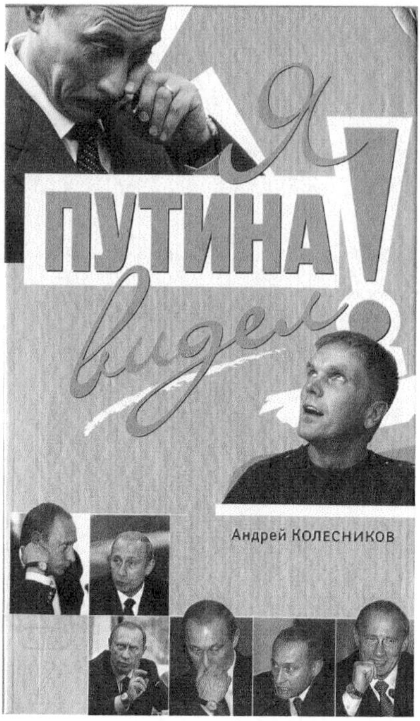

Figure 2.7 The cover of Andrei Kolesnikov, *Ia Putina videl!* Izd. vtoroe, ispravlennoe i dopolnennoe (Moscow: Izd. "EKSMO," 2005).

Source: Used by permission of the publisher.

and *Putin Saw Me!* [Menia Putin videl! 2005] – suggest the degree of self-focus present in most of the reporter's narratives about the Russian President. In these book titles, Kolesnikov's own "I" ("*ia*" and "*menia*") and Putin stand side-by-side, seemingly equal in importance. The covers of the books suggest that Kolesnikov may even enjoy preeminence in relation to his subject: a single image of Kolesnikov appears in the visual center of each cover with the journalist's name inscribed beneath; multiple, smaller photographs of Putin rubbing his eye, wiping his nose, or scratching his ear decorate the upper left corner and the lower border of both covers (Figure 2.7) (Kolesnikov *Ia Putina videl!* and *Menia Putin videl!*). By offering multiple, smaller images of the President engaged in uncouth acts, these covers diminish Putin's stature relative to that of Kolesnikov. Putin appears to lack dignity: he plays the part of baboon, leaving to Kolesnikov the role of the travel-weary nature reporter.

Actor, film director, and cultural figure Nikita Mikhalkov also has closely associated himself with Putin in recent years, as *55*, a 22-minute-long televised greeting card created for the President's fifty-fifth birthday, demonstrates.[28] Aired on the Rossiia television channel on October 7, 2007, this show, narrated by

Mikhalkov himself, offered viewers images of the President at his most decisive: Putin in a helicopter; Putin consoling those who lost loved ones in the *Kursk* submarine disaster; Putin on a bomber plane, on a nuclear aircraft carrier, on a tractor; Putin reuniting the Russian Orthodox Church; Putin delivering his scathing Munich speech; and Putin winning the winter Olympics for Sochi. In many respects, however, the program focused more on the person of its narrator than on the putative subject of the homage. For minutes at a time, it showed close-ups of Mikhalkov seated in a faux-rustic interior, describing the president's significant achievements and admirable personal characteristics. In a tone usually reserved for lecturing ungrateful children, Mikhalkov solemnly reviewed Russia's desperate state in the late 1990s and the many positive changes that, he argued, had taken place as a result of Putin's resolute leadership. Apparently overcome by emotion at the end of the program, Mikhalkov fought back tears and delivered a dramatically subdued "Happy Birthday" to his idol.

Mikhalkov's birthday greeting provoked considerable controversy when it aired, inspiring a number of pointed critical responses in the popular press. Most notably, in a column that *Izvestiia* initially refused to publish, journalist Irina Petrovskaia compared *55* to *Story of a Communist*, an infamous 1976 cinematic tribute to Brezhnev on his seventieth birthday.[29] The many similarities between the two homage are obvious, but, as Petrovskaia herself pointed out, one difference also stands out: unlike its precursor, *55* takes a "deeply personal attitude to its hero" (Petrovskaia 2007). In the film, Mikhalkov foregrounds himself and the special connection that he has to the Russian president, from time to time even referring to private conversations. The pedantic tone that Mikhalkov employs throughout much of the tribute suggests that he believes himself to possess special knowledge that sets him apart from most of his audience. In exhorting, he acknowledges the obvious: the kind of unity and consensus that characterized public rhetoric surrounding the person of the great leader in the Stalin era does not exist in regard to Putin. Playful, ironic speech, and horrified protests about the resurgence of the worst sort of authoritarian pretension reverberate through the public sphere alongside reverent semi-official tributes.

The program *55* and the criticism it inspired illustrate the ways in which the Putin phenomenon at times resembles but ultimately diverges from earlier personality cults. Although individual Putin texts, like Mikhalkov's film, may closely mimic specific cultic monuments from the Soviet era, they operate in a very different cultural environment. The contemporary Putin craze as a whole does not display the monolithic quality that characterized its most obvious historical precursors and hence cannot act in the same way as formalized, highly predictable ritual. If anything, in its ambiguity and dialogic, polyvalent character, contemporary Putin mania reveals a collective loss of faith in absolute truths and metanarratives, which imbues all communicative acts with an inherent subjectivity and creates opportunities for role play, mischief-making, and experimentation. The Putin phenomenon represents the product of distinctly contemporary social and communicative relations and, as such, speaks less of unadulterated hero-worship or even organized promotion than it does of rhetorical and philosophical indeterminacy and of a new mode of performativity available to contemporary Russians. Graeme Robertson's recent remarks on contemporary Russian political culture ring true: "Putin's regime is indeed not your grandfather's authoritarianism. Russia is not sinking back into the past but is creating something new: a postmodern mixture of old school methods and new political technologies" (Colton *et al.* 2009: 556).

Conclusion

By pointing out the ways in which contemporary Putin mania differs from Soviet cults of personality, we in no way mean to suggest that Putin himself has no authoritarian inclinations, or that contemporary Russian society is moving in an entirely positive direction. Certainly, many of the Russian government's policies and decisions give serious cause for concern. In his current position as prime minister, Putin obviously retains much of the authority he exercised as president. His decision to run for president again in 2012 suggests that he has no intention of relinquishing power any time soon, and that he may indeed, as many of his ardent supporters hope, remain de facto leader for life, working around term limits by happily swapping titles with a favored lackey and governing from whatever position he happens to occupy.

Certainly, Putin's current satellite Medvedev, despite the hopes that he once inspired in some observers, now seems unlikely ever to step outside the shadow of his powerful mentor or to challenge his supremacy. Although Medvedev has enjoyed consistently good approval ratings since his election to the presidency, his image has never given rise to the kind of effusive popular response associated with Putin. Aside from tourist staples such as presidential nesting dolls and a few formal portraits, little in the way of Medvedev paraphernalia has emerged. On YouTube, a constantly expanding array of amateur videos savagely and insistently mocks the president as Putin's stooge, pet, or creature: he appears as the prime minister's favorite teddy bear, his orangutan, or the half-human result of an ambitious laboratory experiment in the halls of power.[30] He plays Pinky to Putin's Brain and Samwise Gamgee to his Frodo; his face morphs magically into that of the comedic staple Mr. Bean; his diminutive stature renders him an unlikely lover.[31] A satiric video created by a team from Perm' for Klub veselykh i nakhodchivykh (Club of the Sunny and Smart) (KVN), a televised collegiate humor competition, has enjoyed enduring popularity on YouTube since it was first posted in 2008, earning close to a million and a half views. By adding new dialogue to a famous scene from the Soviet comedy *Kidnapping, Caucasian Style* [Kavkazskaia plennitsa 1967], the team transformed the film so that it appears to show Medvedev despondently yielding to the urging of a political operative and agreeing to run for president in a fixed election that will leave real power in Putin's hands.[32]

More recent videos continue the trend of subordinating President Medvedev to Prime Minister Putin. The animated television series "Mul't lichnosti" – the title plainly referring to the phrase "cult of personality" – portrayed the two men as dancing bobblehead dolls that play the tambourine and accordion in its 2010 and 2011 New Year's programs on the state-sponsored Channel One. In these comedic videos, the Putin–Medvedev team satirizes itself and the year's political events in rhymed couplets, with the figure representing Putin often taking a more assertive line and showing up the Medvedev bobblehead (Barry 2009).[33] More recently, an amateur video of Medevdev awkwardly dancing to the pop song "American boy" went viral the day after Putin's publicity machine released images of him, in full hockey regalia, shooting pucks on the ice with Russian teens.[34] These examples reinforce the notion that Medvedev's political identity functions as a prop and foil for Putin's, and that the Medvedev presidency, as many pundits have suggested and Putin himself has at times hinted, was never more than a stopgap measure designed to evade constitutional restrictions: the younger politician serves as a place holder until Putin himself can legally return to the office in 2012.[35]

Putin's continued dominance in Russian political life and ascendancy in the realm of popular iconography should not, however, lead us to assume that the leader cult he has inspired will ever morph into a structure more akin to its historical predecessors. Unless it is prepared to turn its back on modern communicative technology and the capitalist marketplace entirely and to introduce isolationist policies as strict as those in North Korea (an option likely to appeal to few political actors), the Russian state will not be able to establish the degree of control over public culture that typified the Stalin, or for that matter, even the Brezhnev period (Viktorov *et al.* 2008). If leader cults remain an important element in post-Soviet Russian political culture, they will, regardless of who is in power, in all likelihood, continue to operate according to very different rules from those of their Soviet precursors, privileging producers, and consumers even over the ostensible object of veneration.

Notes

This chapter combines research initially presented by the authors at the 2007 AAASS Annual conference and partially funded by the American Council of Teachers of Russian, the University of Oklahoma, and Williams College. An earlier version of this chapter appeared as Cassiday and Johnson (2010). Some material incorporated in this chapter appeared in a different form in Johnson (2009). The authors would like to thank Brian Kim of Stanford University for research assistance and Bruce Wheat of Williams College for technical assistance with illustrations.

1 "*Twelve moods of Putin* hits Russia," *BBC News*, December 6, 2001. Available at: http://news.bbc.co.uk/2/hi/europe/1694236.stm (accessed June 13, 2008).
2 For deeper analysis of Putin's celebrity status in the visual arts, see Goscilo (2011).
3 "Presidential Performance," *Centre for the Study of Public Policy, University of Aberdeen*, at: http://www.russiavotes.org/president/presidency_performance.php?S776173303132=0306304502cb8f276a25dfef6d30d0a9 (accessed June 13, 2007).
4 See "Presidential Performance" website for poll results.

5 Detailed analysis of the effect of Putin's personality, as well as Medvedev's own emerging identity as a leader, on voters during Russia's 2008 elections can be found in Colton and Hale (2009).
6 See also the March to April 2009 confidence rating posted by VTsIOM at http://wciom.com/news/ratings/confidence-in-political-leaders.html (accessed May 24, 2009) and the chart showing the rise and fall of confidence ratings for Putin, Medvedev, and other political figures from 2006 to present on the same site at http://wciom.ru/index.php?id=169 (accessed November 1, 2011).
7 In recent publications, both Stephen Kotkin and Graeme Robertson have suggested that some claims regarding "the extent to which Russia has been transformed into an authoritarian state under Putin" may have been exaggerated (Colton and Hale 2009; March and Robertson 2009: 555; Kotkin 2009: 551).
8 The earliest use of the phrase "cult of personality" that we have found in conjunction with Putin appears in Safire (2000).
9 E.B. Shestopal echoes this sentiment in her conclusion that by the end of the 1990s, "a demand for a new type of politician, who was in no way similar to Yeltsin, took shape: he had to be young and healthy, more intellectual, less spontaneous, etc." (Shestopal 2004: 506). Similarly, Andrei Rogatchevski in his examination of fiction featuring Putin finds that the president is portrayed "as an empty vessel that could be filled with any substance, or perhaps a chameleon which adapts well to any environment," while Goscilo analyzes the profusion of Putiniana as the logical result of "the rich potential of his vacuity" (Rogatchevski 2010: 163; Goscilo 2011: 41).
10 Shestopal comments, "The parameter of masculinity in the image of Putin was one of the key factors of his attractiveness at all stages of his presidential career" (Shestopal 2008: 354) (see Chapter 8 by Helena Goscilo).
11 The fishing photo can be found at "Dos'e sobytii. Poezdka v Respubliku Tyva. Fotoreportazh." August 13–15, 2007. Available at: http://www.kremlin.ru/events/photos/2007/08/140910.shtml (accessed November 6, 2007). Information on the Mussolini photo can be found in Falasca-Zamponi (1997): 73–74. The authors thank Erika Wolf for bringing the Mussolini photograph to their attention. For the photo of Mao, see "Iconic Photos: Mao Swims in the Yangze." Available at: http://iconicphotos.wordpress.com/2009/04/25/mao-swims-in-the-yangze/ (accessed March 25, 2010). More recently, topless photos of Barack Obama created a stir in the US media (Warner 2009). More topless photos of Putin appeared in the summer of 2009 after a vacation spent swimming, boating, and horseback riding in Siberia, for example, "Putin bares torso in Siberian vacation shots," *CNN.com*. Available at: http://www.cnn.com/2009/WORLD/europe/08/05/putin.holiday/index.html?iref=storysearch (accessed May 5, 2011).
12 "Putin reportedly saves TV crew from tiger," *MSNBC.com*, September 1, 2008. Available at: http://www.msnbc.msn.com/id/26493825/ (accessed September 2, 2008).
13 "Politicheskaia zagadka/On u El'tsina – ne rastet,/U Ziuganova – stoit,/U Zhirinovskogo – padaet,/U Iavlinskogo – koleblet sia,/U Luzhkogo – zastyl,/U Fedorova – ne podvizhen,/U Gorbacheva – sovsem malen'kii,/ U Bryntsalova – voobshche nikakogo,/A u Putina podnimaetsia./Chto eto? Reiting!"
14 "Half of Russian women consider Putin a Super-Man," *Pravda.ru*, May 7, 2004. Available at: http://english.pravda.ru/russia/history/07-05-2004/5498-putin-0 (accessed June 13, 2008).
15 "Half of Russian women consider Putin Super-Man."

16 See also "Film shows Putin the Russian love machine," *Asiaone*, February 6, 2008. Available at: http://www.asiaone.com/News/Latest%2BNews/Showbiz/Story/A1Story 20080206-48570.html (accessed June 13, 2008).

17 For websites with Putin jokes, see, for instance http://www.vladimirvladimirovich.com/anekdot.php (accessed June 13, 2008) and http://smeshok.com/main/humor/anekdots/politics/putin/index-00001.shtml (accessed June 13, 2008).

18 "'Ne speshite ee khoronit': Politicheskaia satira v Rossii perezhivaet novyi pod' 'em," *Obshchaia gazeta*, June 27, 2007. Available at: http://www.og.ru/articles/2007/07/27/25011.shtml (accessed August 28, 2007).

19 "Eshche odna prichina, po kotoroi Putin – nash prezident. V ego lichnosti soedinilis' dva liubimykh personazha anekdotov – Shtirlits i Vovochka."

20 *Fan-klub Vladimira Vladimirovicha Putina* at http://putin-loh.narod.ru (accessed March 3, 2008).

21 For a more detailed examination of works of fiction featuring Vladimir Putin, see Rogatchevski (2010) and Chapter 6 in the present collection.

22 For a history of the use of the phrase "cult of personality" in Russian, see Plamper (2004: 22–33).

23 A partial list of these joke products is provided at http://groups.google.ee/group/fido7.su.humor/browse_thread/thread/8738d8ce2fbf9ada/5da1c50c1d9636e1?lnk=st&q=%D1%8D%D0%B9%D0%BD%D0%BE+%D1%80%D0%B0%D1%85%D1%8C%D1%8F%8F&rnum=1&hl=ru (accessed June 22, 2008). Anna Krylova also mentions the three-person "Lenin is with us" bed in her study of the changes in political humor from the late Soviet to the post-Soviet period (Krylova 1999: 249).

24 Graeme B. Robertson notes specifically that new communicative technologies and globalization have made "information harder to control" and have limited the ability of antidemocratic regimes to isolate their citizens: "Closed, highly repressive regimes, such as Turkmenistan under Saparmurat Niyazov or North Korea under Kim Jong Il [...] feel increasingly like remnants of the late, unlamented totalitarianism of the twentieth century" (Robertson 2009: 546–547).

25 The authors thank Lilya Kaganovsky for suggesting that Putin functions as a reflecting surface for a Lacanian mirror stage within contemporary Russian culture.

26 Goscilo comments on Putin's status as a trademark or brand (Goscilo 2011: 35).

27 "Putin repuet" at http://www.youtube.com/watch?v=fuI22V-bs_8 (accessed February 14, 2008).

28 Stephen M. Norris discusses this show and Mikhalkov's tendency to glom onto Putin (Norris 2011: 120–123).

29 See "Nesravnennyi Nikita Sergeevich," *Grani.ru*, October 12, 2007. Available at: http://grani.ru/Culture/Cinema/m.128586.html (accessed October 22, 2007). Petrovskaia's column finally appeared in *Izvestiia* alongside one by the newspaper's culture editor Elena Iampol'skaia as Petrovskaia (2007) and Iampol'skaia (2007).

30 "Moi pliushevyi Mishka (Dmitrii Medvedev)" at http://www.youtube.com/watch?v=MCXjx_MLLGg&feature=related; "Proiskhozhdenie prezidenta Medvedeva" at http://www.youtube.com/watch?v=Mi8xywbjoFg&feature=related (both accessed May 25, 2009).

31 "'Putin i Medvedev': Pinki i Brain" at http://www.youtube.com/watch?v=Ee4i9ojtiOk&feature=related; "Prikliucheniia Frodo Putina i Semuaiza Medvedeva. Fil'm pervyi" at http://www.youtube.com/watch?v=FsPINioywsU&feature=related; "Morph Medvedev to Mr. Bean" at http://www.youtube.com/watch?v=bRdAWoAVfCc&feature=related;

and "Medvedev i ego krasavitsa zhena v miniatiure" at http://www.youtube.com/watch?v=U9EEcjP7PPA&feature=related (all accessed May 25, 2009). Medvedev is 5'4" tall, a full three inches shorter, by most accounts, than Vladimir Putin, who also scarcely counts as a giant.

32 "Medvedev: Kak eto vse nachalos'" at http://www.youtube.com/watch?v=OJqMK7s0LCI (accessed May 31, 2009).

33 The 2010 cartoon of Putin and Medvedev can be viewed at http://www.youtube.com/watch?v=PlW-8fJwOmU, while the 2011 version is available at: http://www.youtube.com/watch?v=j7oBv4LItNs&feature=related (both accessed May 6, 2011).

34 The video of Medvedev dancing can be viewed at http://www.huffingtonpost.com/2011/04/20/dmitry-medvedev-dance_n_851675.html, and the video of Putin playing ice hockey is available at: http://www.huffingtonpost.com/2011/04/18/vladimir-putin-ice-hockey_n_850492.html (both accessed May 6, 2011).

35 "Putin says he may run for president again in '12," *MSNBC.com*, December 3, 2009. Available at: http://www.msnbc.msn.com/id/34253039/ (accessed May 6, 2011).

Bibliography

AFP. (2004) "Stuffed Rabbits for Putin a Hot Item in Russian Markets." *BNET Research Center*, January. Available at: http://findarticles.com/p/articles/mi_kmafp/is_200401/ai_kepm351293 (accessed October 29, 2007).

Associated Press. (2007) "Putin's Bare-Chested Photos Set Russia Abuzz." *International Herald Tribune*, August 22. Available at: http://www.iht.com/articles/ap/2007/08/22/europe/EU-GEN-Russia-Putins-Image.php (accessed June 13, 2008).

Barry, E. (2009) "Making a Little Fun of Russia's Powerful." *The New York Times*, December 31. Available at: http://www.nytimes.com/2010/01/01/world/europe/01moscow.html (accessed May 6, 2011).

Blomfield, A. (2009) "Vladimir Putin Turns His Hand to Painting." *The Telegraph*, January 14. Available at: http://www.telegraph.co.uk/news/worldnews/europe/russia/4240597/Vladimir-Putin-turns-his-hand-to-painting.html (accessed January 19, 2009).

Borisova, I.P. (2004) *Connie's Stories*. Moscow: Detskaia literatura.

Boym, S. (2001) *The Future of Nostalgia*. New York: Basic Books.

Cassiday, J.A. and E.D. Johnson. (2010) "Putin, Putiniana, and the Question of a Post-Soviet Cult of Personality." *Slavonic and East European Review* 88(4): 681–707.

Colton, T.J. and H.E. Hale. (2009) "The Putin Vote: Presidential Electorates in a Hybrid Regime." *Slavic Review* 68(3): 473–503.

Colton, T.J. *et al.* (2009) "Responses: Political Science, Democracy, and Authoritarianism." *Slavic Review* 68(3): 552–556.

Danilova, S. (2007) "Stan' takim, kak Putin!" *Komsomol'skaia Pravda*, August 8. Available at: http://www.kp.ru/daily/23954/71877/print/ (accessed July 2, 2008).

Davies, S. (2004) "Stalin and the Making of the Leader Cult in the 1930s." Balázs Apor *et al.*, eds. *The Leader Cult in Communist Dictatorship*. New York: Palgrave Macmillan. 29–46.

de Certeau, M. (1984) *The Practice of Everyday Life*. Trans. Steven Rendall. Berkeley, CA: University of California Press.

Dobrenko, E.A. (1997) *The Making of the State Reader: Social and Aesthetic Contexts of the Reception of Soviet Literature*. Trans. Jesse M. Savage. Stanford, CA: Stanford University Press.

Dobrenko, E.A. (2001) *The Making of the State Writer: Social and Aesthetic Origins of Soviet Literary Culture*. Trans. Jesse M. Savage. Stanford, CA: Stanford University Press.

Ennker, B. (2004) "The Stalin Cult, Bolshevik Rule and Kremlin Interaction in the 1930s." Balázs Apor *et al.*, eds. *The Leader Cult in Communist Dictatorship*. New York: Palgrave Macmillan. 83–101.

Falasca-Zamponi, S. (1997) *Fascist Spectacle: The Aesthetics of Power in Mussolini's Italy*. Berkeley, CA: University of California Press.

Glasser, S.B. (2003) "Putin's Cult of Personality: From Portraits to Toothpicks, Russian Leader Captures the Day." *Wall Street Journal (Europe)*, March 16, A3.

Goscilo, H. (2011) "The Ultimate Celebrity: VVP as VIP Objet d'Art." Helena Goscilo and Vlad Strukov, eds. *Celebrity and Glamour in Contemporary Russia: Shocking Chic*. London: Routledge. 29–55.

Harding, L. (2009) "Putin Painting Fetches £750,000 in Charity Auction." *The Guardian*, January 19. Available at: http://www.guardian.co.uk/world/2009/jan/19/vladimir-putin-art-auction (accessed January 19, 2009).

Hellbeck, J. (2006) *Revolution on My Mind: Writing a Diary under Stalin*. Cambridge, MA: Harvard University Press.

Humphrey, C. (2002) *The Unmaking of Soviet Life: Everyday Economies after Socialism*. Ithaca, NY: Cornell University Press.

Iampol'skaia, E. (2007) "Ne prostyie chisla." *Izvestiia*, October 15. Available at: http://www.izvestia.ru/comment/article3109310/ (accessed October 22, 2007).

Ivanova, N. (1997) "Nostal'iashchee. Retro na (post)sovetskom teleekrane." *Znamia* 9: 204–211. Reprinted as "Nostal'iashchee." *Nostal'iashchee: Sobranie nabliudenii*. Moscow: Raduga, 2002, 54–69.

Johnson, E.D. (2009) "Putin and Emptiness: The Place of Satire in the Contemporary Cult of Personality." *The Harriman Review* 16.4 and 17.1: 1–6.

Kaganovsky, L. (2008) *How the Soviet Man Was Unmade: Cultural Fantasy and Male Subjectivity Under Stalin*. Pittsburgh, PA: University of Pittsburgh Press.

Kishkovsky, S. (2008) "Moscow Journal: A Love Letter to Putin (but It's Not Addressed to Him)." *The New York Times*, February 6. Available at: http://www.nytimes.com/2008/02/06/world/europe/06russia.html (accessed June 10, 2008).

Kolesnikov, A. (2005a) *Ia Putina videl! Izdanie vtoroe, ispravlennoe i dopolnennoe*. Moscow: Eksmo.

Kolesnikov, A. (2005b) *Menia Putin videl! Izdanie vtoroe, ispravlennoe i dopolnennoe*. Moscow: Eksmo.

Konradova, N. (2006) "Ideologiia v shkolakh: v poiskakh kul'ta lichnosti?" *BBCRussian.com*, September 13. Available at: http://news.bbc.co.uk/hi/russian/in_depth/newsid_5336000/5336686.stm (accessed September 3, 2007).

Kotkin, S. (2009) "Comment: From Overlooking to Overestimating Russia's Authoriarianism." *Slavic Review* 68(3): 548–551.

Kramer, A.E. (2009) "Putin's Grasp of Energy Drives Russian Agenda." *The New York Times*, January 28. Available at: http://www.nytimes.com/2009/01/29/world/europe/29putin.html (accessed March 10, 2009).

Kravtsova, M. and A. Matveev. (2002) "Proekt 'Putin'." *ArtKhronika*. Available at: http://www.artchronika.ru/archive/042002/president.shtml (accessed September 3, 2007).

Krylova, A. (1999) "Saying 'Lenin' and Meaning 'Party': Subversion and Laughter in Soviet and Post-Soviet Society." *Consuming Russia: Popular Culture, Sex, and*

Society since Gorbachev. Ed. Adele Marie Barker. Durham: Duke University Press. 243–265.

Lacan, J. (2006) "The Mirror Stage as Formative of the *I* Function as Revealed in Psychoanalytic Experience." *Écrits: The First Complete Edition in English*. Trans. Bruce Fink. New York: W.W. Norton & Co. 75–81.

Lahusen, T. (1997) *How Life Writes the Book: Real Socialism and Socialist Realism in Stalin's Russia*. Ithaca, NY: Cornell University Press.

Levy, C.J. (2008) "It isn't Magic: Putin Opponents Vanish from TV." *The New York Times*, June 3. Available at: http://www.nytimes.com/2008/06/03/world/europe/03russia.html?pagewanted=1&;_r=2&hp (accessed February 14, 2009).

Lipman, M. (2004) "Moscow Postcard: The Putin Toothpick." *New Yorker*, March 8. Available at: http://www.newyorker.com/archive/2004/03/08/040308ta_talk_lipman (accessed June 30, 2011).

March, L. (2009) "Managing Opposition in a Hybrid Regime: Just Russia and Parastatal Opposition." *Slavic Review* 68(3): 504–527.

March, L.and G.B. Robertson. (2009) "Responses: Political Science, Democracy, and Authoritarianism." *Slavic Review* 68(3): 552–556.

Mareu, F. (2008) "The Politics of Double Exposure." *TheMoscowTimes.com*, June 20. Available at: http://www.moscowtimes.ru/article/1010/42/368397.htm (accessed June 24, 2008).

Merinov, A. (2004) *Putinki: Kratkii sbornik izrechenii prezidenta (Pervyi srok)*. Moscow: Ekho Buk.

Miachin, E. *et al*. (2004) *Skazki pro nashego prezidenta*. Moscow: Izd. "Russkaia sem'ia."

Morgan, D.S. (2010) "Vlad the Crooner: Putin Sings 'Blueberry Hill'." *CBS News: World*, December 12. Available at: http://www.cbsnews.com/8301-503543_162-20025421-503543.html (accessed May 6, 2011).

Motyl, A.J. (2010) "Ukrainian FEMENists against Putin." *World Affairs: A Journal of Ideas and Debate*, November 8. Available at: http://www.worldaffairsjournal.org/new/blogs/motyl/Ukrainian_FEMENists_against_Putin (accessed May 6, 2011).

Muller, J.P. and W.J. Richardson. (1982) "Introduction." *Lacan and Language: A Reader's Guide to Écrits*. New York: International Universities Press. 1–25.

Nadkarni, M. and O. Shevchenko. (2004) "The Politics of Nostalgia: A Case for Comparative Analysis of Post-Socialist Practices." *Ab Imperio* 2: 487–519.

Norris, S.M. (2011) "Family, Fatherland, and Faith: The Power of Nikita Mikhalkov's Celebrity." *Celebrity and Glamour in Cotemporary Russia: Shocking Chic*. Ed. Helena Goscilo and Vlad Strukov. London: Routledge. 120–123.

Ol'bik, A. (2002) *Prezident*. Donetsk: Stalker.

Osborn, A. (2009) "Crisis Dents Russian Leaders' Popularity." *Wall Street Journal*, February 18. Available at: http://online.wsj.com/article/SB123489424483501551.html (accessed February 18, 2009).

Oushakine, S. (2000a) "In the State of Post-Soviet Aphasia: Symbolic Development in Contemporary Russia." *Europe-Asia Studies* 52(6): 991–1016.

Oushakine, S.A. (2000b) "The Quantity of Style: Imaginary Consumption in the New Russia." *Theory, Culture & Society* 17(5): 97–120.

Oushakine, S.A. (2007) "'We're Nostalgic but We're not Crazy': Retrofitting the Past in Russia." *The Russian Review* 66(3): 451–482.

Pereviazkin, D. (2001) *Anekdoty pro Putina*. St. Petersburg: Izdatel'stvo Bukovskogo.

Petrovskaia, I. (2007) "Ne prostyie chisla." *Izvestiia*, October 15. Available at: http://www.izvestia.ru/petrovskaya/article3109309/ (accessed September 14, 2009).

Plamper, J. (2004) "Introduction: Modern Personality Cults." Klaus Heller and Jan Plamper, eds. *Personality Cults in Stalinism – Personenkulte im Stalinismus*. Göttingen: V&R unipress. 13–42.

Putin, V. *et al.* (2009) *Uchimsia dziudo s Vladimirom Putinym*. Moscow: OLMA Media Grupp.

Rees, E.A. (2004) "Leader Cults: Varieties, Preconditions and Functions." Balázs Apor *et al.*, eds. *The Leader Cult in Communist Dictatorships: Stalin and the Eastern Bloc*. New York: Palgrave MacMillan. 3–26.

Robertson, G.B. (2009) "Managing Society: Protest, Civil Society, and Regime in Putin's Russia." *Slavic Review* 68(3): 528–547.

Rodina, O. (2010) "Studentki razdelis' dlia Putina." *Women.ru*, October 7. Available at: http://www.woman.ru/stars/events/article/58047/?startLeaflet=2&;posLeaflet=1 (accessed May 6, 2011).

Rogatchevski, A. (2010) "Putin in Russian Fiction." Ronald J. Hill and Ottorina Cappelli, eds. *Putin and Putinism*. London: Routledge. 161–188.

Sabonis-Chafee, T. (1999) "Communism as Kitsch: Soviet Symbols in Post-Soviet Society." *Consuming Russia: Popular Culture, Sex, and Society Since Gorbachev*. Ed. Adele Marie Barker. Durham, NC: Duke University Press. 362–382.

Safire, W. (2000) "Essay; Putinism Looms." *The New York Times*, January 31. Available at: http://query.nytimes.com/gst/fullpage.html?res=9403EFDD163FF932A05752C0A9669C8B63 (accessed June 13, 2008).

Schwirtz, M. (2008) "Putin's Tips for What to Do When Negotiations Collapse." *The New York Times*, October 7. Available at: http://www.nytimes.com/2008/10/08/world/europe/08putin.html?_r=2&;sq=putin%20judo&st=cse&oref=slogin (accessed October 13, 2008).

Shestopal, E.B., ed. (2004) *Obrazy vlasti v postsovetskoi Rossii: Politiko-psichologicheskii analiz*. Moscow: Aleteia.

Shestopal, E.B., ed. (2008) *Obrazy rossiiskoi vlasti. Ot El'tsina do Putina*. Moscow: ROSSPEN.

Shevchenko, O. (2002a) "'Between the Holes': Emerging Identities and Hybrid Patterns of Consumption in Post-socialist Russia." *Europe-Asia Studies* 54(6): 841–866.

Shevchenko, O. (2002b) "'In Case of Fire Emergency': Consumption, Security and the Meaning of Durables in a Transforming Society." *Journal of Consumer Culture* 2(2): 147–170.

Sil, R. and Chen C. (2004) "State Legitimacy and the (In)significance of Democracy in Post-Communist Russia." *Europe-Asia Studies* 56(3): 347–368.

Singer, N. (2007) "The U.S.S.R. is Back (on Clothing Racks)." *The New York Times*, November 27. Available at: http://www.nytimes.com/2007/11/27/world/europe/27designer.html?_r=1&;oref=slogin (accessed June 10, 2008).

Smits, I., director. (2003) *Poetins Mama: Een film van Ineke Smits*. Produced by Pieter van Huystee Film and Denis Vaslin (Volya Films). Netherlands: DVD View.

Teterin, V. (2005) *Putin.dok: Deviat' revoliutsionnykh p'es*. Moscow: Kolonna.

Tsvetkova, M. (2011) "Putin's Approval Rating Falls to Lowest Since 2005." Reuters, March 24, 2011. Available at: http://in.reuters.com/article/2011/03/24/idINIndia-55846320110324 (accessed November 1, 2011).

Viktorov, V. *et al.* (2008) *Vladimir Putin: Luchshie raboty 33 fotografov, rabotavshikhs Prezidentom Rossii v 2000–2008*. Moscow: Khudlit.

Warner, J. (2009) "A Hot Time in Washington." *Opinionator*, May 14. Available at: http://warner.blogs.nytimes.com/2009/05/14/president/ (accessed May 31, 2009).

White, S. and I. McAllister. (2003) "Putin and His Supporters." *Europe-Asia Studies* 55(3): 383–399.

Whitmore, B. (2007) "'National Leader' Idea Gains Strength in Russia." *Radio Free Europe/Radio Liberty*, November 18. Available at: http://www.globalsecurity.org/wmd/library/news/russia/2007/russia-071118-rferl01.htm (accessed June 13, 2008).

Yurchak, A. (2006) *Everything Was Forever, Until It Was No More*. Princeton, NJ: Princeton University Press.

Zhulina, O., director. (2008) *Potselui ne dlia pressy*. Produced by Anatolii Voropaev. Moscow: DVD Land and Videobaza.

3 Putin as the Father of the Nation

His family and other animals

Tatiana Mikhailova

The secrets of his success

From the early 2000s to the present, the former Russian president and current prime minister, Vladimir Putin, has maintained an incredible approval rating, ranging from 70 to 80 percent. According to data provided by the Levada Center in 2011,[1] Putin's rating remained steady after his presidential terms, even through the economic turmoil of the world financial crisis, as all other crises, for that matter. Putin's high rating never depended on his actual politics or on the situation in the country – an anomaly that led his critics to brand him "the Teflon president,"[2] meaning that nothing negative ever sticks to him. Government under Putin as its prime minister may be prompting protests (as was the case, e.g., during the "Day of Wrath" in March 2010, when thousands of frustrated citizens rallied against government in 20 Russian cities, from Kaliningrad to Vladivostok), but Putin's rating remains unshaken. This seemingly unique symbolic status is, in fact, hardly unique in the context of Russian cultural history: indeed, using a profitable economic situation, nostalgia for lost Soviet imperial power, and anti-western and xenophobic sentiments, Putin [with the help of an able public relations (PR) team] has managed to restore the image of the Leader as the Father of the Nation in the post-Soviet condition. This association, at least in the Russian context, necessarily implies not only a politician's intellectual abilities and experience, but also (and mainly) those who are associated with the patriarchal model of fatherhood. Yuri Levada has described the following synthetic image of Putin, based on polls of the Russian population:

> A former KGB officer with a confident walk and shy smile, a tough administrator of disarming simplicity, a market-oriented reformer willing to increase state control over the market, and a touching father who can fly a jet and uses military slang in his speech.
>
> (Fartyshev 2004: 35)[3]

Quite telling is the combination of seemingly contradictory features – military, controlling, yet caring – in this representation. However, this contradiction derives from the representation of the father figure in the patriarchal tradition. This model of the state leader goes back to the prerevolutionary image of the Russian monarchs, but, most importantly, it seems to restore cultural stereotypes associated with Stalin as the stern yet loving father to all Soviet people (see Chapter 2 by Cassiday *et al.*, Chapters 1 and 8 by Goscilo, Chapter 6 by Rogatchevski, Chapter 5 Ryazanova-Clarke).

The association between Putin's reign and monarchic/patriarchal representations of the leader is already inscribed in the mechanism of the transition of power in post-Soviet Russia and in the overall neofeudal structure of the political system that emerged in Russia after the collapse of the Soviet Union.[4] In a dynastic mode, President Yeltsin appointed Putin as his successor in 1999, and, in 2008, Putin similarly appointed his own successor, while remaining the actual center of political power. As Vladimir Shlapentokh reminds us, "the succession of power based not on kinship but on the choice of the current leader from a few candidates [is] a practice that was elaborated in the Roman Empire" (2007: 164).

When employing cultural stereotypes associated with the Father of the Nation, Putin has definitely managed to add something new to this image. One of Putin's innovations in this tradition is associated with issues of male sexuality, which were never promoted in relation to the Father of the Nation in Russia before Putin assumed office. In Eliot Borenstein's apt formulation,

> The Yeltsin years considerably lowered the bar [of public expectations] for the country's next leader: Putin's specific policies and actions arguably matter far less than his reassuring symbolic function as "a real man" who can husband the nation's resources and promise a return to greatness.
> (2007: 227)

Putin has emerged as an example of fitness and health that both women and men find very appealing. In some photos made readily available to the public gaze, Putin happily poses bare-chested, showcasing his well-developed musculature as a visual manifestation of virility (see Chapter 8 by Goscilo). This is just one instance of the way the almost 60-year-old, 5' 5" Putin is modeled as the paragon of potency (and, as I argue later, of omnipotence). Such an emphasis on paraded flesh echoes the aesthetics of glossy magazines and contributes to the phenomenon of Putin's popularity.

There are numerous pop-culture testaments to his masculine potency (see Goscilo; Cassiday *et al.* in this volume), and one illuminating example is found in the song "How girls in the village had no orgasms" [*Kak u devok na sele ne bylo orgazma*] by the band Neschastnyi Sluchai. The song was written for a popular theater production called *Election Day* (Den' vyborov 2003), produced by Neschastnyi Sluchai and the Moscow theater Kvartet I. The show's unfading success led to a movie with the same title in 2007. Though several musical numbers from the original show did not make it into the movie version, the song about orgasm-deprived girls did. A pseudo-folk song in a joyful, chastushka-like style, it addresses the problem of one unhappy village where girls could not experience sexual satisfaction. None of the attempted stimuli – doctors and old witches' remedies, gay entertainers, Andrei Makarevich with his culinary show, even a steamy night with Sergei Shoigu, Minister of Emergency Situations – worked. Once he learned of the problem, Putin certainly could not leave the unfortunates unattended and speeded to the rescue: "The girls looked out the window:/And there – closer and closer,/Putin in a kimono/Approaching on his mountain skis./The girls rushed outside,/*Au naturel* . . ./He glanced at them,/And they were done . . ."[5] Although the song obviously mocks the cult of Putin, it nevertheless accurately pinpoints the most prominent and novel aspect of Putin's representation in contemporary culture – his media positioning as a hyperbolic force of virility, whose machismo is so potent as to be magical. Perhaps, the flattering aspect of this image can serve as an explanation for Putin's unshakable tolerance of bawdy humor and rumors of this kind. He certainly seems less tolerant of other kinds of jokes about his person, the most memorable example being his reaction to Mikhail Saakashvili's alleged "Liliputin" (Lilliputian) joke, referring to Putin's diminutive stature, which some interpreted as one of the triggers for the Russian–Georgian war in August 2008 (see "Saakashvili Testifies Before War Commission" 2008).

An erotic calendar produced by female students at the Moscow State University posing in flimsy underwear as a birthday gift for the nation's beloved leader belongs to the same cultural realm (see "Russian Students Create Erotic Calendar for Putin" 2010). Here, one can detect the transformation of the comic heroines from Neschastnyi Sluchai's mock folklore into the country's future elite. Analyzing these calendars, Elena Gapova argues that the real reason for the popularity of Putin's mass-media image lies not in his sex appeal but in the model of the state his image represents:

> A strong nation-state uses political violence and is based upon powerful military institutions; the political category of "national citizenship" is interpreted as the right of those who bear arms and defend *patria.* These "male" categories – citizenship, militarism, violence – are formed around "male" institutions (armies, state "verticals," intelligence services) and "male" practices (wars, revolutions, state violence, big oligarchic business). This state project promotes a corresponding type of manhood associated with the political elite [. . .].
>
> (2011: 5)[6]

In tandem with the representation of Putin as the strong and sexually appealing Father of the Nation, Putin's actual family was effectively removed from public view starting with the early years of his reign. It is doubtful that the public would recognize his daughters' faces, for they certainly have changed since the publication of the book *First Person* (*Ot pervogo litsa* 2000), which included their photos. Only a few would know their names, since in the media and especially on TV very little has ever been said about them. As Simon Shuster argues in his article in *Time* magazine,

> [t]he Western principle that the people have a right to know has not been broadly embraced in Russia, and there is nothing like the US Freedom of Information Act to press the government for answers. Instead there are strict laws against libel, state control of most mass media and a prevailing sense left over from Soviet and czarist times that a strong leader – or *vozhd'* – should remain aloof from the masses if not totally inscrutable.

Putin's wife, Liudmila, rarely makes public appearances, and when she does, betrays obvious discomfort and stiffness. Typically, she either attends protocol meetings or is shown in confined spaces – in church or at home – that recall patriarchal models of a woman's role. In any case, she invariably functions as Putin's appendage rather than as an independent subject. Moreover, almost every such appearance is accompanied by scathing criticism, predominantly in Internet-based media and social networks, mocking her dresses as ill-fitting, unfeminine, etc.[7] These circumstances suggest the existence of a spoken or unspoken ban on information about Putin's family, at odds with the media representation of Western leaders', as well as Gorbachev's and Yeltsin's, families.

It is telling, however, that *First Person* – a collection of interviews with Putin and his close circle compiled prior to his first presidential term – contains an interview with Liudmila Putina. The marginalization of Putin's wife and the complete disappearance of his children from public view developed once he came to power. Both derive from the transformation of Putin's image through the years of his reign and his ever-growing popularity.

On the flip side of this process, Western pundits were amazed by the indifferent reaction of the Russian public and media to rumors of Putin's affair with the Olympic gymnastics champion Alina Kabaeva and his alleged desire to divorce his wife Liudmila so as to marry his supposed mistress. Both American and European commentators (see, for instance, Halpin and Owen 2008; Goldman 2008) seemingly failed to understand that these rumors nicely fit the paradigm of the supermale already laid out for Putin, and therefore caused no symbolic crisis.

Despite these accents in Putin's media representation, some analysts emphasize the "soft and gentle" manner of Putin's authoritarianism (see Fartyshev 2004: 21). This aspect of Putin's image resonates with public polls: according to the Levada Center data of 2007–2010, the most valued feature of an ideal man is "being caring" (*zabotlivost'*), according to 29–32 percent of respondents, followed by such qualities as independence (17–22 percent), fidelity (26–30 percent), compassion (5–8 percent), "strength to resist unfavorable circumstances" (25–27 percent), housekeeping skills (29 percent), and even sex appeal (3 percent). It would be superfluous to argue that the model of an ideal man is inevitably projected onto the representation of a political leader posing as the Father of the Nation.

Similar results are confirmed by other polls. For instance, a survey conducted by the Department of Political Psychology at Moscow State University in 2004 demonstrated that in the eyes of the Russian public, "the ideal president is associated with a 'caring, strict, and loving [. . .] leader as father'" (Shestopal *et al.* 2004: 32), and that Putin's image corresponded to these expectations well.

Furthermore, 29 percent of the respondents to the survey "find feminine traits in his image, while the indicator of his masculinity, as discerned by way of the respondents' association of him with certain smells, stood at only 18 percent" (Shestopal *et al.* 2004: 53).

The question arises: how are the "caring" and even "feminine" aspects of the image of the Father of the Nation channeled through Putin's media representation, if his family is completely removed from public view? I argue that Putin's "caring" side finds an odd manifestation that, in effect, significantly transforms his entire public image, diverting it from conventional totalitarian models and toward the postmodern culture industry.

The Beastmaster

It is symptomatic that in contrast with the minimal public representation of Putin's family members, everyone knows that Putin has a dog – a Labrador named Koni. This Labrador serves as Putin's attribute not only in children's pictures of him, where Koni is depicted as Putin's sidekick, but also elsewhere, and with more obvious importance than the human members of Putin's family. Koni definitely holds an important place in the public's imagination as a metonymy of Putin's power (see Figures 3.1 and 3.2).

For instance, the 36-year-old writer Zakhar Prilepin's description of Putin's meeting with young representatives of the creative intelligentsia in 2007 devotes a lengthy paragraph to Koni, admitting that he kept "a lock of Koni's hair" to commemorate this meeting and mark his adoration of the President:

> A few minutes later, I noticed with horror that Anastasiia [Chekhovskaia, a young playwright also attending the meeting– TM] – as it seemed to me – was caressing the President's leg. No, I didn't see her hand underneath the table, but I deduced accurately from her shoulder movements that Anastasiia's hand was administering gentle strokes. The situation was worsened by the fact that the President briefly glanced with tenderness at the playwright's hand, yet didn't interrupt his speech.
>
> But then there was a glimpse of a dog's furry black ears, and with relief I realized that the dog had approached unnoticed and placed her head right between the President's leg and the playwright's. It was the dog's head that Anastasiia was caressing. [. . .] Then the dog came up to Valeriia [Pustovaia – a young literary critic] and me, and I also stroked her. A few black hairs from the dog's head remained in my hand, and I saved them in my notebook as a memento.
>
> (Prilepin 2007)[8]

In the romantic tradition, lovers used to keep locks of their beloveds' hair as a sign of their undying devotion. The erotic associations surrounding this gesture are emphasized in Prilepin's text by the framing of Koni's appearance with the mistaken suspicion that a female playwright is stroking the President's leg under

Figure 3.1 Putin with his Labrador Koni (June 14, 2002).

Source: http://president.kremlin.ru/dyn_images/img23934.jpg.

Figure 3.2 Putin with Koni and one of his horses (July 26, 2002).

Source: http://president.kremlin.ru/dyn_images/img23932.jpg.

the table. Prilepin is obviously bothered by this suspicion ("noticed with horror"/ *s uzhasom uvidel*) and feels uncomfortable. In this context, his keeping of a dog-hair memento appears as a peculiar, even disquieting, extension of the romantic tradition. The situation is even odder than it seems at first sight, since Prilepin is a former activist of the banned National Bolshevik party that regularly protested Putin's politics and was cruelly persecuted for its activities. Prilepin's second novel, *San'kia*, which brought him into the public spotlight, vividly describes their struggle (Prilepin 2006). Here, Prilepin's recollection of the meeting with Putin, crowned by his acquisition of the weird souvenir, reads like the testimony of an orphaned child who has finally found his father, and Koni's hair appears as the metonymy of this newly found sense of belonging to the great family.

I spend so much time on Prilepin's reaction to Putin's dog because it seems typical of the public's perception of this politician. The example of Prilepin is especially symptomatic, since he openly declares his allegiance to the antigovernment opposition. However, without any prompts, he eagerly projects his attraction to Putin onto Putin's dog, establishing emotional contact with Putin through this substitute image.

Generally speaking, animals play a remarkably significant role in Putin's media representation. The prime minister's website on the portal of the Russian government features several photo albums of Putin, and at least 18 out of the 201 pictures in the "Casual" [Bez galstuka] album depict him with various animals – horse, puppy, bear, moose, and even one stuffed toy – yet none with his wife (see Putin's official website 2011). A Google search for "Putin and animals" brings a staggering number of results, especially in comparison with other leaders. Obviously, Putin likes animals and, more importantly, he likes to be filmed and photographed with them. What is even more significant, is that during these sessions, unlike in his usual political appearances, Putin beams with happiness and openly expresses pleasure at physical contact with animals. Even fish seem to delight him (Figure 3.3).

It would not be an exaggeration to say that in the eyes of the public, Putin is indeed associated with animals; they have become a crucial part of his image. Whether these elements of Putin's representation were intentionally designed by his spinmasters or were spurred by "popular demand" is impossible to determine. As in any political representation, a politician's "image consists of how voters perceive him, perceptions based upon both the subjective appraisals made by the voters and the message (utterances, attributes, qualities, etc.) transmitted by the candidate" (Newman 92). In other words, a convincing political image emerges in the sphere where political messages meet public expectations. Ultimately, the materialization of a recognizable political image signifies a successful dialogue between two intentions: how a politician wants to be seen and how the public wants to see him.

One may argue that the reason for the persistent representation of Putin with animals is not political but personal: "The guy likes animals. So what?" Notably, Putin's love for animals does not translate into official policy: while his participation in the International Tiger Conservation Forum of 2010 in St. Petersburg was

Figure 3.3 President Vladimir Putin relaxing on Cayo Blanco islet, Cuba (December 17, 2000).

Source: http://www.kremlin.ru/events/photos/2000/12/137684.shtml.

widely publicized and his photographs with coparticipant Leonardo Di Caprio flooded the media, it was Putin who during the first months of his presidency signed the decree to end the existence of Russia's federal environmental protection committee, whose main function was to protect endangered species (see "Putin's Animal Antics Questioned in Russia" 2011).

Bruce Newman maintains, "As with brand images, political images do not exist apart from the political objects (or their symbolic surrogates) that stimulate political thoughts, feelings and inclinations" (42). Hence, if animals constitute an important part of Putin's media representation, then they function as symbolic surrogates for "political thoughts, feelings, and inclinations." How may one define these thoughts, feelings, and inclinations?

Putin's love for animals frequently manifests itself in the form of a kiss. Obviously, the kiss of a political leader is not just a kiss. As Karen Harvey (2005) writes in her book *The Kiss in History*, a "kiss can convey social, political and cultural meaning" (11). If previous Soviet leaders obviously found great pleasure in kissing other political leaders, as immortalized by Dmitrii Vrubel's famous painting *The Kiss of Death between Brezhnev and Honecker* (1989), Putin prefers to kiss animals, which suggests not only the "social, political, and cultural meaning" of these kisses, but also a certain transgression of existing models of power. As much may be deduced from the attention paid to Putin's animal kisses by Russian humorists and caricaturists (Figure 3.4).

Figure 3.4 "And how about a kiss?"

Source: Photo by Sergei Elkin. Courtesy of Sergei Elkin.

One of Putin's kisses, shown on all Russian TV channels in August 2007, portrayed him kissing a sturgeon and then releasing it back into the water (Figure 3.5). At least two elements are notable in this episode: first, the sturgeon as a source of black caviar is typically associated with the natural riches and exoticism of Russia; second, as the RTVi commentator Mikhail Osokin ironically mentioned, Putin's kiss turned out to be deadly – the poor fish got so excited that it bumped its head against the boat and died. Why would Putin kiss a sturgeon? To my knowledge, there are no rituals, archaic or otherwise, that involve the kissing of fish. However, one could interpret Putin's kiss as a sign of veneration toward what is sacred in Russia. It is possible, in other words, that Putin or his media team intended the kiss to symbolize the sacralization of Russia's unique natural resources as the source of its greatness. The death of the poor fish was just a nasty spoiler to this elevated gesture; no resurrection followed.

Probably in order to fix the ironic effect of this encounter, a more complex story of another Putin kiss was created. In September 2008, while visiting a wildlife preserve in Siberia, Putin allegedly saved a TV crew from a tigress attack by shooting her with a tranquilizer gun. As he departed, Putin kissed the sleeping tigress – an image shown on several TV channels. This time, too, Putin's kiss was ironically associated with the animal's death – albeit temporary and caused by a tranquilizer. Putin's act was justified by the supposed danger

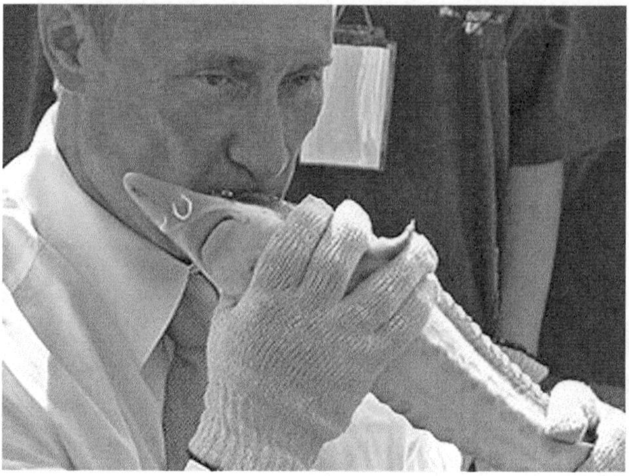

Figure 3.5 Putin kisses a sturgeon (Astrahan, August 2007).
Source: http://www.kremlin.ru/events/photos/2007/12/137664.shtml.

to the lives of the journalists (if one dismisses the lingering suspicion that the tigress had been released onto some journalists to give Putin a photo op). In this episode, not veneration, but control over natural resources and tenderness for the tamed element were spotlighted, with Putin, not the tigress, as the hero of the hour.

However, this story did not end there. It also had a sequel. Two months after Putin's encounter with the tigress, journalists from the Kremlin pool were invited to Putin's country residence for "important news." None of them had a clue what the story was about, and they were kept waiting for almost 4 hours. Eventually, Putin appeared in front of the journalists and commanded that they "avoid squealing" [*ne pishchat'*] and speak quietly. After these mysterious precautions, the journalists were introduced to an appealing tiger cub delivered to Putin as a birthday gift (the name of the donor was not revealed). A symbolic connection between the first and the second tiger episodes could hardly be avoided; yet, no one dared to address it because of its tangibly comical effect, especially if one considers the timing of this news release – in the midst of the political campaign for increasing Russia's birthrate. The kiss Putin planted on the tigress apparently had a magical effect: exactly as in the aforementioned song by Neschastnyi Sluchai, it demonstrated his ability to impregnate Russian nature and its female representatives – an extraordinary power, of which the tiger cub served as living proof. Furthermore, on February 11, 2009, a major regional newspaper, *Vladivostok*, ran a front page story under the headline "After the encounter with Vladimir Putin, a tigress gave birth to three cubs" [*Posle vstrechi s with Vladimirom Putinym tigritsa rodila troikh tigriat*] (Figure 3.6).

После встречи с Владимиром Путиным тигрица родила троих тигрят

Владивосток

В «Луч» просится бывший спартаковец!

Figure 3.6 A local newspaper, *Vladivostok* (February 11, 2009). The headline reads: "After the encounter with Vladimir Putin, a tigress gave birth to three cubs."

Putin's tender attention to animals, which did not end with the tigress episode, was obviously intended to revitalize Russian nature. As the Agency France-Presse states, "The Severtsov institute's program, which studies animals in the Red Book of endangered species" and other especially important animals of Russia "currently lists six mammals, most of which were tagged, patted, or kissed by Putin" (see "Putin's Animal Antics Questioned in Russia" 2011). Apparently, Putin's mojo makes more practical developments in protecting endangered species almost redundant.

It is quite significant that all these representations of Putin are *visual* in nature. As Carol Gelderman comments, with "video-age image making, the picture takes precedence over the word" (Waterman 1999: 119). In all these encounters, Putin appears as not just the Father of the Nation, but also as the husband of Russia's entire natural world. His sexual virility is represented as a mythological power, manifested in an omnipotent masculine deity, the Beastmaster, who venerates yet tames nature with his mighty kiss and hand. At the same time, the patriarchal features in this representation of Putin are complemented by characteristics reminiscent of feminine deities – symbols of the source of life, nurturing (he is frequently pictured feeding and hugging animals), and death. Through these means, Putin's "soft," caring, and nurturing side is not only emphasized – in accordance with public desires – but placed in a symbolic context where Putin's actual family is substituted with the world of nature; the animals appear as "symbolic surrogates" not only for his wife and daughters, but for all Russian citizens. No wonder that the media tropes associated with Putin's representation with animals inevitably find their continuation outside of the animal kingdom.

The politics of love

The consistency of Putin's media behavior suggests that his mythological image of power is employed at the very least for its subliminal effects. One may even argue that the purpose of Putin's myth-making is to construct new models of patriarchy that are symbolically situated beyond modernity and, hence, beyond any modern models of political behavior. However, it is obvious that such a representation of Putin as national father is not simply patriarchal, for his pseudo-traditionalism displays a transgressive character. The most significant function of Putin's kisses is to mark him as an unconventional leader, as one who disregards the norms of propriety and sets his own transgressive standards of behavior, and, by default – of politics.

This implication is most obvious in the kiss Putin planted on a 7-year-old boy's stomach on June 28, 2006. Certainly, there is nothing new about politicians kissing children. But Putin managed to open a new page in this respected tradition. That the episode with his kiss was shown by both Russian and international TV channels, and also was reproduced on the Internet, testifies to the novelty of the act. The location of this historical kiss is quite important: Putin stops to kiss the child while walking across Cathedral Square in the very heart of the Kremlin – in other words, in the epicenter of Russia's traditional locus of power. Willingly or not, Putin presents this kiss as a statement of his rightful belonging to the Russian lineage of authoritarian rulers. Certainly, the boy is not an animal, but he is obviously treated like one by Putin. In the news release, Putin slowly lifts the child's shirt without asking for permission from the boy's teacher, let alone the boy himself, as though he were the boy's owner. The similarity between a child and an animal in this scene is clear – both are deprived of subjectivity.

A vital aspect of this kiss is where Putin places his lips. A kiss on the naked stomach – and especially on a child's tummy – is extremely intimate. It is not exactly indecent, but it is definitely transgressive, since it is without precedent in Russian social interactions and thus violates societal conventions and mores. Yet, symbolically, this kiss is far from meaningless – a belly is *zhivot* in Russian, which is an old Russian word for "life." Hence, in the very heart of Russian power, Putin demonstrates his authority by a kiss to the epitome of Russia's future life – a little boy's *zhivot*. It is at once a sign of transgressive blessing and of Putin's omnipotence.

If one were to situate such a kiss from a political leader in a country other than Russia, it would not take much imagination to predict the outcome: lawsuits from the parents as well as from various organizations, media outrage about the violation of a child's rights, and the inevitable apologies from the presidential administration and the president. Nothing of the sort happened in Russia. This episode only generated muffled commentaries from political analysts and was soon forgotten. In my opinion, this reaction testifies to the stunning success of Putin's positioning as the *soft and tender Father of the Nation*, having an ultimate and intimate power over all his subjects, human and nonhuman. Certainly, it is the power of love – who would dare think otherwise?

There is one more significant aspect that unites all these examples of Putin's public image. Putin's media appearances with animals, his kisses, etc., perfectly fit into the category of media pseudo-events. According to Daniel Boorstin, these are not real events but, rather,

> spectacles created for the sole purpose of creating an image [. . .] There are some important characteristics of a pseudo-event . . . Its success measured by how widely it is reported . . . The question, "Is it real?" is less important than "Is it newsworthy?" . . . Its relation to the underlying reality of the situation is ambiguous. Its interest arises largely from this very ambiguity . . .
>
> (Waterman 1999: 15)

Characteristically, Putin's encounters with animals or children appear inversely proportional to the intensity of political life in Russia. In the first years of Putin's presidency, when the political struggle was still acute, he was rarely if ever shown kissing animals. However, by the late 2000s, when Putin and his team had established full control over the Russian media and removed all strong political opponents from the field, leaving only those who imitate critical discourse, this media image began to be promoted in keeping with Boorstin's description of pseudo-events. Therefore, Putin's representation as loving master of animals and children not only functions as a necessary counterweight to his tough and cold masculinity, thus completing his image of the Father of the Nation, but adds a new element of entertainment unprecedented in Russian politics.

The transformation of post-Soviet politics into a sphere of entertainment or a form of *Kulturindustrie* has been observed in the performances of popular conservative stand-up comedian Mikhail Zadornov. As Oxana Poberejnaia remarks, despite the fact that Zadornov's kind of humor is always politically colored,

> the function of Zadornov's celebrity in Putin's Russia . . . is to distract people from socioeconomic problems and keep them away from the political process. His celebrity works to preserve the status quo desired by the regime and to negate the population's democratic aspirations.
>
> (2010: 135)

There is nothing novel in the fact that a politician like Putin uses his status to "preserve the status quo desired by the regime." The novelty of Putin's actions lies in the fact that he achieves this goal by operating as an entertainer, not as a politician, using methods typical for the *Kulturindustrie* rather than for political debate. Tellingly, he never engages in debates with his political opponents, who are simply banned from Russian TV channels. Even more telling in this respect is the recent (2011) unprecedented appearance of the prime minister singing the Fats Domino hit "Blueberry Hill" in English (!) and (barely) playing the piano at a charity event attended by Sharon Stone, Kurt Russell, and other Hollywood celebrities (see "Putin Sings, Plays Piano at Charity Event" 2010). The emphasis on the entertaining aspect of Putin's image explains why his mythologization does not produce the effect of a sacralization of power; rather, it desacralizes it by situating Putin within the realm of *Kulturindustrie*.

In this context, one can see how wrong the pundits were when they saw signs of a new "Thaw" in the appearance of Putin and Medvedev as puppets dancing and singing moderately funny limericks during the traditional New Year TV show *Goluboi ogonek* [Blue Flame] in 2010. Evgenii Kiselev on the *Ekho Moskvy* radio station, for instance, said that the show marked "the beginning of the desacralization of power" (Bratersky 2010). However, such "desacralization" is typical for the *Kulturindustrie*, and it is this, seemingly subversive, feature that serves as the foundation of the regime's unshakable stability.

Conclusion

Although Putin is frequently interpreted as a neotraditionalist, this model of power representation has no precedents in the Russian tradition. One may recognize here a synthetic, artificial, and pseudo-traditionalist simulacrum of "ancient patriarchal authority" that reminds us less of Alexander Nevsky, Ivan the Terrible, or Stalin, and more of such pop-culture products as Beastmaster, Tarzan, Mawgli, or Dr Doolittle. The last two are especially popular in Russia thanks to brilliant literary and animation adaptations. These spectacles of power are even ironic in their over-the-top, movie- (or even cartoon-) like qualities. They can be interpreted as the postmodern representations of power that mainly rely, not on political arguments, but on the spectacles that manipulate the public imagination (see Chapter 2 in this volume).

On this basis, one may suggest that Putin-era society represents the ultimate instance of a postmodern society of the spectacle, generating a simulacrum of democracy in which the entertainment provided by politicians offers a surrogate for an (absent) political life. While political analysts cannot stop wondering what Putin's ideology is, the answer to this question can be found in Theodor Adorno's (1975) "Culture Theory Reconsidered" – it is the ideology of the culture industry itself: "The power of the culture industry's ideology is such that conformity has replaced consciousness" (18). As Horkheimer and Adorno explain the concept elsewhere,

> [t]o be entertained means to be in agreement. Entertainment makes itself possible only by insulating itself from the totality of the social process, making itself stupid and perversely renouncing from the first the inescapable claim of any work, even the most trivial: in its restrictedness to reflect the whole. Amusement always means putting things out of mind, forgetting suffering, even when it is on display. At its root is powerlessness. It is indeed escape, but not, as it claims, escape from bad reality, but from the last thought of resisting that reality. The shamelessness of the

> rhetorical question "What do people want?" lies in the fact that it appeals to the very people as thinking subjects whose subjectivity it specifically seeks to annul.
>
> (2002: 115–116)

It is this ideological message that the entertaining effects of Putin's media image actually render – the "political thoughts, feelings, and inclinations" stimulated by the media representation of Putin's power in its inseparable "soft" and "tough" aspects alike.

Notes

1 See http://www.levada.ru/press/2011012703.html (accessed July 22, 2011).

2 The earliest use of this term, I have found, harks back to 2004, during Putin's first presidential term (see Fartyshev, 11).

3 Byvshii ofitser KGB s uverennoi pokhodkoi i zastenchivoi ulybkoi, zhestkii administrator s obezoruzhivaiushchei prostotoi, reformator-rynochnik, zhelaiushchii usilit' gosudarstvennyi kontrol' za etim samym rynkom, trogatel'nyi otets, kotoryi upravliaet reaktivnym samoletom i ispol'zuet v rechi kazarmennye vyrazheniia.

4
> In contemporary Russia as well as in mediaeval Europe personal relationships are often more important than relations based on the formal roles in political, social and economic structures. This means that the most powerful people in the country are not elected officials but close friends of the President (or the king, if we examine the past).
>
> (Shlapentokh 1996: 394)

See also Ericson 2000.

5 Devki glianuli v okno:/ A v okne vse blizhe / Edet Putin v kimono/ I na gornykh lyzhakh. / Devki vyskochili von / V chem ikh mat' rodila./ Pogliadel na devok on. /Tut ikh i nakrylo. Available at: http://www.kvartet-i.ru/phpbb2/viewtopic.php?t=29 (accessed July 23, 2011).

6 Sil'noe natsional'noe gosudarstvo osushchestvliaet politicheskoe nasilie; opiraetsia na moshchnye voennye instituty; politicheskaya zhe kategoriia "natsional'nogo grazhdanstva" myslitsia kak pravo tekh, kto nosit oruzhie i zashchishchaet *patria*. Eti 'muzhskie' kategorii – grazhdanstvo, militarizm, nasilie – vystraivaiutsia vokrug "muzhskikh" institutov (armii, vlastnoi vertikali, razvedki) i "muzhskikh" praktik (voin, revoliutsii, gosudarstvennogo nasiliia, bol'shogo oligarkhicheskogo biznesa.) V gosudarstvennicheskom proekte vyrabatyvaetsia sootvetstvuiushchii tip muzhestvennosti politicheskoi elity, prebyvaiushchei na sluzhbe otechestvu.

7 See, for example, "Liudmila Putina podkrasila volosy i iavilas' na tseremoniiu v sapogakh" (2006) and "Britantsy kritikuiut nariady Liudmily Putinoi" (2003).

8 Spustia neskol'ko minut ia s uzhasom uvidel, chto Anastasiia,- mne tak pokazalos',- gladit Prezidenta po noge. Net, samu ee ruku iz-za stola ia ne videl, no tochno opredelil po dvizheniiam plecha Anastasii, chto ruka eta delaet nezhnye, gladiashchie dvizheniia. Situatsiia usugubilas' i tem eshche obstoiatel'stvom, chto Prezident mel'kom laskovo posmotrel na ruku dramaturga, ne prekrashchaia, vprochem, svoiu rech'. No potom mel'knuli iz-pod stola chernye mokhnatye ushi, i ia s oblegcheniiem dogadalsia, chto

eto nezametno podoshla sobaka, i polozhila golovu rovno mezhdu nogoi Prezidenta i nogoi dramaturga. Sobach'iu golovu gladila Anastasiia. (. . .) Potom eta sobaka prishla k nam s Valeriiei, i ia tozhe ee pogladil, v ruke u menia ostalos' neskol'ko chernykh voloskov s sobach'ei golovy, i ia ikh polozhil v svoi bloknot na pamiat'.

Bibliography

Adorno, Th.W. (1975) "Culture Theory Reconsidered," transl. by A.G. Rabinbach, *New German Critique* 6(Fall): 12–19.

Borenstein, E. (2007) *Overkill: Sex and Violence in Contemporary Russian Popular Culture*, London and Ithaca: Cornell University Press.

Bratersky, A. (2010) "New Cartoon Show Puts Prime Minister Among Men," *The St. Petersburg Times*, January 19. Available at: http://www.sptimes.ru/index.php?action_id=2&story_id=30638 (accessed August 18, 2011).

Britantsy kritikuiut nariady Liudmily Putinoi, 2003 "Britantsy kritikuiut nariady Liudmily Putinoi." (2003) *Grani*, June 26. Available at: http://www.grani.ru/Society/People/Politicians/m.36534.html (accessed August 18, 2011).

Ericson, R.E. (2000) *The Post-Soviet Russian Economic System: An Industrial Feudalism?* Helsinki: Bank of Finland, Institute for Economies in Transition (BOFIT).

Fartyshev, V.I. (2004) *Poslednii shans Putina: Sud'ba Rossii v XXI veke*, Moscow: Veche.

Gapova, E. (2011) "Polnyi Fuko: telo kak telo vlasti," *Nerikosnovennyj zapas* 2. Available at: http://wmich.academia.edu/ElenaGapova/Papers/618796/Polnyi_Fuko_tielo_kak_polie_vlasti (accessed August 18, 2011).

Goldman, R. (2008) "Putin Denies Affair with Beautiful Gymnast," *ABC News*, April 18. Available at: http://abcnews.go.com/International/story?id=4677782&;page=1 (accessed August 18, 2011).

Goscilo, H. (2008) "VVP kak Object d'art," *Neprikosnovennyi zapas* 6. Available at: http://magazines.russ.ru/nz/2008/6/go8.html (accessed August 18, 2011).

Halpin, T. and R. Owen. (2008) "President Putin Denies Affair with Kremlin 'Babe' Alina Kabaeva," *The Times*, April 18. Available at: http://www.timesonline.co.uk/tol/news/world/europe/article3773353.ece (accessed August 18, 2011).

Harvey, K. (2005) *The Kiss in History*, Manchester: Manchester University Press.

Horkheimer, M. and Th.W. Adorno (2002) *Dialectic of Enlightenment*. G. Schmid Noerr (ed.), transl. by E. Jephcott, Stanford, CA: Stanford University Press.

"Liudmila Putina podkrasila volosy i iavilas' na tseremoniiu v sapogakh." (2006) *Vokrug novostei*, February 9. Available at: http://www.vokrugnovostei.ru/news/news17338.html (accessed August 18, 2011).

Newman, B. (1994) *The Marketing of the President: Political Marketing as Campaign Strategy*, London: Sage.

Ot pervogo litsa: razgovory s Vladimirom Putinym. (2000) Moscow: Vagrius. Interviews with N. Gevorkian, A. Kolesnikov, N. Timakova.

Poberejnaia, O. (2010) "'Much Ado and Nothing': Mikhail Zadornov as a Celebrity of Russian Comedy," *Celebrity and Glamour in Contemporary Russia: Shocking Chic*, H. Goscilo and V. Strukov (eds.). London and New York: Routledge, 127–143.

Prilepin, Z. (2006) *San'kia*. Moscow: Ad Marginem.

Prilepin, Z. (2007) "Gospodin President, ne vybrasyvaite bloknot." *Zakhar Prilepin's personal website*, February 20. Available at: http://www.zaharprilepin.ru/ru/columnistika/apn-nazlobu/gospodin-prezident.html (accessed August 18, 2011).

"Putin's Animal Antics Questioned in Russia." (2011) *Asia One*, March 25. Available at: http://www.asiaone.com/News/AsiaOne%2BNews/World/Story/A1Story20110325-269975.html (accessed August 18, 2011).
"Putin Sings, Plays Piano at Charity Event." (2010) *Associated Press*, December 11. Available at: http://www.ndtv.com/article/world/putin-sings-plays-piano-at-charity-event-72009 (accessed August 18, 2011).
"Russian Students Create Erotic Calendar for Putin." (2010) *The Huffington Post*, October 7. Available at: http://www.huffingtonpost.com/2010/10/07/russian-students-create-e_n_754047.html (accessed August 18, 2011).
"Saakashvili Testifies Before War Commission." (2008) *Civil.ge. Daily News Online*, November 28. Available at: http://www.civil.ge/eng/article.php?id=20043 (accessed August 18, 2011).
Schroeder, A. (2004) *Celebrity-in-Chief: How Show Business Took Over the White House*, Boulder, CO: Westview Press.
Shestopal, E.B., T.N. Pishcheva, E.M. Gikavyi, and V.A. Zorin. (2004) "The Image of V.V. Putin in the Consciousness of Russia's Citizens," *Sociological Research* 43: 6 (November–December): 29–56.
Shlapentokh, V. (1996). "Early Feudalism – The Best Parallel for Contemporary Russia," *Europe-Asia Studies* 48(3): 393–411.
Shlapentokh, V. (2007) *Contemporary Russia as a Feudal Society: A New Perspective on the Post-Soviet Era*, New York: Palgrave Macmillan.
Shuster, S. (2011) "When Family is Virtually a State Secret," *Time*, June 16. Available at: http://www.time.com/time/world/article/0,8599,2077627,00.html (accessed August 18, 2011).
Waterman, R.W. (1999) *The Image-Is-Everything Presidency: Dilemmas in American Leadership*, Boulder, CO: Westview Press.

4 Putin's language

Michael S. Gorham

The title of this article echoes the theme of a 1924 issue of the Formalist journal *LEF*, the critical section of which was entirely dedicated to studies of Lenin's language (*LEF* 1924). Vladimir Putin, of course, is no Lenin, and the differences go far beyond language styles, but by contemporary standards, his stature in the public eye has come to assume proportions not unlike that of Lenin. While it would be difficult to make the case for a full-blown personality cult [though some have (Azar 2010)], there is little doubt that something like a cottage industry of Putiniana has emerged since he became president in 2000 (Pribylovskii 2003). While most of these manifestations focus on visual representations of the leader, I maintain that his growing symbolic prominence has a linguistic dimension as well. Part of Putin's success and popularity stems from his ability to speak in terms that resonate with Russian citizens.

It is not that Putin distinguishes himself with exceptional oratorical prowess. On the contrary, most would argue that his rhetoric pales by comparison to that of his Petersburg mentor, Anatolii Sobchak, or the Liberal-Democratic sound-bite machine, Vladimir Zhirinovskii (to take two examples from very different regions of the political landscape). His effectiveness, instead, stems from an ability to speak in a variety of voices depending on the context of his utterance, to shift in and out of language registers or speech styles to reflect the broader ideological and political sentiments of his immediate interlocutors and broader listening and viewing audience – most importantly, his domestic constituency. Putin's description of himself in his former KGB days as "a specialist in human relations" is pertinent to his style of communication today (Putin 2000: 44). Even his detractors have admired this trait in him, formulated perhaps in greatest detail by the kiss-and-tell journalist, Elena Tregubova:

> I was sincerely impressed by what a brilliant communicator Putin was. Although all of his professional receptions [and] interaction with interlocutors were relatively textbook and easily readable, their performances were nevertheless virtuoso. I don't know how – through mimicry, intonation, or looks – but in the course of a conversation he would force me to subconsciously feel as though he were someone who shared my circle of interests.

> Although there was absolutely no logical reason to suppose this. On the contrary – all the facts showed that we were totally incompatible.
>
> I figured out that he was simply an ingenious "reflector" (*otrazhatel'*), who, like a mirror, copied his interlocutors so as to force them to believe that he was the same as them (*svoi*). I subsequently had numerous opportunities to observe this phenomenal gift of his during meetings with leaders of other countries, whom he wanted to warm up to him. It's impressive even in several official photographs that successfully capture the moment – the Russian and the American president sitting there and smiling, two Bushes. Or two Schroeders. For about a split second Putin manages to mimic, with frightening precision, the furrowed brow, the bend in the neck, the double chin, and even the facial features of his *vis-à-vis,* and literally mimics them. And he does it so smoothly that his interlocutor doesn't notice it at all, just catches a buzz.
>
> (Tregubova 2003: 166–167)

Beyond this unique chameleon-like style of communication, on closer examination of Putin's unscripted public performances (for the purposes of this study, mainly press conferences, interviews, and publicly broadcasted "conversations" with the Russian people), one finds a short list of high-frequency speech profiles that help give linguistic shape to the president's public persona.[1] These profiles, which I label here *technocrat*, *delovoi* ("doer"), *silovik* ("strong man"), *muzhik* ("good ol' boy"), and *patriot*, not only provide insight into the linguistic underpinnings of Putin's political success. To the extent that popular political leaders can be seen as reflections of national sentiments, the voices outlined here also suggest some of the dominant linguistic identities that currently compete for symbolic authority in today's Russia. As Pavel Shirov, the co-director of *Comrade President* [Tovarishch prezident 2004], a television documentary of Putin, puts it:

> Each of us has our own Putin that has formed in our heads. Someone sees him as a person who'll bring back the younger and happier days. Someone else sees him as a man who wants to turn Russia into a great, developed power. Yet someone else sees him as a father figure who will provide everything, as is usual in this country.
>
> (Vylegzhanin 2004)

Ol'ga Kryshtanovskaia uses nearly an identical formulation in her own account of Putin's popularity, although, unlike Tregubova, she attributes it not to any special communicative skills on his part: "Another reason for Putin's success is that he is ideologically amorphous: neither left-wing nor right-wing . . . [A]n undefined president has a chance of being liked by everyone . . . Everyone sees in him whatever s/he wants to see. Putin is a mirror" (Shipitsyna 2004). Similarly,

Helena Goscilo (2011) has suggested that the diversity stems from an essential vacuity or emptiness in Putin's personal demeanor, that "he impresses sooner by his ABSENCE of qualities," and that this feature allows Russians to see their own, personally tailored Putin in him. Be it through the absence of defining features or some unique endowments, the Russian leader can be seen as both a source and a mirror (or *otrazhatel'*, as Tregubova puts it) of effective models of political discourse.[2]

Technocrat

As might be expected, the vast majority of Putin's language can be categorized as the relatively neutral discourse of a competent, if not eloquent, functionary, or technocrat. This in itself is noteworthy, as he is arguably the first Russian president to display such competency. The hundreds of pages of transcripts I have looked at document Putin's mastery of both bureaucratic and diplomatic jargon in a manner that does not draw negative attention for its deficiencies. He is as proficient with the terms, facts, and figures that serve as the verbal framework for the normal day-to-day functioning of the state as he is with the more refined language of international diplomacy. In contrast to the later Yeltsin years, in particular, his proficiency stands out in the eyes of the Russian population, who finally have a leader of whom they can be proud (or at least not ashamed). "He's normal! He's not an embarrassment," Kryshtanovskaia remarks in describing the sentiment as reflected in public opinion polls (Shipitsyna 2004). Respondents to a 2004 focus-group study of Putin's popularity offer similar praise for his oratorical skills: "He speaks well," "He talks normally, concisely, strictly," "He speaks without notes," "He speaks well and knows how to speak."[3]

An excerpt from Putin's response to a question (at a 2003 press conference) about tax reform exemplifies what might be called his linguistic "default setting":

> Что касается перераспределения налоговой нагрузки, то это – одна из основных задач Правительства в текущем году и в следующем, потому что нам нужно создавать лучшие экономические условия для развития перерабатывающих отраслей производства и высокотехнологичных отраслей. В этой связи Правительство планирует ряд осмысленных, на мой взгляд, действий, пока очень скромных и, наверное, недостаточных, но осмысленных. Они заключаются в том, что с 1 января следующего года планируется понизить, как я уже говорил, налог на добавленную стоимость на два процента, отменить налог с продаж, который будет иметь значение не только для торгующих организаций, но в конечном итоге должен сказаться и на производстве. Будут улучшены структура НДПИ (налог на добычу полезных ископаемых) структура ряда других налогов, в том числе и налогообложение физических лиц. В частности, предполагается изъять из налогооблагаемой базы сумму, которая будет истрачена гражданами на приобретение недвижимости: квартир,

домов, земельных участков. *Поскольку Вы так наморщили лоб, я понял, что я выражаюсь туманно. Я поясню.* Если Вы в течение года из ваших доходов истратили определенную сумму на приобретение жилья, скажем, дома, квартиры, то когда Вы будете заполнять налоговую декларацию, Вы сумму, которую истратили, не будете учитывать при налогообложении. У Вас налоги не будут вычитать из этой суммы. В общем и целом запланирован и ряд других осмысленных, повторяю, действий в сфере налогообложения.[4]

Given the string of nominal phrases (*pererasspredelenie nalogovoi nagruzki, razvitie pererabatyvaiushchikh otraslei proizvodstva*), technical jargon (*nalog na dobavlennuiu stoimost', struktura NDPI, nalogooblagaemaia baza fizicheskikh lits*), and frequent use of the passive voice (*planirovat'sia, skazat'sia, budut uluchsheny, predpologaetsia, budet istrachena*), the passage bulges with bureaucratese. Yet it not only shows a mastery Putin's predecessor lacked, but also demonstrates his ability to recalibrate his language to fit the perceived proficiency level of his audience, pausing midstream to translate the technocratic into layman's terms.

Proficient as he is in the languages of bureaucracy, however, and relieved as his countrymen may be about this elementary mastery, it is not for this language that Putin is most renowned. It is not the fluid discourse of the functionary that distinguishes him or his linguistic identity as a leader. Despite their proportionally infrequent occurrences, it is Putin's more stylistically marked, colorful, popular, and even vulgar turns of phrase that give full shape to his linguistic persona (in Russian, *iazykovaia lichnost'*) and provide insight into the sorts of speech genres that enjoy particular authority in Russia's language culture today. And it is to these I now turn, starting with the discourse of the *delovoi* (doer).[5]

Delovoi ("doer")

The "doer" linguistic profile can be understood as a more actively positive alternative to that of the technocrat. Here action words and metaphors dominate, as do references that privilege deeds over words. Putin's responses to frequent questions about his political biography (particularly during his early tenure as president) often redirect attention from any sort of political ideology or philosophy to the concrete actions he has taken as president:

> А по сути, мне кажется, о человеке нужно судить не по тому, что он сам о себе говорит, а по тому, что он делает. Давайте посмотрим и проанализируем, что происходило в сфере политической, экономической, в сфере строительства государства. [followed by a nine-paragraph list of accomplishments – MSG] [. . .] Все это реальные факты из российской политической действительности последних полутора лет, а из этого вы, пожалуйста, сделайте сами вывод: кто такой господин Путин.[6]

On a more pragmatic level, this impression translates into a heightened level of trust on the part of a populace tired of empty political promises. Respondents to a 2004 focus-group session on the president's performance gave Putin high marks for matching deeds to words: "He's done everything he promised"; "He doesn't toss around words errantly – if he promises to do something, he does it"; "He doesn't make empty promises"; "He doesn't waggle his tongue – he does what he says. . ."[7]

On the surface, the "doer" sees language and public speaking at best as a necessary evil, for words have a tendency to veil or complicate meaning.[8] Particularly in Russia, as one political commentator notes, where the word has either been used infamously (in politics) as a smoke screen for abhorrent behavior, or sacredly (in literature) as a conduit for proclaimed higher truths, the direct, one-to-one correspondence between signifier and signified in Putin's speech is joltingly alien. As one commentator noted,

> How can you pronounce concrete words and leave the simultaneous impression of clarity and ambiguity (*nedoskazannost'*)? He is an oddball (*chuzhak*) in the traditional political culture of Russia, where people are accustomed to catching a pile of meaning behind the words and looks of bossdom. With him, it is just the opposite: a word means no more than it means. In our civilization, where a poet is more than a poet and a plumber is more than a plumber, where there's too much informality, Putin prefers to act rather than interact.
>
> (Oreshkin 2000)

To this cultural level of interpretation, the presidential biographer (and Putin apologist) Roy Medvedev adds a sociological one that is no less relevant for understanding Putin's speech practices. According to Medvedev, Putin's penchant for deeds over words represents a pronounced shift from a charismatic, revolutionary mode of political discourse to one oriented more toward national rebirth:

> But there have been leaders (*vozhdi*) who have given birth not to words, but to action. These are people who have manifested colossal internal energy, an extraordinary concentration of will, decisiveness, and indefatigability. It appears that precisely this huge internal energy and indefatigability, as well as the call for the rebirth and elevation of Russia, has engendered a special relationship today among many Russian citizens to Vladimir Putin.
>
> (Medvedev 2004: 529)

If the Weberian charismatic leader uses spoken language to override written law and incite the populace to revolution, the post-revolutionary voice of restoration eschews such divisive stratagems, taking action instead to restore a modicum of authority and legitimacy to institutions of state power. Revolutionary speech was entirely appropriate for Putin's former boss, Sobchak, who delivered eloquent and spontaneous lectures on parliamentary democracy during the riveting live broadcasts of the First Congress of People's Deputies in 1989, or for the populist Boris Yeltsin, who stood atop tanks to decry the illegitimacy of Gorbachev's kidnappers; but not so for Russia's second president.[9] Putin is concerned not with tearing down past systems and institutions, but rather with raising a nation from the rubble of revolution – a mission that is reflected linguistically in the revival and melding of the three more organically Russian speech styles discussed in the following sections: *silovik*, *muzhik*, and *patriot*.[10]

Silovik ("strongman")

Putin's strongman persona finds linguistic substantiation in his tough talk, primarily invoked around issues concerning the breakaway republic of Chechnya, terror, and crime. Substandard, often vulgar lexicon peppers his language on these themes and ratchets up a rhetoric of violence, confrontation, and aggression. Consider, for example, the single most notorious speech replica to this day associated with Putin, uttered during a September 1999 press conference in Astana, Kazakhstan, when he was still prime minister to Yeltsin: "Мы будем преследовать террористов всюду. Если в туалете поймаем, то и в сортире их замочим."[11] More than any of Putin's utterances, the "*mochit' v sortire*" pearl demonstrates the profound impact an off-color comment (*sortir* being a colloquial synonym for outhouse, *zamochit'* a verb from criminal slang roughly equivalent to "bump off") can have on the career of a public official and even the mindset of a nation. Public response to it was immediate and strong; while some purists took the prime minister to task for degrading the great and mighty national tongue, others viewed it as the ideal campaign slogan for the 2000 elections (Radzikhovskii 1999). According to the sociologist Yurii Levada, "with that comment he enchanted (*obaial*) the people, showed his decisiveness, his approachability. And many people believed that he would really be able to achieve what nobody else thus far had been able to do."[12] In the 12 years since the pronouncement, despite Putin's failure to bring an end either to the Chechen conflict or terrorism in general, *mochit' v sortire* has earned a place in the standard lexicon of the national press, appearing in headlines of articles on topics totally unrelated to the original. A 1999 article on aggressive advertising strategies in *Commercial Petersburg* appeared under the title "Advertiser Will Bump off Consumer Even in the Bus and the Outhouse" (*Reklamodatel' zamochit potrebitelia dazhe v avtobuse i sortire*); the title of a 2000 *Literary Gazette* article uncovering local government corruption in Sochi announced, "A Poor Pensioner Is 'Bumped off in the Outhouse' by Sochi Authorities" (*"Zamochili v sortire" bednogo pensionera sochinskie vlasti*).[13]

Putin's encounters with terror only worsened from the time he assumed the presidency, and while he never repeated his infamous phrase about bumping off terrorists, his discourse on terror still relied selectively on nonstandard expressions and metaphors of violence to frame the issue. "С этими людьми," he commented in a government meeting from 2003, "бесполезно проводить профилактическую работу, их нужно выковыривать из подвалов и пещер, где они до сих пор прячутся, и уничтожать."[14]

In a 2002 press conference in Brussels, Putin invoked a different but equally graphic prophylactic procedure in response to a question from a French journalist who apparently demonstrated excessive sympathy for Islamic radicals:

> Если вы хотите совсем уж стать исламским радикалом и пойти на то, чтобы сделать себе обрезание, то я вас приглашаю в Москву. У нас многоконфессиональная страна, у нас есть специалисты и по этому "вопросу," и я рекомендую сделать эту операцию таким образом, чтобы у вас уже больше ничего не выросло. [15]

Be it a sign of a castration complex or simply a juvenile sort of jocularity, Putin's preoccupation with the male organ is clearly linked to notions of violence and punishment. And it is not reserved for external enemies. Putin euphemistically calls up the image of grabbing oligarchs by the testicles when commenting to the Italian media in November 2003 about Mikhail Khodorkovsky's belated attempt to settle back taxes:

> Вот сейчас ему предъявили конкретное обвинение. Он говорит: "Ну ладно, согласен, давайте сейчас заплачу." Вот такая торговля, такой сговор, он недопустим. Все должны раз и навсегда для себя понять: надо исполнять закон всегда, а не только тогда, когда схватили за одно место.[16]

Whether bumping off, castrating, or grabbing someone by the testicles, all actions involve physical violence meted out to the enemy, internal or external. More generically violent pronouncements predominate as well. In less ethnically charged instances involving criminal justice, Putin employs tough talk as a means of casting himself in the role of superhero and cop, as in his reference to the death penalty as "a gift to me, since it makes it easy to keep score."[17] At times this voice spills over into a populist mode more reminiscent of the *muzhik* speech genre, where he lets his personal emotions show through ("Когда смотришь на это, кажется, что своими руками бы задушил. Но это эмоции").[18]

This verbal suppression of baser emotions and impulses appears quite frequently in the president's tough talk, the speech-act equivalent to what in boxing is known as "pulling a punch" or restraining oneself at the last minute from following through with full force. It may also be understood in rhetorical terms as a form of praeteritio, a rhetorical figure in which the speaker announces the intention of not speaking about something (and thereby, in fact, speaking about it). In either case, if on the surface such utterances reject a certain primitive and brutal approach to resolving crime, terror, government inefficacy, or corruption, their very mention gives them some degree of legitimacy as a valid reaction to perceived misdeeds and injustices. Putin essentially acknowledges existing codes of proper behavior (note, in the previously quoted Khodorkovsky tax-evasion comment, his opting for the euphemistic "*odno mesto*" rather than the more direct "*iaichiki*," or "balls"), while at the same time violating them. Putin plays both sides in his comment on George W. Bush's characterization of Osama Bin Laden as a "villain" (*zlodei*) ("Я думаю, что он еще очень интеллигентно выражается. У меня есть другие определения, но я не могу в средствах массовой информации их использовать"),[19] and even in comments on leadership style within the state apparatus itself: "Самое простое – махать шашкой, рубить головы и выглядеть на этом фоне крутым руководителем."[20] In the case of the *mochit' v sortire* comment, Russian reading audiences actually saw the rhetorical gesture brought to life in the form of Aleksandr Ol'bik's action–adventure novel, *The President* [*Prezident* 2002], which features Putin, as president, secretly joining a division of special forces to root out Chechen leaders in a remote mountain hideaway in the Caucasus (for an extended discussion of the novel, see Chapter 6 by Andrei Rogatchevski). The book's climax describes the president face-to-face with one of the leading Chechen warlords, Garaev, in the very locale invoked in his 1999 threat:

> Swiftly retreating along the corridor, he adjusted the barrel of his submachine gun and "inscribed" a large portion of its contents into Garaev's stomach. Garaev was not able to grab onto the ringlet with his teeth, as he had no more strength left for the extraction of the pin. He took several steps, his muddied consciousness leading him to the side, into an open doorway, where he fell to his knees and, losing his balance, collapsed face forward, stretched out, exhaled a mix of air with bloody ichor, and froze in perpetuity.
>
> When the president stepped through the doorway of the room, he realized that he had come upon a bathroom.
>
> (Ol'bik 2002: 427)

That a single sound bite can serve as the premise for an entire action novel attests to the power of language, not through frequency of usage but through the expressiveness of the metaphor employed just once.

Muzhik (the "good ol' boy")

Arguably Putin's most expressively marked voice, the language of the *muzhik*, bears some resemblance to that of the *silovik* in its penchant for colloquialisms, substandard forms, and slang. But if *silovik*-speak evokes images of violence and toughness with the intent of sending a strong message to one's enemies, the discourse of the *muzhik* is softer and folksier in tone, geared more toward speaking to the common sense of the people, or *narod*. Proverbs, aphorisms, and metalinguistic references along the lines of "*kak v narode govoriat*" ("as the common folk say"), pepper Putin's speech, as do folksy witticisms and good-natured irony. The voice of the *muzhik* appears in a number of contexts, but particularly in discussions of domestic issues of everyday popular concern – salaries, jobs, education, public health, and pension reform. To cite only a few:

> On the positive influence of education in weaning the alcoholic off the bottle: Вообще, нужно, чтобы у человека были перспективы в жизни, чтобы он их видел. И тогда он будет стремиться к их реализации и “слезет,” как в народе говорят, со стакана.[21]

> On the need for a cautious approach to agricultural trade and reform: Мы не должны действовать по примеру, когда хвост вытащили – нос увяз, а нос вытащили – хвост оказался в грязи.[22]

> On the distinction between proper and improper forms of privatization: Вопрос в том: что приватизировано и то, что будет приватизироваться, – все должно происходить в рамках единого федерального закона, по единым правилам, а не так, как это было до сих пор – через пень колоду. Если мы помним, был принят соответствующий Указ Президента Бориса Николаевича Ельцина по этому вопросу. На основе этого указа, который просто продекларировал приватизацию сельхозугодий, на местах начали принимать свои законы – кто в лес, кто по дрова.[23]

> Justifying Russian protectionism by alluding to protectionist trade practices in other countries: Это не значит, что я против этой либеральной экономики. Но это значит, что во многих других странах часто руководствуются русской поговоркой “своя рубашка ближе к телу.”[24]

> On accusations regarding arms sales to rogue states: Вы знаете, у нас есть такая поговорка, может быть, она не очень хорошо звучит, но, наверное, будет к месту: мы считаем, что котлеты и мухи должны находиться друг от друга в разных местах. Вот давайте мы мух от котлет будем отделять.[25]

By citing proverbs, Putin injects a tone of commonsense folk justice that at once brings him closer to the mentality of the *narod* and gives his views a legitimacy based on a seemingly unassailable domain of the Russian national tradition.[26] Ingrained as they are in the lexicon of the national tongue, proverbs and aphorisms create an illusion of permanence that makes them less susceptible to question.

Given that antipathy toward the new rich in Russia today is concentrated among those with lower levels of income and education, it is unsurprising that this voice of time-honored folk justice dominates Putin's comments on the so-called “oligarchs” and their shady involvement in privatization and the mass media. Here one also finds considerable overlap with the discourse of the *silovik* – particularly in references to corruption, thievery, and enforcement. One of the folksier assessments of the crimes perpetrated by the oligarchs, delivered in a 2002 joint press conference with French President Jacques Chirac, plays with parallels to village thievery and hooliganism that cannot help but resonate with almost any Russian:

> Знаете . . ., когда у нас человек украдет мешок картошки либо водки напьется и с соседом подерется, он или хулиган, или вор. Его сажают в тюрьму. А если человек украдет сотни миллионов долларов, он уже политический деятель, его трогать нельзя. Вот у нас таких деятелей оказалось в ходе перестройки экономики и перехода к рыночным отношениям очень много . . .[27]

If anything, the oligarch comes away looking worse than the local village hooligan, not only because he is beyond the reach of justice, but because the object of his lust – cold, hard currency (and foreign, at that) – has far less sentimental value than vodka or potatoes to the average Russian listener. Putin plays off this corrupt passion for excessive amounts of cash in his use of colloquial intensifiers with the stem verb "*vorovat'*" ("to steal") in the following dictionary-like definition of the oligarch he offered in a 2003 Kremlin press conference: "Олигарх в том смысле, в каком мы обычно употребляем это слово, это человек с *наворованными* деньгами, который и дальше продолжает *разворовывать* национальное богатство, используя свой особый доступ к органам власти и управления."[28]

In a Kremlin press conference that same year Putin goes one step further to offer derogatory impersonations of oligarchs (and their representatives in the media), which, through his use of substandard coinages, even criminal slang, underscore the morally destitute nature of their activities.

> Несколько губернаторов уже приходили ко мне. Рассказывают, что представители СМИ приходят и говорят: "Гони 250 тысяч долларов, слова плохого не услышишь в ходе предвыборной кампании, правда, и хорошего не напишу, но гарантирую тебе, что не поддамся на уговоры, провокации, меня никто не купит зато." Это что такое? Это шантаж называется.[29]

The use of the slang "*goni*," the fact that the sum is in dollars rather than rubles, the use of the informal *ty* in addressing a regional governor, the mere reference to shady notions of "persuasion" and "provocation," and the use of colloquial word order ("*slova plokhogo*," "*nikto ne kupit zato*"), when combined, create a distinct if not direct link to the language and practices of a crime boss.

At times, in fact, the godfatherly voice of ironic contempt, family allegiances, veiled threats, and retribution are detectable in Putin's own direct speech, as in the following commentary on Vladimir Gusinskii, given in a 2001 interview with representatives of the American media:

> [Г]осподин Гусинский получил почти миллиард и не отдал, и не собирается. Бегает между Израилем и Вашингтоном и чувствует себя хорошо, и покупает группы влияния в Соединенных Штатах, с тем чтобы осуществлять, разворачивать деятельность против нас. Деньги пусть отдаст. Много других вопросов подобного рода.[30]

Here the rhetoric does more than portray the oligarch in question as an alien and fugitive crime boss (underscored by the derogatory use of "*gospodin*," "*begaet*," and "*chuvstvuet sebia khorosho*"); Putin casts himself (and either his "family" or Russia by extension) as an opposing clan through his use of the personal pronoun in "*deiatel'nost' protiv nas*," through the implication that he and his clan have limited ability to bring Gusinskii to justice themselves ("*Den'gi pust' otdast*"), and finally through the elliptical suggestion that scores on several counts nevertheless need to be settled ("*Mnogo drugikh voprosov podobnogo roda*"). In this context, Putin's colorful reference to Khodorkovsky's seeking compromise only when "they'd grabbed him by the testicles" comes across as the logical next step – the violent execution of the settling of scores.

In all cases, the voice of the *muzhik* functions to delineate Putin as "one of us" (*svoi chelovek*), someone cognizant of the concerns of the people, who shares their commonsense (albeit masculine) perspectives. That folk wisdom often appears in conjunction with a discourse of folk justice, which, however tough, is but a logical extension of that affinity, particularly in a time when the population yearns most of all for a strong leader capable of bringing order to chaos. As one analyst put it:

> According to sociological studies, the "strong government" promised by Vladimir Putin is interpreted in mass consciousness first and foremost as "fair government." [. . .] This is a concrete peculiarity of our social psychology: the growth of trust in power (*vlast'*) is accompanied by a growth in paternalistic attitudes.

In contrast to the late Yeltsin, whose authority was perceived as weak, and thus all had to fend for themselves, under the "strong statist" Putin, "more and more people have begun to depend on state patronage" (Petkhov 2000). *Muzhik* is to *silovik*, then, as *batiushka* is to tsar.

Patriot

In a sense, Putin's patriotic voice carries over this melding of strength, fairness, and populist affinities into the area of national identity, and in so doing, brings another set of emotions into play – pride and shame – with the intent of restoring the dominance of the former over the latter. Given the degree to which Russia's image suffered in the 1990s, the restoration process begins with a direct and forceful rejection of images of the nation as an impoverished beggar or has-been superpower:

> В отличие от прежних времен Россия сегодня сотрудничает с Западом не потому, что хочет понравиться или что-то получить взамен за свою позицию. Мы не стоим с протянутой рукой и ни у кого за это ничего не просим. Я провожу эту политику только потому, что считаю, что это полностью соответствует национальным интересам России, а не для того, чтобы кому-то понравиться . . .[31]

Parallel to this metaphorical rejection of weakness, Putin offers a positive image of a virile Russia ("Должен заметить, руки у России все крепче и крепче. Их не выкрутить даже таким крепким партнером, как Евросоюз"[32]) and at times takes on a more aggressively defiant tone, as in his verbally invoked non-verbal gesture ("giving the finger") in response to the idea that Russia would give Kaliningrad to Germany to pay off debt – again, the rhetorical strategy of praeteritio that has the effect of extending the very gesture he proclaims to be suppressing.[33]

Putin struck a more cautious note in his remarks at the opening ceremony of the Civic Forum in 2001, but drew a direct connection between citizenship and the gradual restoration of national pride:

> Еще пока трудно признаться самим себе, что у нас кое-что, говорю специально очень аккуратно, кое-что начинает получаться. Наступает время, когда жизнь в России постепенно становится более или менее достойной. Быть гражданином России становится престижно, тем более что в России понятие "гражданин" всегда значило гораздо больше, чем юридически оформленная связь с государством. И потому гражданственность и патриотизм от одной лишь записи в документе не появляются.[34]

Attempts at restoring a sense of national pride prove more difficult in the face of more shameful events and indicators such as national disasters and poverty. We see Putin making such an attempt in a televised interview in the wake of the *Kursk* submarine explosion, where he first establishes his own position as a committed, strong leader (using the first-person "I will be" three times), then draws an associative link between himself and the military, the *narod*, and the nation:

> Никаких огульных расправ под влиянием эмоциональных всплесков и под влиянием стечения обстоятельств не будет. Я буду с армией, буду с флотом буду с народом. И вместе мы восстановим и армию, и флот, и страну. Нисколько в этом не сомневаюсь.[35]

When he discusses Russians' perception of themselves and their own nation, Putin's patriotism assumes a moralistic rather than pugilistic tone, with maternal and familial metaphors predominating. In a 2003 speech to a domestic audience, he addresses the issue of national pride and shame, couching it in moral terms akin to the attitude and loyalty one feels toward one's own mother:

> Я считаю, что мы всегда имеем право гордиться своей страной, а стыдиться своей страны – все равно, что стыдиться своей матери. У меня родители были простыми людьми, у мамы не было даже среднего образования. Я ее очень люблю. Никогда их не стыдился, потому что знал, что они делали для меня все, что могли, и даже больше. Я это видел. У меня не было никаких сомнений. Отношение к стране

> должно быть такое же. Если чего-то не нравится – нужно исправлять. Это не от страны зависит, а от нас. Нечего на зеркало пенять, коли рожа крива – помните? Так что если и должно быть стыдно, то только за самих себя.[36]

Here Putin combines a variety of strategies to appeal to the listener, playing off his own "common beginnings," the well-worn link between mother and motherland (*Rodina-mat'*), and calling upon a folk aphorism ("Don't blame the mirror for the crooked mug") that most educated listeners would recognize as a literary reference to Nikolai Gogol's *Inspector General* [Revizor 1836].

Given the metaphorical ties to family and the people, as well as the maternal and paternal bonds, the voice of the patriot often emerges in autobiographical contexts. For instance, Putin declares his affinity with the "rank-and-file Russian citizen" by recalling his childhood years in a communal apartment, and underscores his national service credentials through references to his time in the KGB ("Все-таки в органах безопасности, в разведке культивировалось самое главное – это патриотизм и любовь к Родине").[37] It is not coincidental that the greatest overlap of his two most positively marked voices – the *muzhik* and the patriot – occurs in these autobiographical contexts, linking mother to motherland and citizenship to state. In the following extended excerpt from an interview with the French press, Putin the philosopher considers the paradox of his having been a baptized KGB agent. The commentary combines the colloquial voice of the *muzhik* and the humble Christian with the patriotic verve of a Soviet citizen, generously sprinkled with organic metaphors of national identity:

> Вся жизнь состоит из противоречий. Там, где кончается противоречие, там наступает небытие. Это говорит о том, что Россия так же, как и другие части Европы, не порождение чего-то искусственного, а страна со своей историей, со своим настоящим и будущим. Это говорит о том, что сохраняются исторические культурные корни народа, и истребить их невозможно. Они, если образно выразиться, как трава в крупном мегаполисе, пробиваются через асфальт.
>
> У меня мама была верующая. Это было не то, чтобы не модно, как сейчас, это было даже опасно в бывшем Советском Союзе. И она не то, чтобы тайно, но не афишируя это, окрестила меня в церкви. И нет ничего удивительного в том, что она дала мне крест с собой, чтобы освятить его на Гробе Господнем в Иерусалиме.
>
> У нас не было никакого другого государства, кроме коммунистического. Каждое государство имеет набор инструментов, набор каких-то механизмов, которые делают его государством. Один из этих инструментов – Служба внешней разведки, где я имел честь работать. Это была интересная работа. Это ничуть не мешало мне. И то, что меня мама крестила в церкви, когда мне был примерно год, я даже не знаю точно, сколько мне было тогда, ничуть не мешало мне выполнять обязанности офицера внешней разведки.[38]

In one of his more contemplative statements on the nature of Soviet and post-Soviet identity, Putin taps into the essential "contradiction" that all law-abiding (if not card-carrying) Soviet citizens faced after the collapse. He maneuvers through it rhetorically by ignoring potentially awkward truths about the degree to which he actively pursued and publicized his affiliations to Orthodoxy, by elevating the issue of contradictory lifestyles into the realm of the existential (in the well-established tradition of positing the enigma of Russianness and the Russian soul), and by casting this dilemma in terms of a tension between two parallel identities: one that is organic, maternal, popular, and Christian versus one that is mechanical, paternal, official, and Soviet. As an offshoot of the weed that pushed through the pavement of the Soviet metropolis and thrived in that environment without rejecting his roots, Putin offers a model of reconciliation and rebirth for those who share his existential predicament in the post-Soviet era.[39]

But lest we begin to view Putin as the kind of philosopher-*intelligent* who likes to ponder larger issues of the sort that arguably led to the disappearance of the Russian democrats from the political (and linguistic) radar screen, we should remember that the dominant voice that regularly stands out in Putin's linguistic repertoire is that of the technocrat. Tellingly, in a response to one of the more philosophical and identity-laden questions of the post-Soviet era ("What should the national state idea be in Russia?"), it is to this voice that Putin so mundanely reverts:

> А я уже говорил по этому поводу. Что является главным на сегодняшний момент? Развитие экономики, обеспечение высоких темпов ее развития. [. . .] Самая главная идея – обеспечение темпов роста экономики. От этого зависит будущее страны в прямом смысле этого слова. Обеспечение конкурентоспособности страны во всех сферах, во всех областях.[40]

While there is certainly no mistaking Putin for Nikolai Berdiaev, he is true to his linguistic identity: a functionary proficient in the primary verbal tools of the technocratic trade; willing to stand up to the rogues who threaten the security and integrity of the nation; able to speak to the people in their own language and appeal to their need for stability and justice; and not adverse to invoking tried and true patriotic images of the past and linking them with the prospect of economic hope and national pride.

A leader's linguistic identity emerges not so much from some formula of proportional frequency of the various voices or speech genres employed, but rather from those voices and genres that listeners and readers come to identify most readily with that leader. In Putin's case, while the vast majority of his utterances are not particularly memorable stylistically (though basic competence and minimal eloquence are not to be underrated, given the shoes he filled), the genres of the *delovoi*, *muzhik*, *silovik*, and patriot are most often invoked in commentaries on his speech practices (e.g., *Putinki* 2004). Each of these locutionary functions, which in reality often is intermingled with others, finds strong resonance among the majority of a population that is tired of both the perception and reality of a passive, weak, and corrupt Russia. According to a 2004 public opinion survey, more than 50 percent of the Russian population believed that life in Russia had improved over the course of Putin's first term. When asked to list the strongest virtues of the president, respondents singled out three: 23 percent noted his "strong persona" (*silnaia lichnost'*); 17 percent noted his "style of public behavior" (*stil' publichnogo povedeniia*); and 15 percent noted his stature as a "man of deeds" (*chelovek dela*). When asked to elaborate, those attributing his success to his style most often singled out the fact that he is "a good orator, [. . .has the] ability to express his thoughts well."[41] From a linguistic perspective, this perception helps to account for Putin's popularity and success – even when his actual actions and policies garner less support and appeal (see Bavin 2004). By integrating seemingly contradictory profiles, he symbolically enables the sort of national revival of identities, both organic and instrumental, that suffered during the tumultuous years of the Yeltsin era.

Notes

1 The data for this study come from hundreds of pages of transcribed foreign and domestic press conferences, interviews, and public forums held between January 2000 and May 2004.

2 Some (e.g., Furman 2000) go so far as to claim that the times, not the leaders, dictate the language of public discourse, although one could still argue that it takes an astute leader with a deft command of language both to determine the necessary language of the times and to implement it in a convincing manner.

3 "V. Putin i ego deiatel'nost' v otsenkax rossiian (April 8, 2004)," Fond Obshchestvennogo Mneniia. Available at: http://bd.fom.ru/report/map/projects/dominant/dom0414/domt0414/domt0414_2/d041409 (accessed April 14, 2004).

4 As for the redistribution of the tax burden, this is one of the main tasks of the government in the current year and next year, because we need to create the best economic conditions for the development of manufacturing sectors of production and sectors of high technology. In this regard, the government is planning a series of what I believe to be sensible actions – very modest, for now, and probably insufficient, but sensible. They consist of, beginning January 1 of next year, planning to lower, as I have already said, the value-added tax by 2 percent, eliminating the sales tax, which will significantly impact not only trading organizations, but which should also ultimately impact manufacturing. The structure of the NDPI [the tax on the extraction of commercial minerals] and the structure of a series of other taxes will be improved, including tax burden on sole proprietors. In part, it has been suggested that the sum that citizens will spend on the acquisition of real estate – apartments, houses, land – be exempted from the tax base. *Judging from the way you wrinkled your brow, I see I am expressing myself opaquely. Let me try to explain.* If, in the course of the year you spend a certain sum from your income on housing, such as a home or apartment, then when you fill out the tax declaration the amount that you spent would not count as a tax liability. You will not have taxes taken out from that amount. All in all, a series of other sensible actions in the area of tax assessment are planned. [Emphasis added – MSG] "Stenograficheskii otchet o press-konferentsii dlia rossiiskikh i inostrannykh zhurnalistov." June 20, 2003. Available at: http://archive.kremlin.ru/appears/2003/06/20/1237_type63380type63381

type82634_47449.shtml (accessed May 12, 2011). All quotes from Putin that are a sentence or more in length appear in the text in the original Cyrillic, with English translations provided in footnotes. All English translations are mine.

5 Although for the sake of analysis I organize these voices into five different and discrete linguistic models or identities, the models frequently appear blended or in proximity to one another.

6 Essentially, it seems to me, you have to judge a person not by what he says about himself, but by what he does. Let's look at and analyze what has happened in the spheres of economics, politics, and state construction [followed by a nine-paragraph list of accomplishments – MSG]. [. . .] These are all real facts from the Russian political reality of the last one and a half years and it is from this, if you please, that you yourselves should draw conclusion about who Mr Putin is. "Stenograficheskii otchet o rasshirennoi press-konferentsii dlia rossiiskikh i inostrannykh zhurnalistov." July 18, 2001. Available at: http://archive.kremlin.ru/appears/2001/07/18/0000_type63380type82634_28591.shtml (accessed May 12, 2011). Cf. (after defending his democratic credentials in the face of stereotypes about the KGB) "У нас есть такая поговорка, у нас говорят, что о человеке судят не по тому, что он говорит сам о себе, а по тому, что он делает." (We have a saying, in Russia they say that a man is judged not by what he says about himself, but rather by what he does.) "Interv'iu amerikanskoi telekompanii 'Ei-bi-si.'" November 7, 2001. Available at: http://archive.kremlin.ru/appears/2001/11/07/0003_type63379_28692.shtml [accessed May 12, 2011]).

7 Quoted in "V. Putin i ego deiatel'nost' v otsenkakh rossiian" (April 8, 2004).

8 In this regard, of course, one would need to note Putin's long-standing penchant for action photo-ops – be they of him extinguishing peat fires, tranquilizing tigers, commandeering figher jets, or plumbing the depths of Baikal in a submersible – where words are absent altogether, ceding authority to the power of the image. For detailed analysis of these, see Chapters 1 and 8 by Goscilo and Chapter 2 by Cassiday *et al.*

9 Interestingly, Medvedev claims that "while Sobchak (as mayor of St. Petersburg – MSG) paraded his oratorical skills at social receptions, Putin (as Sobchak's first deputy) did the day-to-day routine work that really made the 'second capital' tick" [Rafael' Guseinov, "Chetyre goda v Kremle," *Trud* 84 (May 7, 2004), 3].

10 For more on Putin as an emblem of post-revolutionary restoration, see Aron (2004).

11 We will follow the terrorists everywhere. If we catch them in the toilet, if you'll pardon the expression, then we'll bump them off in the outhouse sooner or later. That's it. The issue is completely closed. (Transcribed by the author from a video recording of the comment in *Putin: Stairway to Power* [2003], Films for the Humanities and Sciences.)

12 "Putin mozhet delat' vse, chto zakhochet," *Segodnia* (February 28, 2000).

13 *Delovoi Peterburg* (December 13, 1999); *Literaturnaia gazeta* (June 14, 2000). The phrase has also predictably provided fodder for neo-Nazi, nationalist groups who see an ally in Putin [e.g., "Mochi ikh, Putin! Sait v podderzhku Prezidenta." Available at: http://suicide.lenin.ru/putin/ (accessed May 12, 2011)].

14 Conducting preventive work with such people is useless. They need to be dug up from the cellars and caves where they hide to this day and be destroyed. "Vstupitel'noe slovo na soveshchanii s chlenami Pravitel'stva." July 7, 2003. Available at: http://archive.kremlin.ru/appears/2003/07/07/1520_type63374type63378_48375.shtml (accessed May 12, 2011).

15 If you want to convert to Islamic radicalism completely and undergo a circumcision, then I invite you to Moscow. We have a multi-confessional country and specialists in that "area," and I'd recommend that you perform the operation in such a way that

nothing would ever grow there again. "Vyderzhki iz stenograficheskii otcheta o press-konferentsii po itogam vstrechi na vysshem urovne Rossiia – Evropeiskii soiuz." November 11, 2002. Available at: http://archive.kremlin.ru/appears/2002/11/11/0001_type63377type63380type82634_29553.shtml (accessed May 12, 2011).

16 So now they've leveled a concrete indictment against him. And he says, "Well, okay, I agree, let me pay them [taxes – MSG]." This kind of trading, this kind of secret deal is impermissible. Everyone must understand once and for all: you've got to obey the law always, and not just when they've got you by the testicles. "Interv'iu ital'ianskim informatsionnomu agentstvu ANSA, gazete *Kor'ere della sera* i telekompanii RAI." November 3, 2003. Available at: http://archive.kremlin.ru/appears/2003/11/03/2200_type63379_54926.shtml (accessed May 12, 2011). I must note that Russia's hands are stronger and stronger. Even a strong partner like the European Union can't pry them open. "Vystuplenie na vstreche s predstaviteliami delovykh krugov Rossii i Germanii." October 9, 2003. Available at: http://archive.kremlin.ru/appears/2003/10/09/1325_type63376type63377_53768.shtml (accessed May 16, 2011). "Stenogramma priamogo tele- i radioefira ('Priamaia liniia' s Prezidentom Rossii)," December 24, 2001. It's still difficult to admit to oneself that things, and I'm speaking very carefully on purpose, are beginning to work out for us. The time is coming when Russia's gradually becoming more or less worthy. Being a citizen of Russia is becoming prestigious, especially since in Russia the concept of "citizen" has always meant much more than a legally codified link to the state. And that's why citizenship and patriotism don't originate in just a notation in a document. "Vystuplenie na otkrytii Grazhdanskogo foruma." November 21, 2001. Available at: http://archive.kremlin.ru/appears/2001/11/21/0001_type63374type63376type82634_28709.shtml (accessed May 16, 2011). There will be no sweeping reprisals under the influence of emotional outbursts or under the influence of the given set of circumstances. I will be with the army, I will be with the navy, and I will be with the people. And together we'll restore the army, the navy and the country. I have absolutely no doubt about this whatsoever.komanii RAI. November 3, 2003. Available at: http://archive.kremlin.ru/appears/2003/11/03/2200_type63379_54926.shtml (accessed May 12, 2011).

17 Quoted in *Putinki* (2004), 147 from an interview with *Izvestiia* (from ITAR-TASS, March 13, 2002).

18 When you look at this, you feel you could strangle them with your own hands. But that's emotions [getting in the way]. "Vyderzhki iz stenograficheskogo otcheta o vstreche s prezidentom Vsemirnogo banka Dzheimsom Vulfensonom i uchastnikami II Global'noi konferentsii po problemam pravosudia." July 9, 2001. Available at: http://archive.kremlin.ru/appears/2001/07/09/0000_type63376type63377_28580.shtml (accessed May 12, 2011).

19 I think he actually expressed himself quite delicately. I have other designations but I can't use them in the media. "Interv'iu amerikanskoi radiostantsii 'Neshnl pablik redio.'" November 16, 2001. Available at: http://archive.kremlin.ru/appears/2001/11/16/0000_type63379_28703.shtml (accessed May 15, 2011).

20 It's the easiest thing to rattle your sabre, chop off heads, and, against this background, look like a tough leader. "Stenograficheskii otchet o press-konferentsii dlia rossiiskikh i inostrannykh zhurnalistov." June 20, 2003.

21 In general, a person needs to have prospects in life and to see them. And then he'll strive to realize them and "come down off the bottle," as the common folk say. "Stenogramma priamogo tele- i radioefira ('Priamaia liniia' s Prezidentom Rossii)." December 24,

2001. Available at: http://archive.kremlin.ru/appears/2001/12/24/0001_type82634 type146434_28759.shtml (accessed May 12, 2011).

22 We don't want to get into a situation where you pull the tail, the nose gets stuck, pull the nose, the tail ends up in the dirt. "Vstrecha s pensionerami," January 27, 2004.

23 The issue of what's been privatized and what will be privatized: everything must take place within the framework of a single federal law, according to a single set of rules – not as it was done earlier, in a slipshod manner (*cherez pen' kolodu*: literally, "falling over a stump into a log"). We should recall that there's a corresponding decree by President Boris Nikolaevich Yeltsin on this issue. On the basis of this decree, which simply declared the privatization of farmland, laws began to be passed on the local level as to how it would be divvied up (literally, who goes to the woods, and who to the woodpile). "Stenograficheskii otchet o press-konferentsii dlia rossiiskikh i inostrannykh zhurnalistov." June 24, 2002. Available at: http://archive.kremlin.ru/appears/2002/06/24/1158_type63380type63381type82634_29002.shtml (accessed May 16, 2011).

24 That doesn't mean I'm against this liberal economics. But it means that, in many other countries, the Russian saying "every man for himself" (literally, "one's own shirt is closer to the body") is often at work. Ibid.

25 You know we have a saying that might not sound very nice, but probably applies here: we believe that the cutlet and the flies should be separate from one another. Let's separate the flies from the cutlets. "Interv'iu nemetskoi telekompanii ARD." September 19, 2001. Available at: http://archive.kremlin.ru/appears/2001/09/19/0002_type63379_28636.shtml (accessed May 12, 2011).

26 In one of the earliest linguistic analyses of Putin's speech to appear in print, Irina Volkova (2000) argues that the "infusion" of folk sayings in his speech is a conscious strategy by Putin's "image-makers" to invite associations between "the speech behavior of our hero with famous images engrained in the mass consciousness. In the current case – the *chekist* who embodies the classical virtues of fighters of the invisible front: a passionate heart, a cool head, and clean hands."

27 For us, you know, when a man steals a sack of potatoes or gets drunk on vodka and picks a fight with a neighbor, he's either a hooligan or a thief. He gets sent to jail. But if a man steals hundreds of millions of dollars, well, he's a politician and you can't touch him. There were very many of these types who appeared over the course of the restructuring of the economy and transition to market relations. "Zaiavlenie dlia pressy i otvety na voprosy v khode sovmestnoi press-konferentsii s Prezidentom Frantsii Zhakom Shirakom." January 15, 2002. Available at: http://archive.kremlin.ru/appears/2002/01/15/0002_type63377type63380_28774.shtml (accessed May 16, 2011).

28 An oligarch, according to the common use of the term, is a person with *stolen* money who continues to *vandalize* national riches, using his special access to the organs of power and management. [Emphasis added – MSG] "Stenograficheskii otchet o press-konferentsii dlia rossiiskikh i inostrannykh zhurnalistov." June 20, 2003. This is the same sort of defining-the-enemy technique seen in his repeated use of "Eto prosto *bandity*" ("They're *bandits*, plain and simple") with regard to Chechen separatists. Putin's reference to "national riches" here also appeals to listeners' patriotic sentiments.

29 Several governors have already come to me. They tell me how representatives of the media come and say, "Drum up 250 thousand dollars and you won't hear a bad word during the primary campaign – true, we won't write anything good either, but I guarantee you I won't give in to fast talk or provocation, nobody will buy me out." What's

this? It's called blackmail. "Stenograficheskii otchet o press-konferentsii dlia rossiiskikh i inostrannykh zhurnalistov." June 24, 2002.

30 Mr. Gusinskii got almost a billion and didn't give it back and doesn't plan to. He runs back and forth between Israel and Washington and feels good and buys the influence of groups in the United States with the intention of carrying out and setting in motion acts against us. Have him give the money back. There are many other questions along these lines. "Beseda s rukovoditel'iami predstavitel'stv vedushchikh amerikanskikh SMI." June 18, 2001. Available at: http://archive.kremlin.ru/appears/2001/06/18/0002_type63376type63380_28569.shtml (accessed May 16, 2011).

31 In contrast to former times, Russia today collaborates with the West not because it wants to be liked or to get something in exchange for its position. We don't stand with hand outstretched and we don't ask anyone for anything [as reward]. I conduct this policy only because I think it fully corresponds to Russia's national interests, not to be liked by someone. "Stenogramma vstrechi s predstaviteliami germanskikh i rossiiskikh SMI." April 7, 2002. Available at: http://archive.kremlin.ru/appears/2002/04/07/0000_type63380type63381_28859.shtml (accessed May 16, 2011). Cf. Putin's comment about Russia under Yeltsin as being "like the seven people with spades while we are alone with a spoon" (*. . . semero – s soshkoi, a my odni s lozhkoi*). (Putin actually inverts the codified proverb, "*Odin s soshkoi – semero s lozhkoi*" ["One with a spade, seven with spoon in hand"], but in each case those holding the spoons are seeking handouts from others doing all the work.) "Interv'iu telekanalam ORT, RTR i 'Nezavisimoi gazette.'" December 25, 2000. Available at: http://archive.kremlin.ru/appears/2000/12/25/0000_type63379type82634_28444.

32 I must note that Russia's hands are stronger and stronger. Even a strong partner like the European Union can't pry them open. "Vystuplenie na vstreche s predstaviteliami delovykh krugov Rossii i Germanii." October 9, 2003. Available at: http://archive.kremlin.ru/appears/2003/10/09/1325_type63376type63377_53768.shtml (accessed May 16, 2011).

33 "Stenogramma priamogo tele- i radioefira ('Priamaia liniia' s Prezidentom Rossii)," December 24, 2001.

34 It's still difficult to admit to oneself that things, and I'm speaking very carefully on purpose, are beginning to work out for us. The time is coming when Russia's gradually becoming more or less worthy. Being a citizen of Russia is becoming prestigious, especially since in Russia the concept of "citizen" has always meant much more than a legally codified link to the state. And that's why citizenship and patriotism don't originate in just a notation in a document. "Vystuplenie na otkrytii Grazhdanskogo foruma." November 21, 2001. Available at: http://archive.kremlin.ru/appears/2001/11/21/0001_type63374type63376type82634_28709.shtml (accessed May 16, 2011).

35 There will be no sweeping reprisals under the influence of emotional outbursts or under the influence of the given set of circumstances. I will be with the army, I will be with the navy, and I will be with the people. And together we'll restore the army, the navy and the country. I have absolutely no doubt about this whatsoever. "Interv'iu telekompanii RTR v sviazi s tragediei na atomnoi podvodnoi lodke '*Kursk*.'" August 23, 2000. Available at: http://archive.kremlin.ru/appears/2000/08/23/0000_type63374type63379type82634_28834.shtml (accessed May 16, 2011).

36 It's my belief that we always have the right to be proud of our country, whereas being ashamed of it is just the same as being ashamed of one's own mother. My parents were simple people. My mother didn't even have a high school education. I love her very much. And I was never ashamed of them because I knew that they'd done everything they could for me, and more. I saw that. I had no doubts about it. One's attitude toward

one's country should be the same. If there's something you don't like, you need to fix it. It depends not on the country, but on us. Don't blame the mirror for the crooked mug – remember? So if there's the need for shame, it can only be for ourselves. "Stenograficheskii otchet o besede s finalistami konkursa 'Moi dom, moi gorod, moia strana.'" June 5, 2003. Available at: http://archive.kremlin.ru/appears/2003/06/05/2055_type63376type63381type82634_46848.shtml (accessed May 16, 2011).

37 After all, in the security agencies, in espionage, they cultivated the most important thing – patriotism and love for the Motherland. "Stenograficheskii otchet o press-konferentsii dlia rossiiskikh i inostrannykh zhurnalistov." June 24, 2002; "Beseda s rukovoditeliami predstavitel'stv vedushchikh amerikanskikh SMI." June 18, 2001. Cf. his comment, "Когда был Советский Союз – я был его патриотом" (When the Soviet Union existed I was its patriot). "Stenograficheskii otchet besedy s finalistami konkursa 'Moi dom, moi gorod, moia strana.'" June 5, 2003.

38 All of life consists of contradictions. Where contradictions end, there begins nothingness. This speaks to the fact that Russia, just like other parts of Europe, is not an imitation of something artificial, but a country with its own history, its own present and future. It speaks to the fact that the historical and cultural roots of the people have been preserved and it is impossible to destroy them. To phrase it in terms of an image, they're like a weed in a huge metropolis, poking its way through the asphalt. My mother was a believer. It's not just that it wasn't fashionable back then, as it is now; it was downright dangerous in the former Soviet Union. And she baptized me in the Church – not really secretly, but not advertising it. And there's nothing surprising in the fact that she gave me a cross to bless in the Holy Sepulcher in Jerusalem. We had no other government but the communist one. Each government has a selection of tools, a selection of certain mechanisms that make it a government. One of these mechanisms was the Foreign Intelligence Service, where I had the honor of working. It was interesting work. It didn't bother me in the least. And the fact that my mother baptized me in church when I was around a year old – I don't even know exactly how old I was – in no way prevented me from fulfilling my duties as a Foreign Intelligence officer. "Interv'iu frantsuzskoi gazety 'Figaro.'" October 26, 2000. Available at: http://archive.kremlin.ru/appears/2000/10/26/0000_type63379_28946.shtml (accessed May 16, 2011).

39 As Aron (2004) puts it, Putin himself stands out as a symbol and embodiment of that "very precarious balance between freedom and order, [. . .] old and new" that lies at the core of the "broad, multifaceted post-revolutionary 'restoration' that, in one form or another, has followed every great revolution."

40 I've already addressed that issue. What is the main thing at the current moment? The development of the economy, ensuring a fast pace for its development. [. . .] The most important idea is ensuring the tempo of economic growth. The country's future depends on this in the most direct sense of the word. Ensuring the country's competitiveness country in all spheres, in all areas. "Stenograficheskii otchet besedy s finalistami konkursa 'Moi dom, moi gorod, moia strana.'" June 5, 2003.

41 "V. Putin i ego deiatel'nost' v otsenkakh rossiian."

Bibliography

Aron, L. (2004) "Putin Rides High on Russians' Need for Stability," *Newsday*. May 21.

Azar, I. (2010) "*O kul'te Putina*." Available at: http://www.gazeta.ru/politics/2010/07/08_a_3395661.shtml (accessed July 30, 2011).

Bavin, P. (2004) "Putin – 'svoi chelovek' v Kremle." *Fond Obshchestvennogo Mneniia*. Available at: http://bd.fom.ru/report/cat/policy/president2/ptin/d041428 (accessed October 28, 2004).

Bereza, V. and P. Shirov. (2004) *Tovarishch Prezident*, Ekho-TV.

Furman, D. (2000) "Ot pozdnego El'tsina k rannemu Putinu," *Obshchaia gazeta*. February 10.

Goscilo, H. (2011) "The Ultimate Celebrity: VVP as VIP *Object d'Art*," *Celebrity and Glamour in Contemporary Russia: Shocking Chic*. H. Goscilo and V. Strukov (eds.), London: Routledge. 29–55.

"Iazyk Lenina." (1924) *LEF* 1.

Medvedev, R. (2004) *Vladimir Putin: chetyre goda v Kremle*, Moscow: Vremia.

Ol'bik, A. (2002) *Prezident*, Donetsk: Stalker.

Oreshkin, D. "Pushkin, Putin, Pinoshet!" (2000) *Moskovskie novosti*. December 26.

Petkhov, V. (2000) "Perevod s prezidentskogo na russkii," *Obshchaia gazeta*. July 27.

Pribylovskii, V. (2003) "Putinoslavie: Khronika proslavlenii Putina Vladimira Vladimirovicha," *Rossiia Putina: pristrastnyi vzgliad*. A. Verkhovskii, E. Mikhailovskaia, and V. Pribylovskii (eds.), Moscow: Panorama. 193–204.

"Putin mozhet delat' vse, chto zakhochet." (2000) *Segodnia*. February 28.

Putin: Stairway to Power. (2003) Films for the Humanities and Sciences.

Putin, V. (2000) *First Person: An Astonishingly Frank Self-Portrait by Russia's President*, New York: Public Affairs.

Putinki: Kratkii sbornik izrechenii prezidenta (Pervyi srok). (2004) Moscow: Ekho buk.

Radzikhovskii, L. (1999) "Shchedraia na razrushenie dusha," *Segodnia*. November 10.

Shipitsyna, N. (2004) "Liudi v serom," *Moskovskii Komsomolets*. July 14.

Tregubova, E. (2003) *Baiki kremlevskogo digger*, Moscow: Ad Marginem.

Volkova, I. (2000) "Slovo Putina," *Ekspert*. February 14.

"V. Putin i ego deiatel'nost' v otsenkax rossiian." (2004) April 8. *Fond Obshchestvennogo Mneniia*. Available at: http://bd.fom.ru/report/map/projects/dominant/dom0414/domt0414/domt0414_2/d041409 (accessed April 14, 2004).

Vylegzhanin, R. (2004) "100 Minutes about Vladimir Putin," *Moscow News*. July 14.

Primary sources for Putin quotes

"Beseda s rukovoditel'iami predstavitel'stv vedushchikh amerikanskikh SMI." (2001) June 18. Available at: http://archive.kremlin.ru/appears/2001/06/18/0002_type63376 type63380_28569.shtml (accessed May 16, 2011).

"Interv'iu amerikanskoi telekompanii 'Ei-bi-si'." (2001) November 7. Available at: http://archive.kremlin.ru/appears/2001/11/07/0003_type63379_28692.shtml (accessed May 12, 2011).

"Interv'iu frantsuzskoi gazety 'Figaro.'" (2000) October 26. Available at: http://archive.kremlin.ru/appears/2000/10/26/0000_type63379_28946.shtml (accessed May 16, 2011).

"Interv'iu ital'ianskim informatsionnomu agentstvu ANSA, gazete *Kor'ere della sera* i telekomanii RAI." (2003) November 3. Available at: http://archive.kremlin.ru/appears/2003/11/03/2200_type63379_54926.shtml (accessed May 12, 2011).

"Interv'iu nemetskoi telekompanii ARD." (2001) September 19. Available at: http://archive.kremlin.ru/appears/2001/09/19/0002_type63379_28636.shtml (accessed May 12, 2011).

"Interv'iu telekanalam ORT, RTR i 'Nezavisimoi gazete.'" (2000) December 25. Available at: http://archive.kremlin.ru/appears/2000/12/25/0000_type63379type82634_28444.shtml (accessed May 16, 2011).

"Interv'iu telekompanii RTR v sviazi s tragediei na atomnoi podvodnoi lodke '*Kursk*.'" (2000) August 23. Available at: http://archive.kremlin.ru/appears/2000/08/23/0000_type63374type63379type82634_28834.shtml (accessed May 16, 2011).

'Neshnl pablik redio, 2001"Interv'iu amerikanskoi radiostantsii 'Neshnl pablik redio.'" (2001) November 16. Available at: http://archive.kremlin.ru/appears/2001/11/16/0000_type63379_28703.shtml (accessed May 15, 2011).

"Stenograficheskii otchet o besede s finalistami konkursa 'Moi dom, moi gorod, moia strana.'" (2003) June 5. Available at: http://archive.kremlin.ru/appears/2003/06/05/2055_type63376type63381type82634_46848.shtml (accessed May 16, 2011).

"Stenograficheskii otchet o press-konferentsii dlia rossiiskikh i inostrannykh zhurnalistov." (2002) June 24. Available at: http://archive.kremlin.ru/appears/2002/06/24/1158_type63380type63381type82634_29002.shtml (accessed May 16, 2011).

"Stenograficheskii otchet o press-konferentsii dlia rossiiskikh i inostrannykh zhurnalistov." (2003) June 20. Available at: http://archive.kremlin.ru/appears/2003/06/20/1237_type63380type63381type82634_47449.shtml (accessed May 12, 2011).

"Stenograficheskii otchet o rasshirennoi press-konferentsii dlia rossiiskikh i inostrannykh zhurnalistov." (2001) July 18. Available at: http://archive.kremlin.ru/appears/2001/07/18/0000_type63380type82634_28591.shtml (accessed May 12, 2011).

"Stenogramma priamogo tele- i radioefira ('Priamaia liniia' s Prezidentom Rossii)." (2001) December 24. Available at: http://archive.kremlin.ru/appears/2001/12/24/0001_type82634type146434_28759.shtm (accessed May 12, 2011).

"Stenogramma vstrechi s predstaviteliami germanskikh i rossiiskikh SMI." (2002) April 7. Available at: http://archive.kremlin.ru/appears/2002/04/07/0000_type63380type63381_28859.shtml (accessed May 16, 2011).

"Vstupitel'noe slovo na soveshchanii s chlenami Pravitel'stva." (2003) July 7. Available at: http://archive.kremlin.ru/appears/2003/07/07/1520_type63374type63378_48375.shtml (accessed May 12, 2011).

"Vyderzhki iz stenograficheskii otcheta o press-konferentsii po itogam vstrechi na vysshem urovne Rossiia – Evropeiskii soiuz." (2002) November 11. Available at: http://archive.kremlin.ru/appears/2002/11/11/0001_type63377type63380type82634_29553.shtml (accessed May 12, 2011).

"Vyderzhki iz stenograficheskogo otcheta o vstreche s prezidentom Vsemirnogo banka Dzheimsom Vulfensonom i uchastnikami II Global'noi konferentsii po problemam pravosudia." (2001) July 9. Available at: http://archive.kremlin.ru/appears/2001/07/09/0000_type63376type63377_28580.shtml (accessed May 12, 2011).

"Vystuplenie na otkrytii Grazhdanskogo foruma." (2001) November 21. Available at: http://archive.kremlin.ru/appears/2001/11/21/0001_type63374type63376type82634_28709.shtml (accessed May 16, 2011).

"Vystuplenie na vstreche s predstaviteliami delovykh krugov Rossii i Germanii." (2003) October 9. Available at: http://archive.kremlin.ru/appears/2003/10/09/1325_type63376type63377_53768.shtml (accessed May 16, 2011).

"Zaiavlenie dlia pressy i otvety na voprosy v khode sovmestnoi press-konferentsii s Prezidentom Frantsii Zhakom Shirakom." (2002) January 15. Available at: http://archive.kremlin.ru/appears/2002/01/15/0002_type63377type63380_28774.shtml (accessed May 16, 2011).

5 The discourse of a spectacle at the end of the presidential term

Lara Ryazanova-Clarke

Introduction

On October 18, 2007, Russians were treated to the annual ritual that by then had become a familiar feature of Vladimir Putin's presidency – a 'discursive marathon' lasting approximately 3 hours of simultaneous radio and television broadcasts of President Putin's question and answer session with the general public, known under the title *Direct Line with the President* [*Priamaia liniia s prezidentom*]. Throughout his two terms in the Kremlin, the format of *Direct Line* had remained unchanged since it first aired in 2001, and even after Putin officially stepped down from the presidency and assumed the office of prime minister, he, not president Medvedev, continued to hold the televised forum with the nation, whose title was slightly adjusted to *Direct Line with Vladimir Putin*. Back in 2007, Putin's last year in the presidential office, observers reported the sense of uniqueness they felt in that summative national dialogue. The word "record" [record] was used extensively both in the language of the program and in its media descriptions.[1] Journalists closely following the event noted the record of the longest time spent – precisely 3 hours and 6 minutes; of the highest number of questions received (2.5 million), as well as the record number of answers – 69.[2] The discourse constituting answers to approximately 0.003 percent of the questions that concerned the Russian people was framed as an in-depth conversation with the whole nation. Some media labeled the dialogue between the president and the nation as "going to the people" [khozhdenie v narod],[3] romantically evoking a nineteenth-century phrase, with its historical associations of self-denial and dedication,[4] while others cynically called it "online politics," [onlain-politika][5] and "a replacement for democracy" [zamena demokratii].[6] In any case, it was an intensive exercise in identity narrative to which both information seekers and information givers made their contribution. That the postcommunist identity is narrated on television in this exuberant spectacular form reminds us of Guy Debord's (2002) notion of the society of the spectacle, in which the social life is replaced by its commodified representation, which he calls the pseudoworld.

The objective of this chapter is to identify the main trends and linguistic strategies in the construction of meanings related to national identity characteristics in Putin's Russia, as it emerged in the spectacle of *Direct Line*. With that purpose in mind, I analyze the verbal activities of the participants – the president, the presenters, and the public – relying for my data on the full broadcast transcript of the *Direct Line* (2007), consisting of 21,695 words.[7]

As Benedict Anderson persuasively demonstrated, "nations are not only invented but also reinvented and reimagined" (1983: 26). The collapse of the Soviet Union and the ensuing change of legitimacies brought about a fundamental transformation of the society's perception of the world, which included reimagining, renegotiating, and reconstructing a different, post-Soviet Russian identity.

A growing body of scholarship among the critical perspectives in discourse analysis posits the sociocognitive nature of national identity (Wodak *et al.* 1999; Van Dijk 2002; Chilton and Shäffner 2002; Wodak and Chilton 2005). Being a complex mental structure that contains what is perceived to be shared knowledge, it encompasses "common or similar beliefs or opinions internalised in the course of socialisation," including the distinction of the in-groups from the out-groups, and is linked to emotional attitudes and dispositions – both behavioral and linguistic (Wodak *et al.* 1999: 28).

As Siegfried Jäger put it, "discourse is a flow of knowledge" (2001: 34), and within this paradigm, national identity as a form of knowledge is a discursive construct that emerges from a multitude of language practices and social enactments (Ricoeur 1991; Martin 1995; Wodak *et al.* 1999, 2002; Fairclough 2002; Bourdieu 2004: 78–87; Dolón and Todolí 2008). It is schematically represented in the forms for which a variety of terms have been used: scripts, schemas, or frames (Van Dijk 1977: 13), the term accepted in this chapter. The knowledge frames are constructed when identity discourse reinterprets the world by carving out and highlighting certain identity components in the process. Among such components, Denis-Constant Martin singles out the fields of power, time, and the configuration and reconfiguration of human groups. As he explains,

> [t]he identity narrative channels political emotions so that they can fuel efforts to modify and balance power; it transforms the perceptions of the past and of the present; it changes the organisation of human groups and creates new ones; it alters cultures by emphasizing certain traits and skewing their meanings and logic. The identity narrative brings forth a new interpretation of the world in order to modify it.
>
> (Martin 1995: 13)

Co-construction of the discourse

Identity building sometimes may have a principal actor, although generally it is a process of coproduction involving various motivated parties engaged in the reproduction of the identity components (Wodak *et al.* 1999). The objects of knowledge emerge from co-construction of meanings in interaction and the "other-orientation" of the speakers. In particular, Marjut Johansson points out the represented, interdiscursive character of the coproduced discourse of political interview TV shows, noting that speakers tend to "recontextualize material from other contexts" (Johansson 2006: 217).

The discourse of *Direct Line*, in contrast to that of many political interviews, strikes one as a harmonious, cooperative polylogue. It consists of three main types of participation: (1) presenters' moves of introductory narratives about the linked-up locations or about members of the public standing at mobile cameras; (2) moves by the members of the public asking questions or/and expressing wishes; and finally, (3) Vladimir Putin's answers and comments. All the parties involved notwithstanding, there is no doubt that the president is the key narrative actor in the polylogue. The format of questions and answers and the kind of questions that are easy and comfortable – even at their most daring, hardly probing or contradictory – place Putin in the position of the leading source of knowledge, while the public assumes the role of passive agents seeking, sharing, and reinforcing the knowledge offered by the president.

All *Direct Line* collocutors seem to map the knowledge they produce onto the shared mental frames, or, in Michel Foucault's words, *grids of specification* – the systems according to which objects of the discourse are "divided, contrasted, related, regrouped, classified . . ." (Foucault 1972: 42). An example of such coproduction of knowledge frames may be seen in the question and answer sequence between the history teacher Larisa Kul'kova and Putin (1). Together, Kul'kova and the president coconstruct the mental frame of Russian history as requiring correction and the investment of increased patriotism:

> (1) Kul'kova: Well, as a teacher I'm concerned about the sloppy attitude of society and especially youth, to history. There are masses of shocking examples of historical ignorance.
>
> Putin: I completely agree with you. I also love history very much, and you and I know how, not that long ago, we used to read in textbooks things that could make our hair stand on end. Especially in relation to the interpretations of, say, the results of the Second World War and everything connected to that. However, lately, there has been a certain positive move.[8]

In the beginning of their dialogue, the two participants share the belief that youth have a "wrong historical knowledge" – a belief that contains a shared emotional component. Kul'kova expresses her belief in terms of "concern" [*bespokoit*] for the state of people's knowledge of history, which she categorizes as "ignorance" [*nevezhestvo*]. In this strategy of generalization, she negatively qualifies all of Russian society's view of history as "sloppy" [*nebrezhnoe*], then qualifies the examples that she does not give with the emotionally charged adjective "shocking" and the augmentative noun "masses" [*massa shokiruiushchikh primerov*]. In his turn, the president confirms her belief, emphasizing his agreement with the adverbial "completely" [*polnost'iu*] and constructing commonality through the pronoun phrase "you and I" [*my s Vami*]. He reinforces Kul'kova's negative frame with the emotive metaphorical phrase "could make our hair stand on end" [*volosy dybom mogli vstat'*], which virtually rephrases Kul'kova's adjective "shocking," but also concretizes the expression "sloppy attitudes" by a specific example of erroneous interpretations – that of the results of the Second World War in textbooks.

The knowledge frame coconstructed through negative categorization and articulation of a sense of shock serves as justification for Putin's further announcement of new legislation (2). The new law, which gives the Ministry of Education vetting power over the content of history textbooks, is presented through the topos of contrast, as a "certain positive move" [*opredelennye pozitivnye sdvigi*] (1), a commonsense solution to the coconstructed "problem" of unacceptable historical interpretations. Although Kul'kova talks about "the problem" in the grammatical present tense, Putin reframes it in the past tense, "not that long ago," thereby indicating that by now (under Putin) it has been resolved. Replacing the phrase "wrong interpretations of history" with the noun "defect" [*brak*], associated with the Soviet industrial discourse, Putin goes on to equate censorship with effective flaw prevention, as "natural" as a conveyor-belt operation:

> (2) Putin: But you probably know that a relevant legislative decision has been taken to prevent an obvious defect in this area, increasing the role and significance of the Ministry of Education and Science. Now it will be able to provide relevant expert evaluations as part of the preparation of educational literature.[9]

As the discussion to follow demonstrates, the theme of the Second World War – the single historical event that binds Russian in near-unanimity – exerts a particular rhetorical power that is especially used when the knowledge frames need to be adjusted and presented as shared.

How direct?

Although *Direct Line with the President* was presented to the public as a spontaneous exchange, evidence points to the fact that it was thoroughly prepared and scripted. According to *Moskovskii komsomolets*, a thousand call center operators were vetted and psychologically trained to work on the program.[10] Reportedly, questions were filtered and members of the public underwent a selection process before forming picturesque crowds in front of various outside cameras.[11] The leading anchors for this and the six other annual broadcasts were the trusted newsreaders from the two Kremlin-controlled national channels, Ekaterina Andreeva of *Channel One* and Sergei Brilev of *Rossiia*. Both received the state Friendship Medal (Ukaz Prezidenta 2006) for their service. Locations up and down the country chosen for the linkup were kept secret until the last moment, causing agitated rumors to circulate among newspapers and to breed animosity between the included and the excluded.[12] *Novaia gazeta*, for example, reported with disappointment that despite a widespread conviction that St. Petersburg was tipped to be in the program's geography, the television cameras would not arrive there.[13] Questions started to pour in as early as 5 days in advance, giving the president copious time to look through them and select what he called "the most frequent ones," making it all too clear who ultimately decided what merited an answer and what did not.[14]

Construction of magnitude

The spectacle of *Direct Line* has to be interpreted within the context of the Putin mania, a phenomenon that has been evolving throughout the recent decade, and that combined elements of postcommunist consumer culture with the Soviet-styled personality cult (Cassiday and Johnson, 2010; Goscilo 2011). The text of the *Direct Line*, containing 69 question-and-answer sequences, was broadcast, published, and replicated in full or abridged versions in multiple media forms: on all main television and radio channels, on the Internet, and in the national papers. The scale of coverage was matched by the attempt to intimate that the audience is witnessing a nationwide conversation. Lists and numbers were consistently employed to create the impression of a huge scale, and also, in the good Marxist tradition, to imply "truth," suggesting that Putin deals in empirical reality. In particular, the broadcast of the linkup was regularly interrupted by reports from the call centers, which supplied updates on the number of questions received so far and on the means of their arrival, listing the range of communication tools: telephone, text messages, and the Internet (see (3) below). As (3) demonstrates, numerals, in combination with temporal markers such as "day," "minute," and "around the clock," were used to construct a sense of urgency and the large scale of participation. The temporal adverb "around the clock" [*kruglosutochno*], which evokes the contexts of emergency services, constructs the scale by pointing to the size of the country, with its many time zones, but also by stressing the supreme importance of a potential verbal contact with the president.

> (3) Presenter: Our telephone center is now working for the fifth day; it has been working around the clock to make it convenient for the whole country. And at this moment we've already received two million and (almost) two hundred thousand calls. This is a record.[15]

In contrast to the modest number of people actually involved, the numbers cited by the program aim to persuade the public that those 69 participants whose questions were answered genuinely reflect the nation's opinion. So, for *Direct Line*'s narrative, magnitude also means togetherness, based on what Paul Ricoeur calls "the numerical component of identity," by which "the notion of identity corresponds to the process of identification, understood in the sense of reidentification of the same, which makes cognition recognition: the same thing twice, *n* times" (1992: 116). Numerically, the discourse perpetuates and reinforces national meanings, and on top of that, builds a positive and enthusiastic image of the nation. Presenters interpret the high number of questions as an indication neither of a level of concern the public might have nor of their possible wish to bring the president to account, but only of supportive participation, engagement, and, above all, achievement. The noun "record" indicates that success is measured by the numbers of participants having a silent but numerically recorded conversation with the leader. The speaking participants also play their role in the construction of an illusion of magnitude, for they behave metonymically, emphasizing numbers, framing their questions not as posed by individuals but collectively, and greeting the president on behalf of their region or a group: for example, (4) "Respected Vladimir Vladimirovich! Today we convey our hearty greetings on behalf of seven thousand of the inhabitants of Russkii Island."[16]

Construction of national space

Among the salient dimensions of national identity construction, Wodak *et al.* outline the thematic area of the "national body," comprising recurrent features in the descriptions of geographical space, landscape, and "physical national artefacts" (1999: 30–31). Ever since the Ancient Greeks, rhetoric of place has been used to draw a link between the ground "on which one walks" with the people "of whom one speaks" (Martin 2002: 143). Mikhail Bakhtin's notion of "chronotope" accounts for the specific conception of space pertaining to each historical period. Identifying the Soviet chronotope under Stalin, Evgeny Dobrenko and Eric Naiman (2003) have demonstrated that the Soviet space was a dimension of Stalinist discourse used for symbolic mobilization of Soviet citizens: "This was a country in which [. . .] the notion of space [. . .] was imbued with remarkable ideological prominence." (Naiman 2003: xiv).

The mental geography at the core of the post-Soviet *Direct Line* displays many strategies that borrow and perpetuate Soviet discursive patterns. The program maps Russia as a space divided into the center and the periphery, asserting the pattern by which the knowledge frames are produced in the center and delivered centrifugally to the margins. This mapping can be seen in the distribution of locations and positions of the knowledge givers and knowledge receivers. The president, flanked by the two leading journalists, sits in the central studio in Moscow while the question-asking public occupies the periphery, linked by a television bridge from a number of locations in the streets and squares across the Russian Federation.

In the Moscow-centric national body of Russia, the periphery is often described through its function in respect to the center. Thus in (5), the village of Podkolodnovka is linguistically linked to Moscow by its assumed role of supplying the capital with food. A sense of entitlement is emphasized by the adverb "dutifully" [*ispravno*], while the verbal sequence "has been tasted" [*probovali*] and "has been sampled" [*degustirovali*], cast in the impersonal forms of the third person plural, obviates the subject and may be understood as an expression of the center's sybarite approbation: (5) "Presenter: From here, Moscow receives the dutifully sent produce, vegetables and butter (the butter here is especially delicious; it's been tasted, it's been sampled)."[17]

As in the case of Podkolodnovka, the introductory narratives from other places select the local information in respect to what is centrally defined as matters of national value. For instance, in (6), the narrative of the town of Plesetsk explains that it is mapped onto the national body because it boasts a rocket launching facility at the forefront of the military reequipment of the Russian Army. The presenter, Ekaterina Andreeva, says: (6) "Our television camera is positioned in the region where this morning a significant event took place, and what makes us happy is that everything performed deserves the grade of 'excellent.'"[18] Andreeva's speech move defines what was merely a successful military exercise as an event of national magnitute by labeling it "significant" [*vazhnoe sobytie*]. Her introduction also includes something of a retro-flash: video footage of an exercise rocket launch timed to coincide with the day of the *Direct Line*, its visual foregrounding intended to stimulate memories of achievements by the Soviet space program. The impersonal clause "what makes (us) happy" [*chto raduet*] has no subject and therefore can be understood as Andreeva's speaking on behalf of all participants and viewers, thus creating a "community of joy." Coupled with the evaluative adverb "grade of excellent" [*na otlichno*], in which, again, the subject of evaluation is universalized through omission, these utterances aim to produce the illocutionary force[19] of stirring viewers' excitement and pride in their country.

Moreover, the center–periphery relationship within the "national body" is expressed in personalized terms, insofar as the majority of places in the linkup are introduced as having a close connection to president Putin himself. The Black Sea resort of Sochi, for example, is linked to the successful bid for the Winter Olympics 2014, which Russia won, we are told, not least because of Putin's personal effort. Also, the Dagestani village of Botlikh, which Putin visited in 1999, is presented as an advanced post for the start of the second war with Chechnya, which was instrumental in his first election as president. To convey the idea that these locations have special qualities, the presenters often describe them through the strategy of singularization implemented in (7) by certain adjectives. Thus, the Putin-related locations acquire a special status as "symbolic" or anthropomorphically, as "morally" above the rest: (7) Presenter: "(a) [W]e are approaching this symbolic city, which we have already mentioned today – this is the city of Sochi; (b) Botlikh is not a geographical name, but a moral category."[20]

In defining Russian identity through space, size matters. Large expanses have traditionally been important in the articulation of certain ideas: that of Russian belonging (Milner-Gulland 1999: 4–13; Widdis 2004: 30–49) and as an expression of the Soviet "union" identity (Tolz 1998: 995). The *Direct Line*'s construction of national spaces promotes the idea of national unity and coherence; and it also recasts the country's size as its strength and achievement, as illustrated in (8):

> (8) (a) Vladivostok is the easternmost point of this *Direct Line* . . . From us to you it's 9,302 kilometers. (b) . . . it's already getting dark here. (c) This is, indeed Podkolodnovka, 900 kilometers to Moscow and 250 to Voronezh. (d) The Plesetsk spaceship launch pad is the northernmost spaceship launch pad in the world. (e) This is the western edge of the country – Kaliningrad.[21]

Whereas during the period of "the parade of sovereignties" under Yeltsin, republics and regions demanded more autonomy from the center, the discourse of the show reaffirms Putin's policy of the "vertical of power" toward the regions by foregrounding the positive meanings and "superabundance of emotions" attached to the "breadth of the motherland," borrowed from Soviet discourse (Günther 2003: 82–84). Thus, presenters in their intermedia emphasize deictic elements, use geographical terms qualified by numerals, emphatic qualifiers such as "-most" [*samyi*], or temporal and spatial particles and adjectives such as "already (dark)" [*uzhe (temno)*] – which marks the deictic view of the speaker mentally positioned in Moscow the center, where it is not getting dark – and "from . . . to" [*ot . . . do*], emphasizing vastness.

Through the use of tropes, the presenters create the impression of Russia's enormous expanses as an unbroken whole – an image achieved through a strategy of rhetorical cohesivization. Both Soviet and traditional Russian folkloristic metaphors of covering territory quickly and effortlessly seem to be instrumental in stressing this idea; for example, (9) (a) "We're stepping over the Urals"; (b) "And so we swiftly cross over from the North Caucasus to the banks of the Volga."[22] In addition, cohesivization is also achieved through the regular use of synecdoche, which implies uniformity and representativeness: (a) "Goodbye, Kaliningrad; (b) Ekaterinburg greets you."[23]

While the presenters' speech defines Russian locations, it simultaneously redefines them by attributing to them new qualities and a new status. Though Moscow retains its rank of national center, its standard label of "capital" [*stolitsa*] becomes deterritorialized and used for descriptions of various places that speakers describe as the modern and urban variant of the topos of "the lovely place" (*locus amoenus*), cf. (10). Rather than attributing the characteristic of a multipolar space to the Russian national body, the repetitive metaphorical use of the term "capital" elaborates the semantics of cohesion. The "capital" qualification given to places embellishes the narrative, making the objects they describe appear good to talk about.

> (10) (a) Ekaterinburg, the city that's always called the capital of the Urals, greets you. (b) After [the celebration] of the 1000th anniversary of Kazan, the label of the Eastern capital of Russia has stuck to this city. So, the presenter of the program *Vesti* now reports from the Eastern capital of Russia. (c) Sochi greets Moscow. Indeed, now it's not just a resort town, but also the capital of the Winter Olympics 2014. (d) This is the far west of the country, Kaliningrad, the capital of the Russian Baltics, where Oleg Groznetskii works.[24]

Furthermore, *Direct Line*'s redefinitions serve as verbal forms of political adjustment and recategorization. For example, in the cases of Kazan and Kaliningrad, the "capitals" are linked by the genitive construction to the words Russia [*Rossiia*] or Russian [*rossiiskii*], which both affirm that the arguably contested territories truly belong to Russia. Kazan, the capital of the Muslim republic of Tatarstan, which in the 1990s was reassessing its relationship with Moscow and heading for devolution and autonomy (Robertson 2002; Davis *et al.* 2000), is redefined. In the second case, the toponym "the Baltics" [*Pribaltika*], previously used to refer to the territories that are now Baltic independent states, is reclaimed as Russian.

In paying particular attention to outlying and borderline areas, the discourse delineates what is deemed to be the Russian national essence. At all points of the compass, the linkup includes outposts, marking the frontier, producing the effect of a symbolic mental patrol of the territory and of the watchful awareness of the boundary: (11) "Behind me, beyond the mountain, is Georgia. Opposite it, there's a mountain that unfortunately you can't see. That's where Chechnya starts."[25] The opening question in the program emblematically comes from Russkii [Russian] Island, the easternmost point of the country (12). The island symbolizes both the "edge" and essential Russianness, and the question coming from it sets the tone for a further discursive development. Concerned with the ferry to the mainland and flight prices for reaching central Russia, the question relates to the country's cohesion and the participants' belonging:

> (12) Here in the Far East we say this. There are two Russias: a prosperous one, which stretches up to the Urals, and the other Russia, beyond the Urals, which suffers the islander's syndrome of being stranded . . . If Vladivostok is cut off from Russia, then we, the inhabitants of the Russian Island, are cut from off the city of Vladivostok.[26]

The urge expressed in (12) to establish the connectedness of the national body is reinforced in Putin's promise to bring the summit of the Pacific Region countries to Russkii Island and to build a bridge from the island to the mainland.

Both inclusion and exclusion from the imagined map prove to be potent meaning constructors and shifters. The inclusion in *Direct Line* of Aktau, a town in Kazakhstan, may raise a few eyebrows and cause puzzlement and ambiguity as to how far Russia's national body stretches (13). Participants in the show clearly felt that an explanation of this choice was required, as indicated by a justification strategy marked by the multiple "because" [*potomu cho*] clauses. For justification, discourse participants used ethnic and linguistic rhetoric ("Russian people" [*russkie liudi*], "the Russian language" [*russkii iazyk*]), as well as the circular, self-referential argument that the Kazakhstani watch this program.

> (13) Presenter: Today one of the them [cameras] is fixed in Kazakhstan, and not only because many Russian people live there . . . , not only because in state institutions the Russian language has a status equal to Kazakh, but also because we know that many people there watch *Direct Line with the President* of the Russian Federation.[27]

Speakers' references to Kazakhstan reinforce the sense of ambiguity regarding the position of this country on the imagined map of Russian national discursive knowledge. Specifically, the speakers evade the expected noun "country" [*strana*], while often defining it negatively in relation to Russia, as "not Russia," or "outside of Russia": (14) "(a) Andreeva: our mobile television stations work not only in Russia; (b) Putin: Since we're talking to those who happen to be outside the Russian Federation."[28] Another frequent reference to Kazakhstan as a place in the post-Soviet space [*postsovetskoe prostranstvo*] (15) is suggestive of a territory not yet finally shaped and defined by the qualifier with the root "Soviet," reminding listeners of the time when it was within the Soviet Union. Similarly, the choice of the word "republic" [*respublika*] in Putin's comments contains ambiguity, for this was Kazakhstan's label as a constituent part of the Soviet state.

> (15) (a) Presenter Bobrov: The Kazakhstani Aktau greets you directly from the shore of the Caspian Sea. The town's extremely interesting, and in many ways unusual and unique in the post-Soviet space; (b) Putin: the republic's leadership does everything to maintain the current status quo and support the development of the Russian language.[29]

These linguistic negotiations point to the possibility of conceiving blurred boundaries in the Russian national body and of encompassing a global "wider Russian identity" that includes Russian speakers outside the Russian Federation. Such a linguistic treatment of borders is abetted by the discursive prevalence of another strategy – that of perpetuating some entrenched Soviet knowledge frames and the topos of assimilation that finds articulation in expressions stressing commonalities: for instance, references to the common past, assertion of brotherly friendship, and delineation of a common "other," as in (16) "Presenter: Besides, it's not with America, but with Russia that Kazakhstan has many centuries of common history."[30] The evocation of the Second World War is used to build commonalities, borrowing broadly from the Soviet authoritative narrative: (17) "Let's remember the Great Patriotic (war). It's exactly here, on Kazakhstani land, that the legendary battalion of the Panfilovites, which defended Moscow, was formed."[31] The first person plural imperative, "let's remember" [*vspomnim*], initiates the construction of collective memories articulated by the Soviet signifiers of war heroism, including certain collocates ("the legendary battalion" [*legendarnaia diviziia*]) and the elliptic reference to the war omitting the noun, "The Great Patriotic" [*Velikaia Otechestvennaia*]. Another revamped signifier is the story, contained in every Soviet school textbook, of the 28 heroes-Panfilovites, who in November 1941 destroyed 18 Nazi tanks at Dubosekovo. The community of memory about the heroes-Panfilovites, however, can be built only if the participants turn the clock back, to omit the perestroika era, when archival documents opened for the first time exposed the story as a myth created by Stalin's propaganda machine (Tolz 2004).

To sum up, Russian national space emerges from the polylogue of *Direct Line* as an object whose parts constantly are verbally patched and linked together. It is a territory with the defined center and outposts, but despite having clear borders, it also has an ability to stretch beyond them. The knowledge frames of the national space are often informed by those salient elements of Soviet discourse that work, to use Serguei Oushakine's term, as retro-frameworks in the manipulation of memories, defrosting myths, and providing ways of speaking about the nation. As Oushakine explains, languages, frames, and images borrowed from the past signal "a peculiar post-Soviet stylistic block, a particular expressive deficiency of postsocialism" (2007: 481). By borrowing and repetition of the Soviet forms, the deficient discourse of the nation taps into people's retrospective longing for a common repertoire in its attempt to restore the shared symbolic experience.

The construction and reconstruction of time

Attribution of properties to time periods and the construction of a national present, past, and future is another key parameter of the national identity narrative (Wodak 1999: 83–105). Regarding the past, as in the reference to the Panfilovites in the Kazakhstan episode, the participants of *Direct Line* often use the discursive strategy of continuation, which helps in reviving collective memories of the communist period. These include the archetypal symbols of Soviet authoritative discourse, such as the Bolshevik revolution and the Second World War. Putin's recollection of his visit to the Dagestani village of Botlikh at the time when the villagers resisted an attack by Chechen fighters is a case in point. Praising the Botlikh men, in his description of them, the president uses a positively nuanced knowledge schema connected to the October revolution: (18) "and all of them were crisscrossed by cartridge belts, like the revolutionary sailors in 1917."[32]

In (19), the trope of comparison serves the purpose of assimilation between the two periods – the Chechen conflict of Putin's era and the Bolshevik revolution – with the actors in both constructed as fearless heroes. Putin's verbal evocation of the visual image harks back to the Soviet "myth of origin" (Hall 1996: 615) and facilitates recasting the Dagestani villagers in the guise of archetypal Russian masculinity depicted in the figure of the revolutionary sailor in numerous films and paintings. The image from the revolutionary pantheon helps him valorize the Russian side of the conflict, presenting the Dagestani resistance in a generalized manner as the Russian patriotic endeavor.

> (19) Putin: People simply . . . took up arms and rose to defend the interests of Russia and their own homes. This is an exceptional example of patriotism, and, by the way, not only of the local, the Dagestani, but also of Russian patriotism.[33]

The domain of the Second World War is used as another source of positive identity formation. The award of the title "Town of Military Glory" to Rzev a few days before the show[34] seems to be the principal reason for its placement on the map of *Direct Line*'s national body. The symbolic event of the award is entextualized in the moves of the participants, all of whom employ the war theme to talk about the town. The presenter who introduces Rzhev (20) does so standing at the Victory memorial. His speech is represented discourse, which incorporates the recognizable Soviet period war narrative. The markers of this narrative include war-related terms such as "The Great Patriotic War" [*Velikaia Otechestvennaia voina*], "obelisk," "occupation" [*okkupatsiia*], and "veteran." The presenter also borrows from past discourses (1) the linguistic strategy of particularizing the sufferings endured by the town during the war, articulated by the temporal phrase "seventeen months" [*semnadtsat' mesiatsev*], which emphasizes the length of suffering; and (2) cliché collocates highlighting and connecting pain and glory such as "fierce battles" [*ozhestochennye boi*] and "military glory" [*voinskaia slava*].

> (20) Presenter: Behind me is the Victory obelisk. The Victory obelisk reminds us that the history of Rzhev is closely connected with the events of the Great Patriotic War. The town was occupied almost 17 months. Fierce battles took place here. And therefore the news that Rzhev became a "Town of Military Glory" was met by the town's inhabitants, especially by veterans, with joy.[35]

When it comes to his move, Putin echoes the presenter and continues to valorize the Second World War, taking his part in the co-construction of the common memory of the past. His choice of words relies on a high register, on markers of a heroic narrative, such as "warriors" [*voiny*], "did battle" [*srazhalis'*], and "milestone" [*vekha*], which occur in clichéd phrases reminiscent of communist narratives: "the attempt undertaken by Hitler's troops to organize the second large-scale advance on Moscow was averted" [*predotvrashchena popytka gitlerovskikh voisk organizovat' krupnomasshtabnoe nastuplenie na Moskvu*]. Thus, in *Direct Line*'s chronotope, the choice of places and the narratives pertaining to places have a temporal component. The narrative of space highlights selected periods of time as constitutive of national identity and attributes to them qualities such as national heroism and military glory.

While the Soviet-era references are quite positive and nostalgic, the recent past tends to be negatively framed (21). This example shows how the period of Boris Yeltsin's presidency of the 1990s is consistently described within the negative knowledge schema, utilizing the strategy of demontage. In Putin's description of the period, qualities pertaining to the earlier established narrative of the 1990s, such as democratic freedoms and Russia's liberation from Communist ideology, are suppressed or relegated to the background. In their place, a different knowledge frame is constructed, in which the period is described as a time of instability, moral corruption, populism, and governmental inefficiency. In addition, Putin attributes to the time frame the property of shared memories by beginning his move with the imperative "remember" [*vspomnite*]. In comparison with the first invitation to recollect ([*vspomnim*]) in his War heroism narrative, which is formulated in the inclusive first person plural, here the grammar of memory sharing is slightly different. Actualized through the second person form, this becomes a directive from the speaker to the audience regarding what to think about the recent past. The speaker is positioned outside the act of recollecting, as the knower beyond memory. This imperative opens a rhetorically elaborate passage that reveals the speaker's close involvement in the message. Putin continues by liberally filling the knowledge frame about the 1990s with the grammatical category of negativity actualized by negative prefixes: "incapable parliament" [*nedeesposobnyi parlament*] and "impossible to decide" [*nevozmozhno reshit'*], as well as negative clauses: "it wasn't passed" [*priniato ne bylo*]. Additionally, expressions from the arsenal of political castigation are mixed in, as, for example, "populist" [*populistskii*], "to lead into a blind alley" [*zavodit' v tupik*]. He invokes other rhetorical devices, such as the emphatically minimalizing "not even to a miniscule degree" [*malo-mal'ski*] and "not a single one" [ni odnogo]; the colloquial neologism "they took left, right, and center" [*naprinimali*], whose prefix [*na-*] marks the ironically shaded sense of "over the top"; and the anaphoric lexical repetition: "With an incapable parliament, with an incapable Duma" [*pri nedeesposobnom parlamente, pri nedeesposobnoi Dume*].

> (21) Remember the beginning of, and the mid-, 1990s. With an incapable Parliament, with an incapable Duma, it was impossible to take any balanced decision, even to a miniscule degree. But the populist decisions that led the country's economy and its social sphere into a deadend were taken left, right and center, more than necessary. But, in effect, not a single intelligible decision that would spur development of the economy and the social sphere was taken.[36]

In addition, the 1990s are contrasted to the positively constructed subsequent period embracing Putin's two presidential terms. His strategy of positive attributions (*miranda*) is achieved through a combination of figures cited with comments of positive evaluation, which are syntactically broken up into separate sentences or clauses (22). These concise, self-contained propositions increase the relative weight of the message they articulate. Borrowing from the discourse of Soviet planned economy, figures are positively compared with targets, evoking the sense of achievement through over-fulfillment (see Chapter 4 by Gorham). The key words used for the construction of success are lexical elements suggestive of triumphant economic reports: "positive" [*polozhitel'nyi*], "success" [*uspekh*], "record" [*rekord, rekordnyi*], "to grow" [*prirastat'*], and "index" [*pokazatel'*], as well as the comparative adjectival forms "better" [*luchshe*] and "bigger" [*bol'she*]. In addition, Putin engages the relatively new, market-economy vocabulary of economic success, but seems to be in a less familiar territory here. For example, he uses the recent loan word "boom" [*bum*], prefacing the term with the metalinguistic comment "the so-called" [*tak nazyvaemyi*], suggesting some uncertainty in drawing the more obvious elements of capitalism's language into the picture of national identity. The sheer repetition of certain terms is another mechanism by which the president constructs his image of the present. For instance, he uses the noun "growth" [*rost*] 15 times in *Direct Line*, whereas words with the root "*stabil*" – which seems to be the *miranda* label for the status quo occur 12 times: stable [*stabil'nyi*], stabilizational [*stabilizatsionnyi*], stabilization [*stabilizatsiia*], and stability [*stabil'nost'*].

(22) Putin: (a) The results of our work for last year were positive. (b) The main index of success is the growth of the economy. (c) Last year, growth was 6.7%. Not at all a bad indicator. (d) Growth was 7.7% – much higher than the parameters that were in the plan. This alone is quite good. But better still is that we've finally begun to achieve the result that we'd strived for all these years. (e) In the last five years we've added 15% of growth every year. That's a very high indicator. This year's growth will be nearly 25% (24.4%), but the supply of new housing will be even bigger, 34.5% (34.4%). This already looks like a building boom. (f) The gold reserves grew to an all-time record. (g) . . . the stable course of our state's development.[37]

The official and technical bureaucratic flavor of the rhetoric whereby the president constructs the picture of the current national prosperity contrasts to the informal phrasing that frames the voice of the "doubters" subtly incorporated into his speech: (23) "And I'm pleased to note that not once have I massaged any figures or facts. One doesn't need to make it all up [*vysasyvat' iz pal'tsa*], as our folk say."[38] Similar to the instance with the word "boom," his code switching to the informal language is accompanied by a metalinguistic comment justifying the use of the vulgar expression as the language of the common folk. The low tone here, of course, is attributed to imagined critics and operates as a strategy of debunking their position and reasserting the view of Russia's prosperous present as an undisputed truth.

The third part of the time triad – the frame of the national *future* – is also actively constructed by the president, primarily through discursive strategies that emphasize stability and continuity, whereby the future is seen as the continuation of the present, the implementation of today's plans (cf. 24). With the present depicted in terms of success, the future, often through the topos of comparison, simply becomes an even greater success, to a high or even overwhelming degree (25). (24) Putin: "I can only tell you that this work will be continued, to assure you that these measures are being planned and we will implement them."[39] The future is dealt with directly, assertively declared through the future tense, with no subjunctives or any other markers of uncertainty or conditionality.

(25) Putin: (a) Within the framework of the Federal Purpose Programs aimed at the development of the Far East, it's envisaged that substantial sums from the federal budget will be issued. It'll be 500 billion rubles for the next four to five years. That's very big money. We've not issued this kind of money for any program before; (b) So our plans aren't just big, they're grand.[40]

Another way of achieving positive framing of the national future is the expression of Putin's personal confidence in the realization of his goals. In (26), this is keyed by his use of short participles and verbs in the first person singular – "[I'm] certain," [*uveren*], "[I] consider possible" [*schitaiu vozmozhnym*] – with the first person pronoun subject omitted, creating an overtone of a curt, telegraphic style of buoyancy and self-assurance:

> (26) Putin: (a) [I'm] certain that visitors and tourists will come to us even from abroad; (b) [I'm] certain that the number of specialists will increase. (c) At the first stage [I] consider a minimum of a threefold increase [of fertility treatment] possible, and [I] know where to get the money.[41]

Similarly, the performatives of promise, which include iterated modal adverbs expressing certainty, such as "without fail" [*obiazatel'no*], contribute to the confident portrayal of the enhanced future (27):

> (27) Putin: (a) [I] promise, we'll do that without fail. (b) [I] promise you that without fail we'll see this matter through to the end, without fail. The road will be taken care of, and the tunnel will be made, and the social structure will be developed too. (c) "Will there be a banking crisis?" – No, there won't be.[42]

Thus the time dimension of the knowledge frames attributed to the post-Soviet man undergoes revision and reconstruction, with the president functioning as the principal agent of the temporal element in the construction of the national discourse.

Construction of "the other"

Scholars concur that nations, like any social group, fashion themselves or are fashioned in counterdistinction to a significant "other" – an imagined out-group or groups (Mead 1934; Barth 1969: 9; Hall 1996; Neumann 1999; Blum 2007: 63, and others). Putin, together with other contributors to the *Direct Line* polylogue, constructs outgroups as people with negative qualities or as a common national enemy. To that end, they employ elements of "liberalized language use," characterized by register mixing, lexical innovation, and nonstandard elements (Ryazanova-Clarke and Wade 1999; Lunde and Roesen 2006). For example, in responding to a complaint by a Podkokodnovka dairy farmer about local price fixing (28), Putin resorts to a populist gesture and adopts a distancing strategy toward the leaders of municipal governments – his own appointees, who protect the price monopoly. To mark both distancing and negative categorization, he uses the verb "exercise protection rackets" [*kryshevat'*], which, despite having recently gained currency in public discourse, still bears a strong overtone of criminal slang, which is its provenance. To express solidarity with the farmer and construct a category for those who are reprehensible, Putin uses not the neutral contemporary word "middleman" [*posdernik*], but borrows from the lexicon of the 1920s a term with negative connotations: "second-hand dealer" [*perekupshchik*].[43] In both cases, the metalinguistic comments [*tak nazyvaemye; izvinite za moveton*] accompany the speaker's code-shifting, showing the reflective nature of his language choice and his awareness of their rhetorical effect.

> (28) Putin: (a) This tells us that the so-called "second-hand dealers" in many regions and many municipalities act as monopolies; (b) they [leaders – LRC] must create market conditions and not, pardon my French, exercise protection rackets [*kryshevat'*], so to speak, towards those with whom they are linked by special relations.[44]

The liberal language used to define "the other" may also be activated within the already familiar strategy of reviving Soviet knowledge frames. This occurs when both the participant Sibert and the president join forces in the co-construction of the United States within the "enemy" frame (29). Borrowing from the discourse of the Cold War, Sibert, a representative from the Nuclear Physics Research Institute in Novosibirsk, asks Putin's opinion about a comment reputedly made by the former US Secretary of State Madeleine Albright. Allegedly, Albright said that it was unfair for Russia to be sole owner of all its enormous natural resources. Despite the lack of evidence that Albright had ever made this comment and despite Putin's admission that he was unaware of such a remark, this "unexpected question" becomes a convenient discursive trigger for bracketing America as Russia's enemy.

> (29) Sibert: Mr President I want to ask you a question that probably interests many Russians. Not that long ago, the former State Secretary of the United States Albright declared in one of her interviews that it was unfair that the colossal natural treasures of Siberia belonged solely to Russia. Hence the question: what consequences could such declarations have? And what is your evaluation of such declarations?
>
> Putin: An unexpected question, Aleksandr Karlovich. But I do understand that this cannot but worry us, especially those people who live specifically in Siberia. I am not familiar with this statement by Ms Albright, but I know that these ideas reside in the heads of certain politicians. In my view, this is a sort of "political eroticism" that perhaps may afford pleasure to someone, but is unlikely to lead to a positive result.[45]

Regardless of Sibert's obviously spurious claim, the president finds it possible to sympathize with what is described as the concerns of all the people of Siberia – a sympathy expressed by the inclusively used pronoun "us." Moreover, the double negative [*ne mozhet ne volnovat'*] emphasizes the seriousness of this concern. Oddly and rather clumsily, Putin applies to the domain of politics a sexual metaphor in the expressions "political eroticism" and "may afford pleasure" [*politicheskaia erotika; dostavit' udovol'stvie*]. This seems to be a distinctively post-Soviet way of speaking of political issues, which was originally derived from the liberal code and was subsequently appropriated by the new elites.[46] This tool of othering and enemy construction also seems to be reflective of Putin's idiostyle, tested in his earlier dialogue with foreign journalists.[47] Just as in that previous employment of sexual imagery in political speech, here, too, there is an implied threat contained in his hint at some vague negative results of American thinking.

The field of power: construction of authority

The pattern of today's shared subjectivity demonstrated in the discourse of *Direct Line* is close to what Iurii Pivovarov terms the "Russian system." Pivovarov (2002) posits that over the centuries, authority [*vlast'*][48] has been the main substance of Russian history. "The Russian system," according to the historian, is characterized by authority sapping energy out of Russian subjectivity and itself becoming the only socially meaningful subject (2002: 36). Moreover, since the days of Rurik, Russian authority invariably has been "sutured to a physical individual" (2002: 37). Evidential of this thesis, the centrality and singularity attached personally to the president are ingrained in the program starting from its format of "one man talking to millions," which allows Putin to be the central voice in the national narrative. In what at the time seemed to be his farewell talk with the country, Putin emerges as an unquestionable and unchallenged impersonation of authority – not just a president, but a national leader. Though this identification may ominously remind us of Stalin's leader image, as the recent works on Putin's image as a postcommunist communication phenomenon posit, we are perhaps witnessing not so much a revival of the Soviet style monolithic cult of personality, but rather a new mode of performativity. The latter emerges after the loss of faith in national meta-narratives and, like most postcommunist cultural products, is ambiguous and indeterminate, merging authoritarian discourse with its own parody (Cassiday and Johnson 2010: 696; Goscilo 2011).

Dispensing promises and financial commitments, Putin comfortably retrofits the Russian cultural paradigm of a tsar-like figure to whom all citizens desire to confide their problems and dreams. Even in instances of dissatisfaction with aspects of life under Putin, as in the case of Podkolodnovka's dairy farmer, the expressed concern, whether it pertains to the current political system or to the president's appointees, does not seem to affect this dynamic. Whatever the topic of discussion, Putin seems to be in control; he does not flinch from making significant political decisions or meting out justice online. For example, his seemingly spontaneous reactions included a promise to index military pensions and an announcement of a simplification of the "dacha amnesty."[49] Other promises he made concerned issues that cannot possibly depend on the presidential will, such as the level of inflation or a default on the national debt, but he succeeded in creating the impression of his omnipotence as president.

Established as an integral part of Russian national identity discourse, the figure of the president has multiple sides and guises. Seen within the broader context of officially serving the final months of his term, in autumn 2007, Putin's personal position was a major issue of a nationwide discussion. The news that the president had agreed to stand as number one in the membership list of the United Russia party in the December 2007 Duma elections escalated speculations about his future political role. In particular, around the time the program was aired, rumors were circulating about the possibility of a third presidential term, which was not provided by the constitution, and the country was swept by an orchestrated wave of national expression of public love for the outgoing president. A movement called simply "For Putin!" [*Za Putina!*] was created in his support and held mass rallies and meetings requesting him to stay in power.[50] The United Russia party leader, Boris Gryzlov, coined for Putin the title of "national leader" [*natsional'nyi lider*], which was quickly picked up and broadly publicized by the media.[51]

Reverberations of this wider public discourse can be seen in *Direct Line*, where Putin, with the active assistance and reconfirmation of other participants, tries on a variety of linguistically defined roles of authority: a benign ruler, distributing cash on air; a savvy businessman, teaching farmers to produce biofuel; or a father of the nation attending to all human pains (on Putin's multiple "profiles," see Chapters 1 and 8 by Goscilo). The remainder of this chapter examines examples of discursive co-construction of three salient presidential roles – those of a military commander, a competent technocrat, and a cult figure.

A military commander

The linkup with the rocket launch facility in Plesetsk shows how the construction of presidential identity as a military commander is framed as part of the Russian nation. From the start of the Plesetsk episode, all speaking parties, including the president, switch to military language with a high content of such terminology as "uniform of the military detachment" [*forma boevogo rascheta*], "launch pad" [*startovyi kompleks*], "the Topol' rocket" [*raketa Topol'*], "to strike the training target" [*porazit' uchebnuiu tsel'*], and "training ground" [*polygon*]. By switching speech codes to militarese, Putin foregrounds his role as Commander in Chief, a device preempted by the presenter who is the first to use his military title: (30) "Questions to the Commander in Chief, please."[52] This mode of address is matched by other participants who engage in the formal military ritual of self-introduction: (31) "Polunin: Comrade Commander in Chief! Head of the testing department, Colonel Polunin."[53] Discursive co-construction continues when Putin congratulates the soldiers on the successful launch of the missile, and voices in the crowd respond with the anticipated cliché of "We serve our Fatherland!" [*sluzhim otechestvu!*]. This formulaic exchange containing "Fatherland" as the emotive reference to the country binds together discursive elements relating to military achievements, pride in the powerful state, and the authority as its principal addressee.

Instead of asking a genuine question, Polunin urges Putin to speed up the reequipment of the Russian army. This request supports the narrative around the launch of the rocket and elaborates the theme of the reemergence of Russia as a confident military power, which surfaces at various points throughout *Direct Line*. As a co-constructor of this knowledge frame, Putin linguistically associates himself with the military meaning of the national identity, including his demonstration of familiarity with many technical details of weapons and new types of equipment (32).

> (32) Putin: But you and I well know that now the forces are already getting deliveries of "Topol'-M." (b) [We] will pay attention not only to all the nuclear triade, and I mean RVSN [The Strategic Purpose Rocket Forces – LRC], strategic aviation, and nuclear submarine fleet, but also to other kinds of weapons.[54]

His use of the first person plural [*budem udeliat' vnimanie*] with an unclear referent and agentless constructions ("The weapons program has been adopted until 2015" [*priniata programma vooruzheniia do 2015 goda*]) conveys the notion that the re-equipment program has its own velocity of existence and development, strengthening the nation of which the authority is almost a dispersed force, the function, the "attention." The lexical item [sushki] Putin uses to label the fighter jet SU-34 marks his awareness of military slang and creates solidarity with the personnel. The use of the inclusive forms "You and I well know" [*my s Vami khorosho znaem*] and "you also know" [*i Vy znaete*] contain a presupposition of shared knowledge that casts Putin's move about the speed of the weapons reequipment program as the reiteration of existing and shared information. This set of discursive techniques makes the message sound commonsense and normalized – the natural way forward for Russia.

A competent technocrat

Another facet of the presidential identity is that of a competent technocrat who has a firm grip on knowledge of the issues and a phenomenal memory for details and figures. This role is linguistically marked in his speech by a strategy of particularization, implemented by the frequent use of numbers and forms associated with bureaucratic administrative jargon, such as abbreviations and in particular, stump compounds [*sel'khozproizvodstvo*],[55] or elliptical attributive use of dative phrases with the preposition "po" (33). These last forms were among those characteristic of "the Communist Party dialect," which the post-Soviet period retained, broadening their use in bureaucratic registers (Shaposhnikov 1998: 78).

> (33) Putin: In Europe – and we buy a great number of food stuffs as imports from there – an event occurred that had an impact on us: the stoppage of subsidies for primarily agricultural produce has led to price increases in Europe by an average of 15-17%. Here they immediately rose by 25%, and for some products, by up to 40 and even 60%.[56]

On other occasions, Putin hides behind the language of the "competent specialist," notably on the infrequent occasions when he faces uncomfortable questions or has to convey less glorious, more mundane information. In such situations, he often deals metalinguistically with technocratic terminology, glossing or commenting on it. This strategy helps to construct a language persona of someone who has conceptual explanations for issues raised and who is on top of modern vocabulary when it comes to describing Russian society (34):

> (34) (a) In recent years, about 1.5 million people have left these regions. *Depopulation* of this region of the country is taking place. (b) In my opinion, this decision must be made publicly – *transparently*, as it's fashionable to say nowadays . . . (c) But it's not just a matter of [the Far East's] system of communication with the European part . . . There is a *disparity* in electricity tariffs.[57]

A cult figure

Finally, *Direct Line* portrays the national leader as someone who is worth two million questions. On the emotional level, the discourse transmits feelings of love and admiration for the president. The verbal moves of the public on the program demonstrate that they orient their speech to the Putin phenomenon described by Goscilo as post-Soviet commodified celebrity, which has the eerie flavor of a Soviet style cult of personality (2011). For example, they ritualistically begin their speech moves by expressing gratitude to the president, following the cultural paradigm familiar from Soviet times of the paternalistic relations between authority and the population (35):

> (35) Participants: (a) You visited Botlikh in the hardest days of August 1999 . . . Your visit meant very much to us. We felt both support and care at that time; it meant a lot to us then. Thank you very much. (b) My name is Natal'ia Plotnikova. I run a restaurant. First of all, I want to thank you for taking an interest in the life of our town.[58]

The participants' flattering questions (36a) presuppose the addressee's almost superhuman qualities, such as the ability to speak many languages. The indexical "already" in the preamble to the following question marks the sense that Putin's assumed command of French on top of two other foreign languages is, in the speaker's view, above the expected norm.[59] Other members of the public simper over his bravery in deciding to visit Iran despite having received threats to his life, or ask about his presumed punishing, sleep-deprived work schedule (36b).

> (36) (a) You've got a brilliant command of German and you also speak English. In your recent speech in Guatemala, you already spoke in French. So, seeing how busy you are, with a really packed work schedule, how do you manage to learn languages? (b) Brilev: Vladimir Vladimirovich, you've not yet answered one of the endlessly repeated questions: How many hours a day do you sleep?
>
> Putin: Enough to have a possibility to answer your questions.[60]

The presenter Brilev's use of hyperbole – that the question about Putin's sleep pattern is "endlessly repeated" – produces the impression of the nation's overwhelming worry about the leader's presumed shortage of rest, since he overworks. The strategy of evasiveness that Putin assumes in his coquettish answer has the effect of confirming rather than dismissing the question's assumption of sleep shortage. This question-and-answer sequence evokes the image of the ever-watchful leader perpetuated in the mythology of Stalin, a key figure in the personality cult culture (Bogdanov 2007, 2009: 239) (on the personality cult around Putin, see Chapter 2 by Cassiday *et al.*, as well as Chapter 1 by Goscilo).

Expressions of adoration and gratitude, and the assumption of superhuman qualities in the man who personifies authority are not simply silly, insignificant asides; they are built into the emotive fabric of the national discourse. As much is evident at one point (37), when a participant in *Direct Line* displays a quasi-religious veneration for Putin – the woman has no question to ask, but feels a need for "verbal communion" with the president, almost like a believer yearning to touch an object of worship. To verify the president's existence and to know that this status quo is stable in time (the one that obtains now, but also did before) are everything she needs to feel happy and grateful, albeit this state does not prevent her instinctive verbal aggression toward others. This verbal exchange illustrates not only Pivovarov's notion of subjectivity dissolved and absorbed by the authority as the dominant social subject, but also, on a lighter note, Cassiday and Johnson's thesis that the Putin narrative can verge on self-parody:

> (37) Presenter Semenikhina: Hello! Please introduce yourself.
> Participant: I'll not speak to you, only to the President.
> Semenikhina: Vladimir Vladimirovich is listening to you. Ask your question.
> Putin: I'm listening to you. Good day!
> Participant: Is that you?
> Putin: Me. Good day! Yes.
> Participant: Is that truly you?
> Putin: Truly.
> Participant: And before, was that you too?
> Putin: And before it was me, yes.
> Participant: Oh, God, thank you so much for everything. An enormous thank you.
> Presenter Brilev: Managed without a question.[61]

To conclude, the discourse produced in the 2007 shows *Direct Line with the President* in many ways sums up Putin's 8-year rule of Russia. It aims to construct a united Russian post-Soviet identity, to which all the participants make their verbal contribution. The choreographed presenters' intermedia, questions from the selected public, and President Putin's answers all work together to supply the shared and emotionally charged knowledge frames within which Russians can feel and speak about themselves. Components such as specifically imagined time, mythologized space, and authority in the form of Putin mania are the key elements employed for the identity narrative of Putin's Russia. Although illustrative of the Russian post-Soviet condition, the *Direct Line* discourse to a significant extent, functions as a represented discourse, as it often emphasizes connections with and directly borrows from its Soviet predecessor, using them as retro-frameworks to reestablish a common repertoire of meanings. Finally, today's Russian identity narrative, in which a controlled political television show imitates a heartfelt nationwide conversation, is a peculiar postcommunist performance that seems to implement what Guy Debord calls "spectacular power." The discourse of the nation in the *Direct Line* proves to be the discourse of the spectacle, "for the final sense of the integrated spectacle is this – that it has integrated itself into reality to the same extent as it was describing it, and that it was reconstructing it as it was describing it" (Debord 1990: 9).

Notes

1 "Absolute record" [Absoliutnyi record], *Komsomol'skaia pravda*, October 19, 2007; "This last (at least in the current political season) virtual on-line Putin's talk with the country has a record length – nearly three and a half hours" [Eta posledniaia (po krainei mere v tekushchem politicheskom sezone) virtual'naia beseda Putina so stranoi v rezhime onlain prodolzhalas' rekordno – pochti tri s polovinoi chasa]. *Moskovskie novosti* 41, 2007. All translations from Russian are mine.

2 *Komsomol'skaia pradva*, October 19, 2007.

3 *Moskovskie novosti* 41, 2007.

4 The phrase used in relation to the Narodniki [Populist] movement of the Russian *intelligentsia* of the 1860s and 1870s.

5 *Moskovskie novosti* 41, 2007.

6 Orekh, Anton. "Tol'ko on i my," *Ezhednevnyi zhurnal*, October 19, 2007.

7 All *Direct Line* quotations are sourced from the full text of the program available at: http://archive.kremlin.ru/appears/2007/10/18/1259_type82634type146434_148629.shtml (accessed February 11, 2009). Spelling and punctuation follow the transcript.

8 Kul'kova: I menia kak prepodavatelia bespokoit nebrezhnoe otnoshenie obshchestva k istorii, osobenno sredi molodezhi. Massa shokiruiushchikh primerov istoricheskogo nevezhestva.
Putin: Polnost'iu s Vami soglasen. My s Vami znaem – a ia tozhe ochen' liubliu istoriiu, – kak eshche sovsem nedavno my v uchebnikakh chitali veshchi, ot kotorykh volosy dybom mogli vstat', osobenno pri traktovkakh, skazhem, rezul'tatov Vtoroi mirovoi voiny i vsego, chto s etim sviazano. No v poslednee vremia vse-taki opredelennye pozitivnye sdvigi est'.

9 No dlia togo, chtoby ne dopuskat' ochevidnogo braka v etoi sfere, Vy naverno, znaete, priniato sootvetstvuiushchee reshenie i na zakonodatel'nom urovne, povyshena rol' i znachenie Ministerstva obrazovaniia i nauki, kotoroe uzhe v sostoianii budet davat' sootvetstvuiushchie ekspertnye otsenki pri podgotovke uchebnoi literatury.

10 *Moskovskii komsomolets*, October 18, 2007.

11 *Novaia gazeta*, October 18, 2007.

12 Ibid.
13 *Novaia gazeta*, October 18, 2007.
14 *Rossiiskaia gazeta*, October 18, 2007.
15 Piatyi den' rabotaet nash telefonnyi tsentr, rabotaet kruglosutochno – tak, chtoby bylo udobno vsei strane. I vot k etoi minute my poluchili uzhe 2 milliona i eshche pochti 200 tysiach zvonkov. Eto rekord.
16 Uvazhaemyi Vladimir Vladimirovich! My segodnia ot litsa 7 tysiach zhitelei Russkogo ostrova peredaem Vam ogromnyi privet.
17 Moskva otsiuda ispravno poluchaet produkty – i ovoshchi, i maslo (maslo zdes' osobenno vkusnoe, probovali, degustirovali).
18 E. Andreeva: Nasha televizionnaia kamera segodnia ustanovlena v regione, gde segodnia utrom proizoshlo vazhnoe sobytie, i, chto raduet, vse proshlo na "otlichno."
19 In pragmatics, illocutionary force indicates a certain intended impact, or effect of the utterance. The term was introduced by John Austin (1975) and developed by John Searle (cf. Searle *et al.* 1980).
20 (a) U nas na podkhode takoi znakovyi gorod, kotoryi my segodnia odnazhdy dazhe upomianuli, – eto gorod Sochi; (b) Botlikh eto ne geograficheskoe nazvanie, a moral'naia karegoriia.
21 (a) Vladivostok – samaia vostochnaia tochka etoi "priamoi linii... ot nas do vas 9302 kilometra; (b) . . . zdes' uzhe temneet; (c) eto deistvitel'no Podkolodnovka. Do Moskvy 900 kilometrov, do Voronezha – 250; (d) . . . kosmodrom Plesetsk, gde my seichas nakhodimsia, – eto samyi severnyi kosmodrom v mire; (e) . . . eto – krainii zapad strany – Kaliningrad.
22 (a) My pereshagivaem Ural; (b) A my perenosimsia s Severnogo Kavkaza na berega Volgi. See similar imagery in the Lebedev-Kumach's lyrics of the famous Soviet *Song of the Motherland* [*Pesnia o Rodine*] by Issak Dunaevskii (1936): "From Moscow to the very edges, from the Southern mountains to the Northern seas, the man passes by like a master on his enormous Motherland." [*"Ot Moskvy do samykh do okrain, s iuzhnykh gor do severnykh morei chelovek prokhodit kak khoziain neob' 'iatnoi Rodiny svoei."*] Available at: http://enotka.com/music/pesnya-o-rodine-dunaevskii-i (accessed June 19, 2011).
23 Do svidaniia, Kaliningrad; Vas privetstvuet Ekaterinburg.
24 (a) Vas privetstvuet Ekaterinburg, gorod, kotoryi chasto nazyvaiut stolitsei Urala; (b) Posle 1000-letiia Kazani k etomu gorodu prikrepilos' nazvanie vostochnoi stolitsy Rossii. Tak vot, v vostochnoi stolitse Rossii seichas rabotaet vedushchii *Vestei* Mikhkail Antonov; (c) Moskvu privetstvuiut Sochi. Deistvitel'no, teper' eto ne prosto gorod-kurort, teper' eto eshche i stolitsa zimnei Olimpiady 2014 goda; (d) Eto krainii zapad strany – Kaliningrad. I tam, v stolitse rossiiskoi Pribaltiki, rabotaet Oleg Groznetskii.
25 Za moei spinoi za goroi Gruziia. Naprotiv nee gora, kotoruiu vy, k sozhaleniiu, ne vidite. Tam nachinaetsia Chechnia.
26 U nas na Dal'nem Vostoke govoriat sleduiushchem obrazom. Sushchestvuiut dve Rossii: odna – protsvetaiushchaia – do Urala, i drugaia Rossiia – s ostrovnym sindromom otorvannosti – posle Urala . . . Esli Vladivostok otorvan ot Rossii, to my, zhiteli ostrova Russkogo, otorvany ot goroda Vladivostoka.
27 Segodnia odna iz [kamer] ustanovlena v Kazakhstane. I ne tol'ko potomu, chto tam prozhivaet mnogo russkikhk liudei . . ., ne tol'ko potomu, chto v gosudarstvennykh uchrezhdeniiakh russkii iazyk tam imeet status naravne s kazakhskim, no i potomu, chto my znaem, chto tam mnogie smotriat *Priamuiu liniiu s prezidentom Rossiiskoi Federatsii*.

28 (a) Andreeva: Nashi peredvizhnye televizionnye stantsii rabotaiut ne tol'ko v Rossii; (b) Putin: Poskol'ku my razgovarivaem s temi, kto nakhoditsia za predelami Rossiiskoi Federatsii.

29 (a) Bobrov: Vas priamo s berega Kaspiia privetstvuet kazakhstanskii Aktau – gorod interesneishii, gorod vo mnogom neobychnyi i edinstvennyi na postsovetskom prostranstve; (b) Putin: rukovodstvo respubliki delaet vse dlia togo, chtoby podderzhat' takoe sostoianie del i podderzhat' razvitie russkogo iazyka.

30 Vprochem, ne s Amerikoi – s Rossiei u Kazakhstana obshchaia mnogovekovaia istoriia.

31 Vspomnim Velikuiu Otechestvennuiu. Immeno zdes', na kazakhstanskoi zemle, formirovalas' legendarnaia diviziia panfilovtsev, kotoraia zashchishchala Mosvku.

32 . . . a vse oni byli pereviazany pulemetnymi lentami, kak revoliutsionnye matrosy v 1917 godu . . .

33 Liudi prosto . . . vziali v ruki oruzhie i vstali na zashchitu interesov Rossii i svoikh sobstvennykh domov; . . . eto iskliuchitel'nyi primer patriotizma, prichem ne tol'ko mestnogo, dagestanskogo, – rossiiskogo patriotizma.

34 The town was awarded on October 10, 2007. *Byl' novogo Rzheva*, October 10, 2007. Available at: http://www.newrzhev.ru/news.php?news_id=1042 (accessed July 22, 2011).

35 Za moei spinoi – obelisk *Pobeda*. Obelisk *Pobeda* napominaet, chto istoriia Rzheva tesno sviazana s sobytiiami Velikoi Otechestvennoi voiny. Gorod pochti 17 mesiatsev byl v okkupatsii. Zdes' shli ozhestochennye boi. I poetomu novost' o tom, chto Rzhev stal Gorodom voinskoi slavy, vstrechena zhiteliami s radost'iu, osobenno veteranami.

36 Vspomnite nachalo i seredinu 90-x godov. Pri nedeesposobnom parlamente, pri nedeesposobnoi Dume nevozmozhno bylo priniat' ni odnogo malo-mal'ski vyverennogo resheniia. Vot populistskikh reshenii, kotorye zavodili i ekonomiku, i sotsial'nuiu sferu v tupik, v eto vremia naprinimali bole, chem dostatochno. No ni odnogo vniatnogo resheniia, kotoroe by nakhodilos' v strue razvitiia ekonomiki i sotsial'noi sfere, po suti dela, priniato ne bylo.

37 (a) Rezul'taty raboty za proshedshii god byli polozhitel'nymi; (b) Glavnyi pokazatel' uspekha – eto rost ekonomiki; (c) V proshlom godu rost sostavil 6,5 protsenta. Ochen' neplokhoi pokazatel'; (d) Rost sostavil 7,7 protsenta – znachitel'nio vyshe zaplanirovannykh parametrov. Eto samo po sebe uzhe ochen' neplokho. No eshche luchshe to, chto my nachali nakonets dobivat'sia togo rezul'tata, k kotoromu stremilis' vse eti gody; (e) Za poslednie piat' let my prirastali po 15 protsentov ezhegodno. Eto ochen' bol'shoi pokazatel'. V etom godu rost sostavit pochti 25 protsentov – 24,4, a vvod zhil'ia eshche bol'she – 34,5 (34,4) protsenta. Eto uzhe pokhozhe na tak nazyvaemyi stroitel'nyi bum; (f) Zolotovaliutnye rezervy vyrosli do rekordnogo za vsiu istoriiu; (g) . . . stabil'nyi kurs razvitiia nashego gosudarstva.

38 I mne priiatno otmetit', chto ni odnogo raza mnoiu ne byli dopushcheny kakie-to natiazhki. Nichego ne nuzhno vysasyvat', kak govoriat u nas v narode, iz pal'tsa.

39 Mogu Vam tol'ko skazat', chto eta rabota budet prodolzhat'sia. Uveriaiu vas, takie shagi planiruiutsia, i my ikh predprimem.

40 (a) V ramkakh federal'nykh tselevykh program na razvitie Dal'nego Vostoka predusmotreno vydelenie znachitel'nykh summ iz federal'nogo biudzheta. Na blizhaishie 4–5 let eto 500 milliardov rublei. Eto ochen' bol'shie den'gi, my takikh deneg ni na odnu programmu ne vydeliali; (b) Tak chto u nas plany ne prosto bol'shie – oni grandioznye.

41 (a) Uveren, chto i iz-za granitsy poedut k nam otdykhaiushchie i turisty. (b) Uveren, chto ikh kolichestvo [spetsialistov] budet uvelichivat'sia. (c) Na pervom etape schitaiu vozmozhnym uvelichit' eto [iskusstvennoe oplodotvorenie] kak minimum v tri raza i znaiu, gde vziat' den'gi.

42 (a) Obeshchaiu, my eto obiazatel'no sdelaem; (b) Obeshchaiu Vam, chto obiazatel'no my dovedem eto delo do kontsa, obiazatel'no. I doroga budet, I tunnel' budet sdelan, tak zhe kak razvitie sotsial'noi infrastruktury. (c) "Budet li bankovskii krizis?" – Net, ne budet.

43 The Russian National Corpus testifies to the consistent negative connotation occurring in the current use of [perekupshchik]. Cf. some data that explicitly contain this information: "Just to say that those at the depot consider the word 'second-hand dealer' in relation to the middleman to be badmouthing." [Tol'ko vot slovo 'perekupshchik' primenitel'no k posredniku na baze schitaiut ochernitel'nym.] *Trud-7*, March 21, 2007. Available at: http://search.ruscorpora.ru/ (accessed April 18, 2011).

44 (a) Eto govorit o tom, chto tak nazyvaemye perekupshchiki vo mnogikh regionakh i vo mnogikh munitsipalitetakh deistvuiut monopol'no; (b) oni [rukovoditeli] dolzhny sozdavat' rynochnye usloviia, a ne, izvinite za moveton, "kryshevat'" tam tekh, s kotorymi ikh sviazyvaiut osobye otnosheniia.

45 Sibert: Gospodin President, ia khochu Vam zadat' vopros, kotoryi, pozhalui, interesuet mnogikh rossiian. Ne stol' davno v odnom iz interv'iu byvshii gossekretar' Soedinennykh Shtatov Olbrait zaiavila, chto kolossal'nye estestvennye bogatstva Sibiri nespravedlivo prinadlezhat odnoi Rossii. Otsiuda vopros: kakie posledstviia mogut byt' posle takikh zaiavlenii? I kak vy otsenivaete takie zaiavleniia? Putin: Neozhidannyi vopros, Aleksandr Karlovich. No ia ponimaiu, chto on ne mozhet nas ne volnovat', osobenno tekh liudei, kotorye neposderstvenno zhivut v Sibiri. Ia ne znakom s etim vyskazyvaniem gospozhi Olbrait, no znaiu, chto takie idei v golovakh nekotorykh politikov brodiat. Eto, na moi vzgliad, takaia "politicheskaia erotika', kotoraia, mozhet byt", komu-nibud' i mozhet dostavit' udovol'stvie, no vriad li privedet k polozhitel'nomu rezul'tatu.

46 Among post-Soviet politicians, Vladimir Zhirinovsky was particularly renowned for this tactic. In his speeches and in the book *Azbuka seksa*, he referred to Soviet leaders as eunuchs, onanists, etc. (Goscilo 2000).

47 For example, in 2002, at a Brussels summit press conference with foreign journalists, Vladimir Putin famously used a vulgar sexual innuendo in the performative of threat of castration:

> If you completely want to become an Islamist radical and if you are prepared to have circumcision then I invite you to Moscow. We are a multiconfessional country and we have specialists in this matter. So I will recommend him to make this operation in such a way so that you will have nothing growing there. [Esli vy khotite sovsem uzh stat' islamskim radikalom i gotovy poiti na to, chtoby sdelat' sebe obrezanie, to ia vas priglashaiu v Moskvu. U nas mnogokonfessional'naia strana, u nas est' spetsialisty i po etomu voprosu. I ia porekommenduiu emu sdelat' operatsiiu takim obrazom, chtoby u vas uzhe nichego ne vyroslo.]
>
> (Sukhotskii 2004)

48 Pivovarov capitalizes the word.

49 The "dacha amnesty" was a permission given by authorities to summer cottage owners to privatize their property without providing documents for its provenance. This was a solution to the widespread legal problem rooted in the Soviet period, when many people received plots of land given by factories and other enterprises they worked for, built houses there for which no documents were issued.

50 *Moskovskii komsololets*, November 16, 2007
51 *News.Ru.com*. November 7, 2007.
52 Pozhaluista, voprosy k Verkhovnomu Glavnokomanduiushchemu.
53 Tovarishch Verkhovnyi Glavnokomanduiushchii! Nachal'nik ispytatel'nogo otdela polkovnik Polunin.
54 Putin: (a) No my s vami khorosho znaem, chto seichas na vooruzhenie postupaet uzhe "Topol'-M"; (b) I ne tol'ko budem udeliat' vnimanie vsei iadernoi triade – ia imeiu v vidu RVSN, strategicheskuiu aviatsiiu i podvodnyi iadernyi flot, – no i drugim vidam vooruzhenniia.
55 Stump compound contains the truncated forms of two or more words (Wade 2000: 63).
56 V Evrope – a my ottuda zakupaem ochen' mnogo prodovol'stvennykh tovarov po importu – proizoshlo sobytie, kotoroe otrazilos' na nas: prekrashchenie subsidirovaniia v znachitel'noi stepeni sel'khozproizvodstva privelo k povysheniiu tsen v Evrope v srednem na 15-17 protsentov. U nas eto srazu vyroslo do 25-ti, po nekotorym produktam – do 40 i dazhe do 60 protsentov.
57 (a) Iz etikh regionov vyekhalo v poslednie gody poltora milliona chelovek. Proiskhodit depopuliatsiia etogo regiona strany; (b) Po-moemu mneniiu, eto reshenie dolzhno byt' priniato publichno, kak seichas modno govorit', transparentno . . .; (c) No delo ne tol'ko v sredstvakh kommunikatsii s evropeiskoi chast'iu . . . Eto disparitet v tarifakh na elektroenergiiu.
58 (a) Vy pobyvali v Botlikhe v samye tiazhelye dni avgusta 99-go goda . . . Vash priezd dlia nas mnogoe znachil, my pochuvstvovali i podderzhku, i zabotu, togda eto dlia nas oznachalo mnogoe. Spasibo Vam bol'shoe; (b) Menia zovut Natal'ia Plotnikova. Ia restorator. Vo-pervykh, khochu Vas pobnlagodarit' za to, chto Vashe uchastie v sud'be nashego goroda.
59 To the knowledge of the present writer, Putin speaks German fluently and took lessons in English; however, there has been no evidence that he speaks French. At the Nineteenth Session of the International Olymplic Committee in Guatemala in July 2007, he read out his speech in accented English. See the episode of the *Russia Today*'s broadcast of this speech on http://www.youtube.com/watch?v=_aNo3DxWaW4 (accessed July 18, 2011).
60 (a) Vy prekrasno znaete nemetskii iazyk, govorite na angliiskom. I v nedavnem svoem vystuplenii v Gvatemale Vy govorili uzhe na frantsuzskom iazyke. Tak vot kak pri vsei Vashei zaniatosti, v deistvitel'no plotnom grafike raboty Vy uspevaete izuchat' iazyki? (b) Brilev: Vladimir Vladimirovich, Vy ne otvetili na odin iz voprosov, kotoryi beskonechno tam povtoriaetsia: "Skol'ko chasov v den' Vy spite?" Putin: Dostatochnoe kolichestvo, chtoby imet' vozmozhnost' otvechat' na vashi voprosy.
61 Semenikhina: Zdravstvuite! Predstav'tes', pozhaluista.
Otvet: Ia ne budu s vami razgovarivat', a tol'ko s Prezidentom.
S.: Vladimir Vladimirovich Vas slushaet, zadavaite vopros.
Putin: Slushaiu Vas. Dobryi den'!
Vopros: Eto Vy?
P.: Ia. Dobryi den'! Da.
Vopros: Eto pravda Vy?
P.: Pravda.
Vopros: A ran'she tozhe byli Vy, da?
P.: I ran'she byl ia, da.
Vopros: Oi, gospodi, spasibo Vam bol'shoe za vse, ogromnoe spasibo.
Brilev: Bez voprosa oboshlos'.

Bibliography

Anderson, B. (1983) *Imagined Communities: Reflections on the Origin and Spread of Nationalism*, London: Verso.

Austin, J. (1975) *How to Do Things with Words*, Oxford: Oxford University Press.

Barth, F. (1969) "Introduction," *Ethnic Groups and Boundaries: The Social Organization of Cultural Difference*, F. Barth (ed.), Boston, MA: Little, Brown and Co. 9–38.

Blum, D. (2007) *National Identity and Globalization*, Cambridge, MA: Cambridge University Press.

Bogdanov, K. (2007) "Pravo na son i uslovnye refleksy: kolubel'nye pesni v sovetskoi kul'ture (1930-1950-e gody)," *Novoe literaturnoe obozrenie* 86. Available at: http://magazines.russ.ru/nlo/2007/86/bo1.html (accessed March 12, 2008).

Bogdanov, K. (2009) *Vox Populi: Fol'klornye zhanry sovetskoi kul'tury*. Moscow: Novoe Literaturnoe obozrenie.

Bourdieu, P. (2004) *Outline of the Theory of Practice*, Cambridge, MA: Cambridge University Press.

Cassiday, J. and E. Johnson. (2010) "Putin, Putiniana and the Question of a Post-Soviet Cult of Personality," *Slavonic and East European Review* 88(4): 681–707.

Chilton, P. A. and C. Shäffner (eds.) (2002) *Politics as Text and Talk: Analytic Approaches to Political Discourse*, Amsterdam and Philadelphia: John Benjamins.

Davis, H., P. Hammond and L. Nazimova. (2000) "Media, Language Policy and Cultural Change in Tatarstan: Historic vs Pragmatic Claims to Nationhood," *Nations and Nationalism* 6(2): 203–226.

Debord, G. (1990) *Comments on the Society of the Spectacle*, London: Verso.

Debord, G. (2002) *The Society of the Spectacle*, Canberra: Hobgoblin Press.

Dobrenko, E. and E. Naiman. (eds.) (2003) *The Landscape of Stalinism: The Art and Ideology of Soviet Space*, Seattle, WA: University of Washington Press.

Dolón, R. and J. Todolí. (2008) *Analysing Identities in Discourse*, Amsterdam and Philadelphia: John Benjamins Company.

Fairclough, N. (2002) *Analyzing Discourse: Text Analysis for Social Research*, New York: Routledge.

Foucault, M. (1972) *The Archaeology of Knowledge*, London: Tavistock.

Goscilo, H. (ed.) (2000) *Studies in 20th Century Literature*. Special Issue: Russian Culture of the 1990s. 24. 1.

Goscilo, H. (2011) "The Ultimate Celebrity: VVP as VIP *Objet d'Art*." *Celebrity and Glamour in Contemporary Russia*, H. Goscilo and V. Strukov (eds.), London and New York: Routledge. 29–55.

Günther, H. (2003) "Broad is My Motherland. The Mother Archetype and Space in the Soviet Mass Song." *The Landscape of Stalinism: The Art and Ideology of Soviet Space*, E. Dobrenko and E. Naiman (eds.), Seattle, WA: University of Washington Press. 77–95.

Hall, S. (1992) "The Question of Cultural Identity," *Modernity and Its Futures*, S. Hall, D. Held *et al.* (eds.), Cambridge: Polity Press. 274–316.

Jager, S. (2001) "Discourse and Knowledge: Theoretical and Methodological Aspects of a Critical Discourse and Dispositive Analysis," *Methods of Critical Discourse Analysis*. R. Wodak and M. Meyer (eds.), London: Sage. 32–62.

Johansson, M. (2002) "Sequential Positioning of Represented Discourse in Institutional Media Interaction," *Rethinking Sequentiality*. A. Fetzer and C. Meierkord (eds.), Amsterdam: John Benjamins. 249–271.

Johansson, M. (2006) "Constructing Objects of Discourse in the Broadcast Political Interview," *Journal of Pragmatics* 38: 216–229.

Lunde, I. and T. Roesen (2006) *Landslide of the Norm: Language Culture in Post-Soviet Russia*, Slavica Bergensia 6, Bergen: John Grieg.

Martin, D.-C. (1995) "The Choices of Identity," *Social Identities* 1(1): 5–20.

Martin, R.P. (2002) "A Good Place to Talk: Discourse and Topos in Achilles Tatius and Philostratus," *Space in the Ancient Novel*, M. Paschalis (ed.), Eelde: Barkhuis Publishing. 143–160.

Mead, G.H. (1934) *Mind, Self and Society from the Standpoint of the Social Behaviorist*, Chicago, IL: Chicago University Press.

Milner-Gulland, R. (1999) *The Russians*, Oxford: Blackwell.

Naiman, E. (2003) "Introduction," *The Landscape of Stalinism: The Art and Ideology of Soviet Space*, E. Dobrenko and E. Naiman (eds.), Seattle, WA: The University of Washington Press. xi–xvi.

Neumann, I.B. (1999) *The Uses of the Other: The East in European Identity Formation*, Minneapolis, MN: University of Minnesota Press.

Oushakine, S. (2007) "'We're nostalgic but we're not crazy': Retrofitting the Past in Russia," *The Russian Review* 66: 452–481.

Pivovarov, I. (2002) "Russkaia politicheskaia kul'tura i political culture (obshchestvo, vlast', Lenin)," *Pro et Contra* 7/3: 23–50.

Ricoeur, P. (1991) "Narrative Identity." *Philosophy Today* 35(Spring): 73–81.

Ricoeur, P. (1992) *Oneself as Another*. Chicago and London: University of Chicago Press.

Robertson, A.E. (2002) "Yelstin, Shamiev and Dudaev: Negotiating Autonomy for Tatarstan and Chechnya," *Unity or Separation: Center-Periphery Relations in the Former Soviet Union*, D.R. Kempton and T.D. Clark (eds.), Westport, CT: Praeger. 99–142.

Ryazanova-Clarke, L. and T. Wade. (1999) *The Russian Language Today*, London: Routledge.

Searle, J.R, F. Kiefer, and M. Bierwisch (eds.) (1980) *Speech Act Theory and Pragmatics*, Dordrecht, Boston, MA and London: D. Reidel Publishing Company.

Shaposhnikov, V.N. (1998) *Russkaia rech' 1990-kh. Sovremennaia Rossiia v iazykovom Otobrazhenii*, Moscow: MALP.

Sukhotskii, K. (2004) "Putinizmy – 'produmannyi lichnyi epatazh'?," *BBC Russian.com*. March 5. Available at: http://news.bbc.co.uk/hi/russian/russia/newsid_3535000/3535811.stm (accessed March 15, 2007).

Tolz, V. (1998) "Forging the Nation: National Identity and Nation Building in Post-Communist Russia," *Europe-Asia Studies* 50(6): 993–1022.

Tolz, V. (2004) "Sovetskii geroicheskii mif: mekhanika, proshloe, nastoiashchee," *Russkii Globus* 5. Available at: http://www.russianglobe.com/N27/Tolts.SovetskyGeroicheskyMif.htm (accessed June 19, 2011).

Ukaz Prezidenta RF ot 27.11.2006 N 1316. Available at: http://document.kremlin.ru/doc.asp?ID=36473&;PSC=1&PT=3&Page=3 (accessed April 30, 2011).

Van Dijk, T. (1977) "Semantic Macro-Structures and Knowledge Frames in Discourse Comprehension," *Cognitive Processes in Comprehension*, P.A. Carpenter and M.A. Just (eds.), Hillsdale NJ: Lawrence Erlbaum Associates. 3–32.

Van Dijk, T. (1997) *Discourse as Social Interaction*, Vol. 2. London: Sage.

Van Dijk, T. (2002) "Political Discourse and Political Cognition," *Politics as Text and Talk: Analytic Approaches to Political Discourse*, P.A. Chilton and C. Shäffner (eds.), Amsterdam and Philadelphia: John Benjamins. 203–237.

Wade, T. (2000) *A Comprehensive Russian Grammar*, 2nd edition, revised and expanded, Oxford: Blackwell.

Widdis, E. (2004) "Russia as space," *National Identity in Russian Culture: An Introduction*, S. Franklin and E. Widdis (eds.), Cambridge: Cambridge University Press.

Wodak, R. (2002) "Fragmented Identities: Redefining and Recontextualizing National Identity," *Politics as Text and Talk: Analytic approaches to political discourse*, P.A. Chilton and C. Shäffner (eds.), Amsterdam and Philadelphia: John Benjamins.

Wodak, R. and R. de Cillia, *et al.* (1999) *The Discursive Construction of National Identity*, Edinburgh: Edinburgh University Press.

Wodak, R. and P. Chilton (eds.) (2005) *A New Agenda in (Critical) Discourse Analysis*, Amsterdam and Philadelphia: John Benjamins.

6 Putin in Russian fiction

Andrei Rogatchevski

This chapter examines the works of fiction by some 20 authors, published in 2000–11, in which Putin occupies center stage, plays a secondary role, makes a cameo appearance, or is conspicuous by his absence. Written in a variety of genres, these works represent a comprehensive range of political views across a wide geographical spread, including Latvia, Ukraine, and the United States. Whenever possible, different fictional images of Putin are juxtaposed to information taken from journalistic reports, interviews, and memoirs. The chapter's principal objective is to find out why Putin has been recurrently treated as a fictional character, and what, if anything, can be learned from Putin's fictional representations that cannot be learned otherwise – both about Putin himself and about the Russian public discourse on Putin. Because of space constraints, the plot summaries aim to focus on Putin-related episodes only.

Putin's meteoric rise to power has caused an extraordinary public interest in his life story and personality. In the words of his school teacher, Vera Gurevich, Putin's sudden status as Yeltsin's successor "generated many discussions, speculations, different explanations and inventions. He was referred to as a 'blank sheet,' a 'black box,' a 'dark horse,' and, most frequently, the 'unknown Putin'" (Gurevich 2004: 117).[1] Although dubbed "astonishingly frank" by their British publishers, Putin's six interviews with the journalists Nataliia Gevorkian, Nataliia Timakova, and Andrei Kolesnikov, released in 2000 under the title *First Person* [*Ot pervogo litsa*] in an attempt to introduce the new president to his electorate and the rest of the world, arguably portray him as a rather secretive individual,[2] reveal little of profound significance either about his past or about his plans for the future, and could only fuel speculations.[3] Moreover, Putin's personality has proved elusive even to those who have observed him from up close over a number of years. Andrei Kolesnikov, a member of the so-called Kremlin pool of journalists, who from May 2000 covered the president's public engagements for *Kommersant* newspaper, earned praise for being the only one who could do so in a "readable" way (Vasil'ev 2005: 7). He says of Putin's conduct at a meeting with the bereaved relatives of the *Kursk* submarine crew at the Vidyaevo naval base in the north of Russia on August 24, 2000:

> In front of me [. . .] sat a man who was very different from the one I had met when we were working on the *First Person* book. [. . .] Afterwards, I met him at the Chanukah celebrations [in Moscow, on 22 December 2000]. [. . .] I saw some other Putin again. And at the Tatar summer festival Sabantuy [in Kazan, on 24 June 2000], there was yet another one. I almost suspected that I was looking at Putin's doubles – this is how all these people seemed to be so unlike the person who had discussed his life with me in great detail only six months ago. [. . .] It appears that my almost daily observations of Vladimir Putin have set me on a bizarre pursuit of this man. In this situation, to catch up with him would mean to understand him. And, from time to time, I have the feeling [. . .] that I've got him. [. . .] Then it turns out that I've missed him yet again. He's kind of escaped once more. And the pursuit goes on.
>
> (Kolesnikov 2005a: 10–11)

Even Putin's physical appearance has presented a problem for no other person than his wife, Liudmila, when her German friend asked her to describe her husband: "'It's not easy to do. [. . .] He's not tall. You can say that he has fair but not especially thick hair.' Liudmila realized that these features were not really permanent or suitable for identification documents. The description ground to a halt" (Pietsch 2001: 316).

The harder it is to get to the bottom of a statesman's identity, the stronger the desire to do so – by resort to fiction if alternative means seem exhausted.[4] It is curious, however, that one of the earliest fictional treatments of Putin, the novel *Mr Hexogen* (*Gospodin Geksogen*, 2001) by the Communist Party of the Russian Federation (CPRF) member Aleksandr Prokhanov, the editor-in-chief of the nationalist newspaper *Tomorrow* [*Zavtra*], constructs its portrayal of Putin precisely around elusiveness as his dominant trait. Awarded the National Bestseller prize for 2002, *Mr Hexogen* is a *roman à clef* featuring many well-known Russian powerbrokers in easily recognizable guise. Its contemporary setting includes a number of memorable political events in 1999 – such as the downfall of Prosecutor General Iurii Skuratov in April because of a videotaped "honey trap"; the dismissal of Prime Minister Sergei Stepashin in August in the wake of an armed incursion into Dagestan by the so-called Islamic International Peacekeeping Brigade, led by Shamil Basaev and Ibn al-Khattab; and the hexogen explosions (hence the novel's title) that destroyed several blocks of flats in Moscow in September, blamed on the Chechen militants and the ostensible cause of the Second Chechen War – all treated as various stages in the Federal Security Service of the Russian Federation (FSB) plot to replace President Yeltsin (in the novel known as "Istukan," or Dummy) with Putin (referred to as "Izbrannik," or the Chosen One).[5]

Prokhanov describes the Chosen One through the eyes of a fictional character, a GRU (military intelligence) General brought out of retirement to assist the FSB in the implementation of their plot, codenamed "Project Swahili." The General meets the Chosen One in a swimming pool and compares him to "a dolphin in a man's body" (Prokhanov 2002: 272):[6]

> The General would have liked to discover the Chosen One's true self behind his false exterior [*mnimaia vneshnost'*]. But a playing sunbeam reflection split into colored rays of light, and every single one of them went their separate ways and fractured and splintered the Chosen One's image. And it was not clear where the real Chosen One is, or if he exists at all, or whether he is merely a hologram.
>
> (Prokhanov 2002: 279)

However, Prokhanov's Chosen One is not simply a "non-entity" (Warren 2002), as it might be tempting to conclude. The Chosen One is portrayed rather as an empty vessel that could be filled with any substance, or perhaps a chameleon which adapts well to any environment,[7] while trying to convince his associates, whoever they are, that he is one of them and serves their interests better than anybody else could.[8] This smoothes the Chosen One's path to the presidency quite considerably, but does it make him fit to govern? When in the novel's epilogue the Chosen One temporarily takes charge of an airborne jet symbolically named "Russia," he disappears from the cockpit suddenly and mysteriously, without a trace, leaving behind him only a "rainbow disintegrating into pencils of soaring light" (Prokhanov 2002: 474) – and the airplane, piloted by no one.

By contrast, a loyalist book called *The President* [*Prezident* 2002], by Aleksandr Ol'bik, a Russian-speaking writer from Latvia, portrays Putin – under his own name – as a man of flesh and blood, whose decisive actions bring a resolution to the armed conflict in Chechnya. Accompanied by a handful of special agents, Putin hunts down the fictional Chechen rebel leaders Bars, Taipan, and Garaev in their hideaway in the Chechen mountains, prompted by Bars's personal letter challenging the president to come and get him. Putin believes that eliminating the three leaders would deal the Chechen resistance a fatal blow. He arranges for the mission to be carried out secretly during August 10–14, 2000, pretending that he is on holiday in his Bocharov Creek residence (instead, a look-alike takes Putin's place at this summer vacation resort). The mission succeeds, although every member of Putin's group, except for him, is killed in the process. Putin is lightly wounded and has a concussion but still manages to dispose of Taipan and Garaev personally. The timing of the special operation coincides with the *Kursk* submarine disaster, and, according to Ol'bik, Putin does not interrupt his holiday quickly enough to deal with the crisis not because he does not care about the plight of the *Kursk* or because he already knows that the *Kursk* sailors are dead and the rescue mission is futile, but because he cannot recover from his injuries in time.

Ol'bik portrays Putin as a man of action, who knows how to handle weapons and endure difficult weather conditions in the Chechen mountains; an intellectual, who reads Seneca and quotes Rilke from memory (both in translation); a religious person, who cites from the Bible and asks the Russian Patriarch to give his blessing to the secret mission; a man of conscience, who has doubts over the morality of killing the Chechen resistance fighters surreptitiously instead of bringing them before a court of law; and a compassionate person, who can be moved by the sight of a dying enemy (Putin gives a shot of morphine to the wounded Taipan to alleviate his suffering and leaves a loaded Kalashnikov next to him to give him an opportunity to commit suicide, only to face this gun aimed by the treacherous Chechen at Putin himself a little later; see Ol'bik 2002: 196–197, 260, 286, 347–348, 419–422).[9]

It is obvious that in his approach to Putin's image Ol'bik follows, either consciously or subconsciously, the standard set of qualities that, in the eyes of most Russians, a modern Russian politician ideally should possess to win over the electorate: strength, dynamism, discretion, integrity, good education, and personal charm (see Shestopal 2004: 310). As one critic notes, the novel "results in a wish-fulfillment: a brave one comes and sorts everything out, unassisted" (Grigor'eva 2002). However, it is hard to ignore the fact that Ol'bik's idealized portrait of Putin "as Russia's savior from Chechen terrorists" (Paton Walsh 2002), steeped in a time-honored desire of many Russians to have a strong ruler, ultimately does the Russian president a disservice, especially in the long run: if Putin took such a good care of the Chechen problem in the year 2000, why does it persist to the present day?

Ol'bik does a much better PR job for President Putin in his sequel to *The President*, devoted to the 2002 Moscow theater hostage crisis. Co-authored with the Chechen Arbi Indorbaev and published as *Nord-Ost* in Riga in 2005, it appeared under the title *Operation "Armageddon" Is Terminated* [*Operatsiia "Armageddon" otmeniaetsia*] in Moscow in 2006. The standoff at the House of Culture of State Ball-Bearing Plant No. 1 in the Dubrovka area of Moscow, captured by some 40 Chechen militants in the middle of a sold-out performance of the musical *Nord-Ost* on the evening of October 23, 2002, resulted in at least 129 officially reported deaths among some 850 hostages (although other estimates put the death toll at over 200; see, for instance, Putley 2006). Most hostages seem to have died of gas poisoning after an unknown chemical agent was pumped into the House of Culture shortly before a special forces detachment stormed it in the early morning of October 26. In the absence of any subsequent official investigation and public inquiry, what exactly happened both at the theater and, so to speak, behind the scenes, is anybody's guess.[10]

Ol'bik takes full advantage of poetic license, claiming that the Nord-Ost was targeted because the President's daughter Katia was planning to attend the show that night (she had allegedly been invited to the performance by an Internet acquaintance, a member of the radical National Bolshevik Party (NBP); the invitation had been made at the suggestion of his Chechen friend, who later turned out to be one of the attackers; fortunately, Katia did not go to Dubrovka in the end). Moreover, an intercepted telephone call made by a hostage-taker reveals that inside the theater, the Chechens planted a portable nuclear bomb (referred to as "article 500," part of the Soviet Union's arsenal of nuclear weaponry that has gone missing after the country ceased to exist). The bomb is powerful enough to destroy the entire city of Moscow, and the militants are determined to use it if necessary, which makes the situation critical. To incapacitate the hostage-takers, it is decided, upon the Central Intelligence Agency's (CIA) advice,[11] to use an aerosol anesthetic similar to fentanyl, as the best possible solution. Putin appears at the Dubrovka House of Culture in disguise, this time not to engage in the action against the militants personally, as he did in Ol'bik's earlier novel, but to save as many gas-affected hostages as possible (he ultimately saves a total of 12; see Ol'bik and Indorbaev 2005: 364–366, 404, 432–435, 467, 474–475, 490–491).

The intention behind *Nord-Ost* presumably is to counter the impression that the tactics adopted to resolve the Dubrovka incident were heavy-handed. The presence of the nuclear threat is expected to remove all doubts on that score. It also goes a long way to put an emphasis on Putin's tender side by depicting him as a loving family man and a volunteer rescuer, who feels obliged to put himself in the hostages' shoes by testing the aerosol anesthetic on himself before authorizing its use in the theater (see Ol'bik and Indorbaev 2005: 445–446). This is probably meant to contribute toward redressing the balance of Putin's perception by Russian voters, who tend to see him as "a man of deeds rather than words," unable to show or feel emotion and "cagey, dry, constipated, uncommunicative" [*zakrytyi, sukhoi, zakreposhchennyi, skrytyi*] (Shestopal 2004: 371, 363).

Ol'bik's spin on Putin's behalf appears to be unsolicited. In fact, his publishers felt uneasy about ascribing the president's real name to a fictional character, and it took Ol'bik some effort to persuade them.[12] Ultimately, they are unlikely to have been left disappointed, because "the word 'Putin' in a book title guarantees more or less decent sales [. . .], and had the protagonist had a different name, there would not have been much to read" (Grigor'eva 2002). *The President* has been especially successful.[13] Complimentary copies of the novel were sent to the Duma's deputies, which ensured extensive media coverage, including an almost 1-hour long program, *Results* [Itogi], on the TVS channel, with the participation of Prokhanov, the Duma deputy Viktor Semenov, and the founder of the pro-Putin youth movement Marching Together [Idushchie vmeste] Vasilii Iakemenko.

Presumably prompted by a mixture of patriotic and commercial reasons, Ol'bik can hardly be reproached for giving free rein to his imagination. It has often been impossible to separate fact from fiction not only when biographers and journalists tried to uncover the truth about Putin's career as a secret agent (see Voronov, undated), but even when they researched his childhood. Suffice it to mention the persistent rumors that at the age of ninePutin was separated from his real mother, Vera Nikolaevna Putina-Osepashvili, and moved from the village of Metekhi in Georgia, where he resided, to St. Petersburg, to live with foster parents, Vladimir Spiridonovich and Mariia Ivanovna Putin (Vera's distant relatives). The foster parents apparently changed his date of birth from 1950 to 1952 to be able to send him to the first grade in his new school and to conceal his Georgian past from his teachers and classmates (see Pribylovskii and Fel'shtinskii 2004: 152–156).[14]

Certain circumstances of Putin's life – most notably his progression from an unemployed ex-vice-mayor of St. Petersburg to president of the Russian Federation in less than 4 years – are unquestionably the stuff that fairy tales are made of. Russia, however, has a long tradition of suffusing the genre of fairy tales (usually in their literary, not oral, form) with political satire, to voice the author's critical opinion of certain aspects of the regime in an accessible form and to try, at the same time, not to incur censors' wrath [e.g., Mikhail Saltykov-Shchedrin's *Fairy Tales* (*Skazki*, 1869–86) and Maksim Gor'kii's *Russian Fairy Tales* (Russkie skazki, 1912–17)].[15] An early example of the fairy-tale genre targeting Vladimir Putin is Nataliia Babasian's "Gadkii Putenok" ("*putenok*" is an amalgamation of Putin's surname and the Russian word *utenok*, "duckling"; it can approximately be translated as "The Ugly Putling"). "The Ugly Putling" was published in January 2000 on the now defunct Deadline.ru site, almost immediately after Yeltsin's resignation, which had made Putin acting president. A cross between Hans Christian Andersen's "Ugly Duckling" and George Orwell's *Animal Farm*, it tells the story of an unattractive but assiduous duckling (Putin) from a poultry yard, who is noted for his diligence and reliability by the Mole (presumably an allusion to the tycoon Boris Berezovsky, who is widely believed to have helped Putin take over the Kremlin) and the Ginger Cat (modeled, it seems, after the politician Anatolii Chubais, who might have recommended Putin for his first job in the presidential administration; see Pribylovskii and Fel'shtinskii 2004: 166). With their assistance, the duckling is taken to the household of the Old Farmer (Yeltsin) to manage the poultry yard on his behalf. The duckling's unfortunate appearance plays an important part in his promotion because the Old Farmer's protégé is not supposed to be loved by the domestic fowls more than the Old Farmer himself.

A different fairy tale, based on the domestic tradition of the "be careful what you wish for" variety, credits Putin's magic victory in the 2000 presidential contest to the Russian incarnation of Santa Claus, known as Ded Moroz (Father Frost).[16] Dmitrii Bykov's "The G-spot" [*Tochka dzhi* 2000] describes how Mother Russia is compiling a wish list in search for a husband or head of state:

> who should be neither young nor old but in the prime of life; neither bold nor unkempt, with his hair done neatly; and neither a drinker nor a rowdy. He should make money, not debts, and be careful with what he earns (but not at my expense). He should ensure prosperity but not by making me work too hard. [. . .] He should be strict but compassionate. [. . .] He should be somewhat dynamic, [. . .] not lazy. He should talk smoothly but without affectation. He should be shy but decisive. The main thing, he ought to like discipline and be obeyed by everyone. [. . .] It'd be better if this is someone from the military, [. . .] but not entirely.
>
> (Bykov 2005: 232)

Only Father Frost can help with a match to fit these rather contradictory specifications, which he refers to as a "typical God Knows What" [*tipichnoe To,*

Ne Znaiu Chto] (Bykov 2005: 233) – and comes up with Putin, who is duly accepted. Soon after the marriage (i.e., the elections) he finds Russia's G-spot and presses it in such a way that Russia loses the ability to differentiate between freedom and its absence, becomes indifferent to the outside world and even lethargic – until the next presidential elections, that is.

Putin's re-election bid in 2004 saw an attempt to utilize the fairy tale genre in the president's favor. In February that year, the Russian Family (*Russkaia sem'ia*) publishing house put together a book called *Tales about Our President* [*Skazki pro nashego prezidenta*]. It included 11 fairy tales, written by two reputable children's authors, Inna Gamazkova and Sergei Sedov. Illustrated by children's drawings based on the fairy tales' subjects and supplied with a sewed-in bookmark (colored in white, blue and red in imitation of the Russian national flag), the book was clearly aimed at the family audience, perhaps envisaging (grand) parents and (grand) children (re-)reading the tales together, as could be surmised from the rhymed "hint," placed on the last two lines of the penultimate page of the book: "Both old and young/enjoy these fairy tales" [*I star, i mlad / etim skazkam rad!*].[17]

In the book, the president – never mentioned by name but instantly recognizable because he swims with dolphins and practices Judo – does everything one would expect from a fairy-tale hero: he defeats a dragon (to release the German Chancellor, the British Prime Minister, and the American President, swallowed by the beast), a magician (who turned the president's wife, Liudmila the Beautiful, into a gray mouse), and the elements (represented by the Cruel Frost, who turns the finance minister and the defense minister into ice). With the help of a magic assistant (a sparrow spy, who dons a pair of dark glasses), he even gets himself a ghost from a Scottish castle as his English teacher – simply because Scottish ghosts are the only thing the Russian president does not have (see Gamazkova and Sedov 2004: 18–28, 35–39, 56–61).

Given the timing of the book's publication, the election theme features in it fairly prominently. The tales called "A Sparrow in Sunglasses" [*Vorobei v chernykh ochkakh*] and "People, vote!" [*Vybirai, narod!*] describe allegorically Putin's emergence as the country's leader and seem to be engaging in polemics directly both with Bykov's "The G-spot" and Babasian's "Ugly Putling": Putin was allegedly chosen with the assistance of the sparrow spy, not Father Frost; and not for his unattractiveness, which is specifically mentioned in "People, vote!" in relation to the process of succession, but because he was the most modest of all the presidential candidates (Gamazkova and Sedov 2004: 7–12).[18] There are also subliminal messages about the forthcoming re-election: for example, when the president, captured by the Sea King, defeats an octopus in a wrestling contest, he is returned to the Russian Federation in reward, and it is reported that "all people were glad that he turned out to be alive and well, and that a snap election wasn't necessary" (Gamazkova and Sedov 2004: 55).

Tales about Our President might well have been a result of the same drive to reach not merely the existing, but also the future, electorate that brought about, under the aegis of the presidential administration, the development of the "Find out about the President" website, www.uznay-prezidenta.ru, aimed at children aged 6–10. Its launch, attended by Putin himself, took place on January 19, 2004 (see Kolesnikov 2005c: 295–299). As for *Tales*, according to some reports, they were deemed unsuccessful by the presidential administration and did not go on sale – at least not until after the March elections. Rumor had it that somebody was even dismissed because of what was seen as the book's shortcomings (see Tsarik 2006). It is easy to see how the authors' efforts to make their subject look appealing to their target audience could backfire. One tale describes the president overcoming the severe weather conditions, the depravity of the London criminal underworld, and the treacherousness of the British Lord Chancellor (sic!) in order to be able – with the assistance of white bears, flying cranes, and Time, which volunteered to stand still – to arrive in time for an appointment with Her Majesty the Queen exactly as specified (Gamazkova and Sedov 2004: 45–51). Needless to say, it has been widely reported that during his state visit to the United Kingdom on June 24, 2003, Putin was 15 minutes late for the official ceremony of meeting with the Queen at the Horse Guards.[19] The ease with which Putin, after drinking a magic potion, could be mistaken for a witch called Lusha in yet another tale, is also potentially open to misinterpretation (Gamazkova and Sedov 2004: 40–44).

The fact that in 2004 the presidential administration directed their pro-Putin propaganda at the children who would not be eligible to vote for at least another 8 years at the earliest, was one of many signs suggesting that the powers-that-be were considering a "third-term" scenario, that is, Putin remaining in office for longer than the two 4-year terms established by the Russian Constitution. A number of Putin-related novels discuss what exactly such a scenario might involve, whether it is at all desirable, and what might happen if it goes wrong.

The most obvious way of going about the business of keeping Putin in power after his first 8 years in the office would have been to change the Constitution by means of a national referendum. A *roman à clef* called *The Hostage: Operation "Memorandum"* [*Zalozhnik: Operatsiia "Memorandum"* 2006], by the retired "oligarch" Aleksandr Smolenskii of the SBS-Agro Bank and his friend since their military service days, the journalist Eduard Krasnianskii, is written from the viewpoint of those opposing such a referendum. The novel is set in 1999–2006. In 1999, to ensure a smooth transition from the old president, Uralov (Yeltsin), to his successor (never mentioned in the book by his name), a secret memorandum is signed by 15 people – the so-called guarantors, who include the old and the new presidents, several officials from the presidential administration, as well as governors, ministers, and businessmen. The document is intended to ensure, among other things, that the existing constitutional order (more specifically, a maximum of two presidential terms) will be adhered to under the new regime. The FSB catches wind of this several years later, when one of the signatories, Governor Listov, gets drunk, lets the secret out, and is killed for this lapse by a hired assassin.[20] Knowing little about the content of the memorandum apart from the identities of most of its signatories (the tycoons Elenskii and Dukhon, i.e., Boris Berezovsky and Smolensky himself, among them), the secret services suspect an anti-government plot and begin an investigation. Meanwhile, the president is under pressure from his advisers Umnov and Smirnov (possibly modeled on Vladislav Surkov and Igor' Sechin, respectively) to announce a referendum on the issue of the third term. Outsmarting the FSB surveillance, a number of the signatories (such as Uralov, Elenskii, and Dukhon) gather in Normandy – at the estate of the film director Luc Martin (based upon Luc Bresson, of all people), with his ex-wife Milla Majevic (the actress Milla Jovovich) as the hostess – to discuss what to do next. It transpires that the memorandum has a secret appendix (initially known to only six signatories), according to which the new president is bound to ensure that Uralov's daughter Tat'iana (also present at the meeting in Normandy) would become his successor at the end of his second term. With Tat'iana's consent, the signatories decide to revoke this appendix, on the condition that the president abandon the idea of the referendum and of appointing an alternative successor, and instead call for a free and fair presidential election. Otherwise, the signatories threaten to make the memorandum public at a press conference in Paris. Dukhon's friend Bagrianskii (Krasnianskii serving as his prototype) is entrusted with the dangerous task of delivering the original of the memorandum from Russia to France. In an unrelated chain of events, the new president's older daughter, Natasha (modeled on Putin's daughter Masha), chances upon the president's own copy of the memorandum on his desk at his Novo-Ogarevo residence, immediately realizes its significance – and steals it in order to smuggle it to the West with the assistance of her Italian friend Gabriele. Her act is supposed to guarantee that her father observe the letter and the spirit of the memorandum (minus the secret appendix, presumably) in the name of the country's future. *The Hostage*'s open ending leaves the president incumbent undecided whether to call the referendum off and publicly accuse some members of his inner circle (such as Smirnov) of conspiring against the constitutional order or to press ahead with the referendum and denounce some of the memorandum's signatories instead (Smolenskii and Krasnianskii 2006: 11–12, 50, 397–324, 431–448, 457–424, 527–585).

The "hostage" of the title can be applied to many characters in the novel. President Uralov became a hostage to fortune when he took charge of the country that started falling apart, and the same applies to his successor when he agreed to try and clear up the political and economic mess that he inherited from Uralov. Bagrianskii becomes a hostage to his old friendship with Dukhon when he agrees to be the signatories' courier upon Dukhon's request. Even the novel's readers become "hostages to the semi-documentary narrative" (Loshak 2006: 63), invited to keep guessing what, if any, of this actually happened. According to one account, in December 1999, Yeltsin and Putin did sign a confidential formal agreement regulating the transfer of power from the former to the latter, by which Putin, *inter alia*, "undertook responsibility for keeping the Constitution of the Russian Federation intact. In this context, it is likely to have meant that the new president would not remain in his office beyond the two terms" (Medvedev 2007: 108). Were there any other guarantors and/or signatories to this agreement, though? And if yes, were they hunted by the FSB the way *The Hostage* describes? Perhaps most importantly, some readers find it hard to understand "why all the novel's characters (both the positive and the negative ones) attach such an enormous significance to this list of good intentions [i.e., the memorandum AR]" (Arbitman 2007). Judging by how the memorandum is presented in the book, it hardly seems likely that it could be treated as a legally binding document, whether signed or not, and in that sense alone it is not worth the paper it was written on.

There is, of course, a loophole that would allow Putin – or anyone else, for that matter – to become Russian president for the third and fourth time without violating the Constitution, which bans more than two consecutive presidential terms for the same person. As Putin himself clarified in his speech at the industrial fair in Hanover on April 11, 2005, the Constitution "does not forbid anyone to stand for a third non-consecutive presidential election. He added: 'I am not sure I would want to go for it, though'" (Kolesnikov 2005b: 511). Few novelists (and political commentators) shared that uncertainty. In a satirical thriller titled *The President's Last Love* [*Posledniaia liubov' prezidenta* 2004], by the Russian-Ukrainian author Andrei Kurkov, partly set in a not so distant future, Putin hosts an ice-swimming party for foreign heads of state in Moscow in January 2013. The event celebrates the 400th anniversary of the House of Romanov, and Putin has returned as Russian president after missing one presidential term (see Kurkov 2004: 10–12). Yet another satirical thriller, by well-known Moscow journalist Sergei Dorenko,[21] titled *2008* but published in 2005, contemplates a somewhat more exhilarating scenario of a power transfer from Putin to Putin and the end of his second consecutive presidential term.

To stay in power, Putin and his principal financial backer, Roman Abramovich, come up with the following plan. Dmitrii Kozak, a former Deputy Head of the presidential administration and the presidential representative in the Southern Federal Region at the time when the novel went to press, is chosen to stand for election as Putin's successor, to concede power to Putin 4 years later. However, to avoid the danger of Kozak's succumbing to the temptation of retaining power, he will be made ill shortly after his inauguration speech, kept in a hospital for several months, and then pronounced incurable and unable to function. Putin, who could become prime minister by that time,[22] will be summoned back to the presidency by well-orchestrated popular demand. The Chairman of the Constitutional Court will declare that the Constitution is not violated, because Putin's new presidency cannot be considered a third consecutive term in office.

From January 7 to February 4, 2008, when the novel's plot unfolds, the plan is at the initial stage of its implementation, but Putin already wants more. He is looking at various ways of prolonging his life and perhaps even gaining immortality (by recourse to castration or cloning, if necessary). He becomes a devoted follower of Taoism, which teaches that life can be extended, even indefinitely, through various spiritual practices.[23] Putin was once told by an acquaintance that his KGB training, which develops the art of mimicry and resourceful adjustment to any circumstances, is akin to Taoist philosophy, which promotes so-called "effortless doing," that is, achieving the best results by going with the flow, rather than against the current, and maximizing already existing opportunities, rather than creating them from scratch. When in 1999 or 2000, Dorenko, himself a Tao fan, said to Putin that one should let the events unfold naturally rather than organize them, Putin reportedly answered, "That's an extremely efficient way of doing things" (Volchek 2005).

When in a state of trance, caused by inhaling drug fumes, Putin has a vision of Yen-lo Wang, the ruler of Hell in Chinese mythology, which means a bad omen and a warning. To ascertain the exact nature of the warning, Putin arranges for a visit to Manchuria to consult Wang Leping, a Taoist spiritual leader, in the hope that he will provide an explanation of the vision. To the rest of the world, Putin pretends that he is going on holiday to the Altai mountains, to a residence belonging to the family of the "former" Moscow Mayor Yury Luzhkov (who ostensibly dies before the action in the book commences, and is replaced by Kozak as the "next" mayor).[24] Accompanied only by three FSB agents, a doctor, and an interpreter specializing in Chinese, Putin is secretly transported from Altai to China by helicopter.[25] While he is undergoing spiritual training to prepare himself for a revelation contained in the message of the vision, back in Russia the Chechens resistance fighters take control over a nuclear power station in Obninsk (near Moscow) and threaten to blow it up to destroy Moscow by nuclear fallout. The Muscovites flee in panic, and the abandoned Kremlin is taken over by the NBP and their leader, Eduard Limonov, who appoints as his prime minister the oil magnate Mikhail Khodorkovsky (whose arrest in 2003 on charges of fraud and tax evasion, followed by a sentence of 8 years in prison, is widely believed to be politically motivated; in the fictional world of *2008*, Kozak releases him from jail). Putin returns to Moscow from China when it is already too late to make any difference, except for authorizing President Bush's offer of sending US marines to Russia to ensure safety at its civil and military nuclear sites, as well as in all major cities, to avert new terrorist attacks. Thus, the mysterious vision of Yen-lo Wang turns out to signify the catastrophic events with which the book concludes, and the book itself serves as a warning that unforeseen circumstances might interfere with Putin's alleged plans to stay at the helm for as long as possible (see Dorenko 2005: 14, 20, 25–27, 40, 47–48, 76–78, 140–141, 152–154, 163–164, 199–239).[26]

Yet another apocalyptic scenario with Putin's participation is the subject of a diptych by yet another TV and radio journalist, Vladimir Solov'ev. His novels *The Gospel According to Solov'ev* [*Evangelie ot Solov'eva* 2007] and *Apocalypse of Vladimir* [*Apokalipsis ot Vladimira* 2007], set in 2005–07 and linked by the same characters and the continuity of plot, invite comparisons with Mikhail Bulgakov's *The Master and Margarita* and Dan Brown's *Da Vinci Code*. In Solov'ev's books, structured as a first-person narration on behalf of Solov'ev's fictional *alter ego*, Putin has to deal with what appears to be a Second Coming – no more, no less.[27] On a business trip to Detroit to cover an international auto show, Solov'ev meets a Russian émigré called Daniil. Daniil was conceived by his Jewish mother as a result of artificial insemination, administered in the late

1960s in the Soviet Union with genetic material gathered by KGB agents from the Shroud of Turin. After moving to Israel, and then to the United States, Daniil reveals himself as the Messiah to Solov'ev, restoring a blind black boy's eyesight as proof of his supernatural powers. Solov'ev becomes Daniil's right-hand man, an archangel of sorts, and immediately discovers that he also is endowed with some supernatural abilities (he can read people's thoughts in any language, instantly transport individuals anywhere on earth, turn sinners into ashes by heavenly fire, and even make time stop). Applying these useful skills as and when necessary, Solov'ev helps to arrange for Daniil's live appearance on the Larry King show to inform mankind that the Second Coming has arrived.

Well informed as ever, Putin and his administration monitor these developments, which are not yet in the public domain, with grave concern. After all, the Second Coming – if this is indeed what is happening – renders presidential elections and presidential authority superfluous. Putin attempts to establish the alleged Messiah's authenticity and, at the same time, just in case, tries to find out if it is possible for him to become Daniil's apostle and/or one of the 12 kings-cum-prophets who are expected to rule the world on Daniil's behalf. To this end, Putin meets Solov'ev a number of times in an effort to make him influence Daniil's decision. Putin tries to ingratiate himself with both Daniil and Solov'ev by various means, such as appealing to the Russian roots of the former, finding a luxurious flat for the lover of the latter, and warning both Daniil and Solov'ev of assassination attempts on their lives. For his part, Solov'ev asks Putin to ensure Daniil's endorsement as the Messiah by the Russian Patriarch and leading Russian scientists using the striking resemblance between Daniil's DNA samples and those taken from the Turin shroud[28], as well as the Arab leaders' cooperation.

Given that Daniil turns out to be a false Messiah in the end, Solov'ev's ambitious and at times somewhat pretentious literary undertaking seems to be lamenting the well-known fact that the modern world falls under the spell of false prophets only too often, and the mass media should take significant responsibility for this. What has the novel got to do with President Putin? Any Russian ruler can be perceived in a messianic context, because, following a special ceremony of anointing sovereigns as part of their consecration to the office (developed under Ivan the Terrible and in effect since 1584), Russian monarchs become the Lord's Anointed and are associated, first and foremost, with Jesus Christ (see Uspenskii 1998: 20). Paradoxically, Soviet and post-Soviet leaders are no exception, because, as Solov'ev explains,

> Russia is an autocratic country. No matter what you call a supreme ruler, people still think of him as a monarch-like father figure (*tsar'-batiushka*). It's the clever dicks who decide by themselves how to label the form of government in the country, and then shout tirelessly, "It's a democracy!" from every rooftop. And when they get tired, and life starts to go wrong, they criticize everything and name what they see a tyranny.
>
> (Solov'ev 2007b: 65)[29]

Putin, in particular, has been linked by some observers to Christ and the Second Coming, though ironically. When he attended the Kondopoga pulp and paper mill in Karelia on July 21, 2003, a pipe burst and flooded the mill's floor. A journalist describes what happened next, deliberately replacing the sublime with the ridiculous:

> How was the president of the country that has laid a claim to becoming great again, supposed to behave? [. . .] He was supposed to walk on water. And he did. Evil tongues might say that he would have done something different had his re-election campaign not been about to begin. [. . .] Yes, he did walk on water and didn't even get his feet wet, it seems, although it was quite deep. History, as we know, remembers only one similar occasion. And it took place such a long time ago! And we have been waiting for it to happen again so impatiently!
>
> (Kolesnikov 2005c: 22)

In Solov'ev's novels, written in all seriousness, Putin is not a Messiah, but he has to react to the consequences of what appears to be the arrival of a Messiah. He does not mind utilizing a bit of Daniil's charisma when Solov'ev's fictional *alter ego* informs the president's closest aides that Daniil might give Putin his blessing and thus make him "the Lord's Anointed," which would enhance his spiritual authority and enable him to discount the Communist opposition (see Solov'ev 2007a: 199). Solov'ev accepts Putin's handling of the situation as natural for someone who has to balance looking after his country's interests against looking out for his own interests. In his portrayal of the president, Solov'ev seems well disposed, emphasizing Putin's unassuming appearance, which "does not create the impression of an arbiter of people's destinies" (Solov'ev 2007a: 170). In addition, he praises Putin's competence and skill as a communicator,[30] as well as his good taste in fashion accessories, such as wearing a Breguet watch on a simple leather strap (see Solov'ev 2007b: 73).[31] Such praise is hardly surprising from a man who, at the All-Russia Forum for Putin's Supporters on November 21, 2007, said, "We're lucky. We have a strong, clever, talented leader. [. . .] Every Putin supporter has to ask himself a question: 'What have I done not to let my national leader down?'"[32] In the novels' context, however, it is clear that in a battle of wills and wits between Solov'ev's fictional self as a "guarantor of the Second Coming" (Solov'ev 2007b: 95) and his fictional representation of Putin as a guarantor of the Russian Constitution,[33] Putin does not stand a chance, because any secular power would feel defenseless when the Messiah (even a false one) and his messengers begin meting out punishment to sinners without blinking an eye.

In the surreal world of short stories about Putin by the programmer-cum-journalist Maksim Kononenko, published in book form in spring 2005 as *Vladimir Vladimirovich TM*,[34] Putin talks not so much to archangels but directly to God himself. It is never a conversation of two equals, however.[35] In one of his impassionate pleas to God, Putin complains that he is held responsible for every disaster that happens in Russia, while everything actually is in God's hands (see Kononenko 2005: 607–609). In another, he asks why no one loves him unless he promises social security benefits, cheap vodka, and exemptions from the military service. God's answer, "Because you are an *izbrannyi*" (Kononenko 2005: 628), plays on the ambiguity of the word *izbrannyi*, which may be translated as both "the elected one" and "the chosen one." Kononenko's aim is to separate the charisma of the Chosen One, almost automatically ascribed to any Russian ruler who is seen by the majority of the populace as legitimate, from the routine of the country's highest administrative office that in theory could be filled by almost anyone, and to demystify Putin's persona as a result. In his January 27, 2004 interview to Radio Liberty, Kononenko stated, "If there's a danger of [Putin's] personality cult, instead of rallying and picketing against it, one should, as a matter of urgency, stimulate this cult to such an extent that it would collapse under its own weight" (Sokolov 2004).[36] Kononenko does so in the tradition represented by Daniil Kharms (1905–42), known for inventing absurd stories about famous people (see, e.g., Kharms 1999: 536–537, 846–848).

Kononenko's Putin is hapless, absentminded, irritable, and vain, sooner described as a victim of circumstance than a leader in control of his own and other people's fates. As Putin is often perceived as a media-generated phenomenon, in Kononenko's stories his decisions and pronouncements are frequently influenced by television commercials (such as an advertisement for Rama margarine) and popular music (such as songs by Tatu; see Kononenko 2005: 71–72, 258, 524). For his advisers, Kononenko's Putin has the ghost of Stalin and a personal Martian who lives inside the president's head. In his office, surrounded by presidential accessories (a paper knife made of Shamil Basaev's shinbone and an ashtray resembling Boris Berezovsky's skull), he feels quite out of place as "the most useless person in the country." He complains, "Everyone is doing something, either manufacturing spares, or treating illnesses, or pushing drugs. And me? I'm sitting under a national flag playing computer games. [. . .] I won't be able to take this for another five years!" (Kononenko 2005: 161).[37] Prone to escapism, he dreams of going fishing, but the dream never comes true (Kononenko 2005: 158, 398–400).[38] With the Russian Patriarch, he discusses the life of hermits; with the Dalai Lama, life in exile; and with the Martian, life on Mars (Kononenko 2005: 330–331). On the other hand, Kononenko's Putin envies the mayor of Moscow, for whom there is no limit on the number of times he can get re-elected [since 2006, re-appointed – AR], and considers making the presidential term a lifelong commitment. He also contemplates erecting a monument to himself, with a bronze submarine for a pedestal. For his part, the head of the presidential administration is thinking about removing the body of Lenin from the Mausoleum by 2020, to make room for Putin (Kononenko 2005, 80–81, 258–259, 313, 500).

Yet another parallel between Putin and Lenin has been drawn in a thriller called *A Hostile Takeover* [*Reider* 2007], by the barrister Pavel Astakhov, who has been a legal representative of the NTV, TNT, and ORT television companies and fronts the regular television program *An Hour in Court* [*Chas suda*] on REN-TV. His *roman à clef* describes an attempt at a hostile takeover of a privatized provincial enterprise that manufactures equipment for the defense industry. The takeover involves an armed raid on the enterprise, an illegal transfer of the ownership of its shares, and a number of vicious lawsuits instigated under false pretences. It is masterminded by one Petr Spirskii,[39] the illegitimate son of the Supreme Court chairman, the blood relationship introduced mostly to illustrate how Russian laws breed corrupt practices. The director of the enterprise hires the lawyer Artem Pavlov (Astakhov's fictional self) to block the attempt. After many twists and turns in the plot, Pavlov succeeds in doing so and discovers that the takeover has been requested by a local vice-governor. Surprisingly, Spirskii is not the only one who gets his just desserts. Some of those who have not been implicated in the takeover are punished too. President Putin – referred to only by his initials ("VeVe"), but unmistakably identifiable thanks to the presence of his pet Labrador, Connie[40] – personally dismisses the aforementioned Supreme Court chairman (for being related to a criminal) and the governor (for overlooking the takeover plot under his very nose). Such a retribution might appear rather disproportionate to the reader. But this is not the end. On the president's authority, an ex-FSB colonel is dispatched to the enterprise to become the director's first deputy and to oversee its re-nationalization and merger with a state-owned defense concern, under the pretext that the interests of the state are at stake. Thus, an unsuccessful hostile takeover is almost imperceptibly followed by a successful one, by a different party using different methods. When received by the president for the last time in his capacity as a regional leader, the governor, who has nothing to lose, blames Putin for setting an example in hostile takeovers in Russia by presiding over a "state-sponsored raid on the largest privately owned oil firm in the country and reselling it via a shell company" (Astakhov 2007: 376).[41] In a separate scene, Artem Pavlov traces the origins of hostile takeovers in Russia back to no other person than Lenin: "No one has been able to repeat what he has done. To seize a whole country without investing anything, on a promise alone, is an absolute record" (Astakhov 2007: 400). When put together, the governor's and Pavlov's statements, about the law in present-day Russia being turned into a blunt instrument of a Lenin-like expropriation of the expropriators,[42] are critical not only of the peculiarities of Soviet and post-Soviet legal culture, but also of Putin's personal conduct, which seems to be steeped in this culture.[43] These statements acquire a special significance because they appear to be coming, via fictional characters, from Astakhov himself, who is not only a fellow lawyer and an ex-KGB trainee,[44] but also a leader of a pro-Putin movement.[45]

As for the artistic strategies of the works under consideration, they all continue a long line of similar publications about Russian political leaders of the twentieth century,[46] written in the traditions of either realism, or satire, or allegory and fantasy (see Marsh 1989: 7), or a combination thereof. The authors' political stances vary: nihilistic in Bykov's case; unquestionably loyal in that of Ol'bik; deferential, with some reservations, in the works of Solov'ev and Astakhov; "democratic and capitalist à la Yeltsin" (Nazarov 2006) in those of Smolenskii and Krasnianskii; indeterminate in the narratives of Gamazkova and Sedov; right-wing nationalist in Prokhanov's text[47]; left-wing in Dorenko's[48]; and both liberal and conservative from Kononenko's viewpoint.[49] Their ideological loyalties fully explain the authors' approaches to their respective fictional representations of President Putin. Thus, Dorenko's passive and ultimately powerless Putin is at dramatic odds with Ol'bik's Bond-like man of action, just as Ol'bik's Putin, with his extraordinary personality, is the exact opposite of Prokhanov's nondescript Chosen One.[50]

It is curious that in their characterization of Putin, all draw on more or less the same information about him, available either through the mass media or from those close to Putin.[51] None of the authors, however, is averse to playing fast and loose with the facts and making conjectures to suit his particular political agenda. This is only natural. After all,

> fiction writers, given a choice between bare, recorded historical facts – often skimpy, and almost certainly devoid of juicy details – and the colorful lore offered by *petite histoire*[52] and its popularizers, invariably and understandably choose the latter.
>
> (Gasiorowska 1979: 38)

Thus, ignoring all evidence to the contrary,[53] in his two novels about Putin, Ol'bik portrays him as a man very much in love with his wife, and treats her as his confidante. For his part, Kononenko, whose purpose is less to reveal a super-hero's human side (Ol'bik's intention) than to evoke sympathy for an average man out of his depth,[54] also depicts the Putins' relationship as that of a "lovey-dovey couple," but does so in a grotesquely exaggerated way.[55] Dorenko, who sets out to degrade Putin by every means at his disposal, the cruder the better; his Putin sleeps with a prostitute who is destined for Berezovsky's private pleasure in his London exile, while Liudmila is described as a drinker, not particularly happy in her marriage but struggling to make it work.[56]

There is more unanimity displayed in the authors' strategies of describing Putin through the medium of his entourage. Only Ol'bik offers flattering sketches of Prime Minister Kasyanov, FSB chief Patrushev, Defense Minister Sergeev, and Voloshin, Head of the presidential administration. They all appear in his books under their own names, as members of a dedicated and competent team that rescues Putin from the mountains after the success of his mission in *The President*. Interior Minister Boris Gryzlov and the chairman of the Federation Council, Sergei Mironov, are among those whom Putin consults on the best way to resolve the hostage crisis in *Nord-Ost*.[57] Kononenko is more selective; though partial to both Voloshin and his deputy, Vladislav Surkov, he brands Gryzlov and Mironov "androids" (Kononenko 2005: VI). Solov'ev portrays Voloshin as practically a "cross between the Golem and Frankenstein's monster" (Solov'ev 2007a: 168) and concentrates on Voloshin's and Surkov's alleged rivalry. Dorenko, also full of venom, chooses to focus instead on the rivalry between Surkov and Sechin. Smolenskii and Krasnianskii are equally disparaging about the fictional presidential advisers Umnov and Smirnov, thus perpetuating the "old [. . .] myth about [the ruler's] evil counselors" (Chantsev 2007: 294), while presenting the president in a much more positive light.[58]

To sum up, Putin's image in fiction is multifaceted, because every writer tries to present him from his own perspective. One author sees him as a politician prone to hiding behind various masks; another, as a dictator; yet another, as a more or less average person suddenly finding himself in charge of Russia and not always coping well enough; yet another, a kindly father-like tsar encircled and deceived by evil boyars (El'kina undated).

It remains a mystery to what degree, if at all, the fictional Putin in the prose of Prokhanov, Ol'bik, Kononenko, Dorenko, Solov'ev, Astakhov, and Smolenskii and Krasnianskii, not to speak of the fairy tales, resembles the real Putin in any way.[59] The only thing that can probably be said of Putin with some confidence after trawling through his representations in Russian fiction is that there is no Martian living in his head.[60]

On the purely aesthetic side, too, there are few rewards to glean from these works. Most fall under the category of political novel, "in which political ideas play a dominant role or in which the political milieu is the dominant setting" (Howe 1961: 17). According to Irving Howe, such texts do not normally have a high artistic value, for ideology "is abstract, as it must be, and therefore likely to be recalcitrant whenever an attempt is made to incorporate it into the novel's stream of sensuous impression. The conflict is inescapable" (Howe 1961: 20). That is why readers' response to these books often goes well beyond the means of literary criticism.[61] For instance, in November 2005, the Duma Committee for constitutional legislation, at the insistence of the Liberal Democratic Party of Russia (LDPR) Deputy Aleksei Mitrofanov, held a special hearing to decide whether Dorenko's *2008* intrudes too far in Putin's personal life and can be used as a manual for future *coups d'état* (see Troitskii and Melikova 2005).[62] In July 2007, Head of the Moscow Police Department for Investigations, General Ivan Glukhov, asked the Prosecutor Iurii Semin to institute legal proceedings for slander against Pavel Astakhov and his publishers, for *A Hostile Takeover* states that, in pursuit of financial gain, the employees of the Department participate in hostile takeovers (see Zheglov 2007).[63]

There are signs that, from time to time, the Kremlin also decides to take fiction seriously and resorts to litigation (or a threat of litigation, sometimes issued via a third party) to protect itself from criticism that is perceived as having gone too far.[64] It is widely believed that the criminal case against the Ad Marginem publishing house on the charges of distributing pornography by releasing Vladimir Sorokin's novel *Blue Lard* [*Goluboe salo* 1999], initiated by the Moscow city prosecutor's office in July 2002 at the request of the Kremlin-sponsored Marching Together youth action group, was in fact punishment for printing Prokhanov's *Mr Hexogen* (see Tarasov 2002; and Pribylovskii and Fel'shtinskii 2004: 219–220). The case was dropped in April 2003. Ad Marginem, however, ignored the warning from on high and, on Prokhanov's recommendation (see Volchek 2005), published yet another, arguably even more insulting anti-Putin novel, Dorenko's

2008. The fact that Ad Marginem has continued to operate as normal until now should probably be put down to the Kremlin's realization that its attempts to censor works of art tend to rebound,[65] and, with the average print run for modern fiction in present-day Russia ranging from 4,000 to 25,000 copies (depending on the genre; see Margolin 2007),[66] it is wiser to concentrate on exercising control over television broadcasts because they reach a much wider audience.[67] As a result, the situation with Putin in fiction has not yet reverted to the one with the literary image of Lenin in the Soviet days, when it was possible to show him "as a human being, attractive or unattractive, rather than the icon" (Friedberg 1977: 124), only outside the Soviet bloc.[68]

An exceptional case is Lev Gurskii's recent pseudo-biography of Roman Arbitman, a provincial teacher who is said to have saved President Yeltsin from an assassination attempt and was made his successor, that is, Russia's second president, as a result. The book's author, whose real name happens to be Roman Arbitman, deals with the issue of Putin's seeming omnipresence and omnipotence by pretending, in a satirically charged alternative history mode, that in 2000–08 Russia had been ruled by someone else, who, among other things, "for eight years has been a staunch supporter of *glasnost* in Russia; accordingly, not a single programme on the main TV channels has been shut under pressure from the Kremlin" (Gurskii 2009: 31). What appears to be reprisal for Putin's conspicuous absence (he is not mentioned in the book even once) was not long in coming. Under the pretext that the cover design of the Arbitman book was modeled after the well-established series Lives of Remarkable People [Zhizn' zamechatel'nykh liudei], which the book parodied, the Young Guard [Molodaia gvardiia] publishing house that has been producing this series since 1938 sued Gurskii's publishers for plagiarism – and won the case (even though the Young Guard's initial demand of a million rubles, or approximately USD 36,500, in compensation was reduced by the court to 30,000 roubles, or approximately USD 1,000, and the request for pulping the print run of the offending title was rejected; see Edel'shtein 2011).

Both positive and negative portrayals of Putin in fiction (and in other cultural forms)[69] frequently serve as a guarantee of commercial success (Kuznetsov 2005), whether his name is mentioned directly or his identity is merely hinted at in a far from subtle manner. This is clearly not the only reason he remains popular with fiction writers – or, to put it differently, not the only reason journalists and public figures increasingly turn to fiction when they write about Putin. Fiction writers are justifiably attracted not only by Putin's status as an international man of mystery, but also by the safety net of poetic license, which is Vital if one intends to disclose secrets related to a head of state (and other actual persons) with impunity. Hence, the proliferation of *romans à clef*.[70]

Putin's popularity ratings – a factor also responsible for Putin as a subject of choice for fiction writers – have almost always been uncommonly and consistently high.[71] However, "ratings studies do not reveal what is concealed in people's collective unconscious" (Shestopal 2008: 77), while works of art do (see, for instance, Rancour-Laferriere 1989), and that is why rulers' fictional images should be studied alongside their real-life words and deeds.

Notes

1 All translations are mine.

2 According to a statement following the in-depth interviews and opinion polls on the images of power in post-Soviet Russia, conducted – mostly in Moscow – by an interdisciplinary team of experts, led by Elena Shestopal of Moscow University, throughout the 1990s and the early 2000s, "the chief political characteristics of President Putin's image are its enigma and mystery" (see Shestopal 2004: 372).

3 Thus Putin seems happy to talk about accidentally running a man over with his car or about a fire that destroyed his summer house in 1996, but does not provide much detail about the specific nature of his work as an intelligence operative when on a posting in East Germany, except for the admission that he drank a lot of beer (see Gevorkian, Kolesnikov, and Timakova 2000: 34, 64, 113–118).

4 Cf. "Historical personages scantily supported by documents have always been considered fair game by fiction writers" (Gasiorowska 1979: 45).

5 Circumstantial evidence in support of an influential conspiracy theory claiming that there was an FSB trace in the apartment explosions in Moscow, Buinaksk, and Volgodonsk has been gathered in Felshtinsky and Litvinenko 2002. For his part, Putin vehemently and indignantly denies any involvement of the Russian special forces in setting up the explosions (see Gevorkian, Kolesnikov, and Timakova 2000: 137).

6 This image might have been inspired by a well-known photograph of Putin swimming with dolphins (by S. Velichkin and V. Rodionov), which can be seen, for example, in an insert with other photographs of Putin in Kolesnikov (2005a).

7 The author Viktor Shenderovich, who had a chance to observe Putin from a close distance in January 2001, claims that even Putin's eyes can change color from gray to blue to white (see Shenderovich 2002: 34–37).

8 For his part, the film and television critic Iurii Bogomolov has noted that

> everyone sees in Putin what one wants to see: an intellectual thinks of him as an art lover; a General, a benefactor; a liberal, yet another liberal; foreign statesmen, one of their own. [. . .] Such is the structure of his image, that of a great man without a name (*velikogo Anonima*).
>
> (Bogomolov 2004: 30)

9 In addition, this fast-paced thriller describes the Chechen terrorists' attempts to blow up a hydroelectric power station near Volgograd, a nuclear power station in Voronezh, and Putin's cortege on its way to ex-President Yeltsin in his Barvikha residence. All these attempts are thwarted by the consolidated efforts of vigilant civilians and fearless combatants, including Putin's bodyguards.

10 For a detailed account of what is known, see, for instance, Dunlop 2006: 103–157.

11 This detail might have been included in an attempt to remove the full burden of responsibility for the hostages' deaths from the Russian authorities. It also illustrates, in support of Putin's official line, that, in fighting against the Chechen resistance, Russia is making its contribution to the global war on terror as an ally of the United States. Already in *The President*, Putin's undercover mission takes place simultaneously with a similar special operation of US commandos, who hide in the same gorge as Putin's group to assassinate an international terrorist called Emir, who arrives from Kandahar to see Bars and Taipan on an inspection visit (see Ol'bik 2002: 274, 417–418, 436, 460).

12 Ol'bik's own admission in his email to me dated February 20, 2008.

13 Kolesnikov mentions it as "very popular with readers" in connection with Putin's visit on December 16, 2004 to the Kalininskaia nuclear power station (see Kolesnikov 2005b: 360).

14 The name of Putin's father is given here as Platon Privalov.

15 The ambiguous nature of the tales' allegories allows their authors to argue that they comment on human vices in general, rather than launch personal attacks.

16 Other sources ascribe it to vote rigging (see Pribylovskii and Fel'shtinskii 2004: 115–127).

17 The same page indicates that the idea of the book belongs to Evgenii Miachin, the general director of the Pressa publishing house.

18 Cf. "a progressively smaller number of our respondents think of Putin as an honest and modest person. This feature peaked at 70 per cent in November 2003. Merely a year later, it fell to 45 per cent" (Shestopal 2008: 352).

19 See, for instance, Kolesnikov 2005a: 441, 443 and Hamilton 2003. Putin's disregard for punctuality is common knowledge. Some observers suggest that he comes late to most of his business meetings quite deliberately (see Pribylovskii and Felshtinskii 2004: 249). His wife recalls that it was not unusual for Putin to be over an hour late for their meetings during their courtship (see Blotskii 2002: 24).

20 The circumstances of Listov's murder coincide with those of the death of the governor of the Magadan region, Valentin Tsvetkov, shot dead in Moscow on October 18, 2002.

21 In 1999–2000, when he worked for the ORT television company as a news anchor man, Dorenko became instrumental in popularizing Putin's image in the media. He earned the nickname "TV killer" for character assassinations of Yeltsin's and Putin's political rivals Evgeny Primakov and Yury Luzhkov. Dorenko lost his job on television after criticizing Putin's conduct during the *Kursk* submarine crisis, and has been in opposition to the Putin regime ever since.

22 The suggestion that at the end of his second presidential term Putin might become prime minister (after which the new president's role would be largely ceremonial) seems to have been first publicly advanced by the director of the Institute for National Strategy, Stanislav Belkovskii (see Samarina and Kornia 2005).

23 Dorenko must have been inspired by Putin's active and long-standing interest in judo (which is based on Taoist principles; on the character-building qualities of judo, which might well have been indispensable in molding Putin into a future president, see Kolesnikov 2005c: 237; for Putin on judo, see Gevorkian, Kolesnikov, and Timakova 2000: 20). Also, according to a common assumption, Putin's surname derives from the word "put'" (pathway, route, journey) – and "tao" in Chinese means roughly the same. Some observers, however, assert that Putin's surname comes from "puty" (restraints, fetters) (see Sedakova 2007).

24 It has to be said, with the benefit of hindsight, that Dorenko guessed correctly the first name and the place of work of Putin's real-life successor Dmitrii Medvedev. Dorenko also should be credited with emphasizing the importance of the post of Moscow mayor for a transition to governmental jobs at the very top. Currently, the post is occupied by Sergei Sobianin, who might well move higher up in due course.

25 In Russian fiction, there is a tradition of portraying domestic affairs through a Chinese veil, mostly for satirical purposes (cf. Eduard Topol's 1997 novel *The Chinese Thoroughfare* [*Kitaiskii proezd*], depicting Yeltsin and the CPRF leader Gennady Zyuganov as Chinese politicians Yel Tsin and Zyu Gan). Andrei Kolesnikov testifies that, during the Russian President's official visit to China during October 14–16, 2004, Putin's surname was represented by the Chinese characters "pu" and "tsin," allegedly meaning "ordinary, mediocre" and "capital city," respectively (see Kolesnikov 2005b: 270).

26 When still on television, Dorenko liked acting like a prophet of doom. Some of his programs were decidedly apocalyptic. The mention of the NBP can be explained by the fact that the party representatives voiced their support for Dorenko during the defamation law suit brought against him by the then Moscow mayor, Iurii Luzhkov (see Bogomolov 2004: 196–197, 223).

27 According to Kolesnikov, Putin is not a stranger to the "end of the world" discourse. Thus, when meeting his proxies on February 12, 2004 at Moscow University and talking about the state of Russia 4 years earlier, he "painted a picture of a final apocalypse in full swing" (Kolesnikov 2005c: 336).

28 In fact, the DNA match would only "prove" that Daniil was "cloned" with genes from the shroud. Solov'ev does not appear to be questioning whether the person beneath the Turin shroud was Jesus Christ.

29 Incidentally, Putin is thanked for preparing the ground for a restoration of the monarchy in Russia by the main character in a satirical novel written by a British Slavist residing in the United States (Kharington 2004: 419).

30 Cf.

> I didn't have to explain to Putin either about Daniil or the end of the world. He had taken things seriously and had done his homework. What a pleasure to deal with citizens like that! Also, he tactfully keeps his distance and doesn't try to worm himself into my confidence.
>
> (Solov'ev 2007b: 65)

31 In fact, Putin has been reported as wearing a much flashier but probably just as expensive Patek-Philippe Calatrava watch (see Pribylovskii and Fel'shtinskii 2004: 240).

32 See http://rutube.ru/tracks/553302.html?v=4091fe40a52b74f3f2ec5036ab3b2a35 (accessed April 30, 2011).

33 An example is a long theological argument whether or not Daniil is an anti-Christ, in the course of which Solov'ev teleports Putin, much to the chagrin of his bodyguards, from his Novo-Ogarevo residence to a small room in the Winter Palace in St. Petersburg (see Solov'ev 2007b: 79).

34 Parts of it have been circulated on the Internet since the autumn of 2002 and broadcast on the Ekho Moskvy radio station since the end of summer 2004.

35 Yet Putin appeared as a cloud on the mountain and a burning bush in the "Ten Commandments" episode of an NTV program called *Kukly* (a Russian equivalent of *The Spitting Image*) in May 2000 (see Pribylovskii and Fel'shtinskii 2004: 210) and is likened to "God Almighty" (*vsevyshnii*) in Kolesnikov 2005b: 480.

36 For Putin's medium-scale personality cult, see Pribylovskii 2003.

37 Kononenko's book is arranged as a list of entries in chronological order, which often (but not always) respond to various current affairs. This particular entry is dated September 22, 2003.

38 When stationed in Dresden, Major Putin was a member of the local amateur fishermen's association (see Pribylovskii and Fel'shtinskii 2004: 160).

39 The entrepreneur Aleksandr Sabadash, an ex-member of the Federation Council (for the Yamalo-Nenetsky autonomous district), has been named as Spirskii's prototype (see Nesterov 2007). Among other recognizable characters, Mikhail Fridman of the Alpha Group consortium is portrayed in the novel as Mark Frid.

40 Connie has been featuring in many reports on Putin's activities (e.g., Kolesnikov 2005c: 51–52 and Kolesnikov 2005b: 494–495). Putin has reportedly said about her: "I don't know if she's a dog or not. We have warm mutual feelings for each other" (Kolesnikov 2005b: 618).

41 The governor is referring to the December 2004 sale of Yuganskneftegaz (the core production subsidiary of Khodorkovsky's Yukos) to the Baikalfinansgrup, and its subsequent acquisition by the Rosneft oil company (chaired by Igor' Sechin, then a deputy head of the presidential administration).

42 In the case of Yukos, to benefit the Russian state in its function as a competing expropriator, it seems.

43 Cf. Putin's characterization by his former KGB colleague as a "lawyer through and through [*iurist do mozga kostei*], who does not accept any breach of legal principles" (Usol'tsev 2004: 130; Usol'tsev and Putin shared an office in Dresden in August 1985–October 1987). It is possible that this particular feature was what helped to make Putin electable. According to some estimates, in 1999, the majority of Russians (39 per cent) were united by the idea of a strict adherence to the law (see Sedov 1999: 17).

44 In 1991, Astakhov graduated from the KGB Higher School.

45 See, for instance, the anonymous note, "Astakhov priglasil Putina v Luzhniki na forum storonnikov," *Vedomosti*, November 19, 2007.

46 See, for example, Solzhenitsyn 1975; Rybakov 1987 (includes chapters on Stalin); Shnaider 1983 (on Khrushchev); Aksenov 1983 (includes sections on Brezhnev); Topol' 1992 (on Gorbachev); and Limonov 1998 (contains a caricature of Yeltsin).

47 Prokhanov openly admits that he "doesn't care whether Russia is ruled by Fascists, as long as it is a large, forward-moving, and prosperous country" (Danilkin 2007: 610).

48 Dorenko is reported to have joined the CPRF in September 2003.

49 See http://www.anticompromat.org/kononenko/kononbio.html (accessed April 30, 2011).

50 Some of the works discussed in this article seem to exhibit an awareness of other such works. For example, *2008* might well have been conceived in response to a January 2003 entry in Kononenko 2005: 37–39, with Putin speaking Chinese, and is partly a reaction to Ol'bik's *The President*, with shared motifs of Putin's secret mission disguised as a holiday trip and a Chechen attack on the nuclear power station with the assistance of bomb-throwing hang gliders.

51 Thus, Ol'bik saw Putin only on television, while Dorenko knew the man personally and presumably relied on this personal knowledge when working on his fictional image of the president.

52 That is, memoirs, anecdotes, and personal correspondence, if available.

53 A German friend of the Putins recalls that Liudmila Putina described her husband as a "vampire," while Vladimir Putin promised that friend to erect a monument in her honor if she survived 3 weeks under the same roof with Liudmila (see Pietsch 2001: 223, 274; the Russian translation appeared in 2002). Liudmila Putina admits that her husband "has never ever talked to her about his job" (Blotskii 2002: 57).

54 Kononenko's Putin is capable of forgetting about the Dubrovka siege (see Kononenko 2005: 55).

55 In the entry dated November 3, 2004, at his spouse's request, Putin promises to pull strings to re-elect George W. Bush as the US president, and in the entry of March 8, 2005, to bring peace to Chechnya as a present to her on International Women's Day (see Kononenko 2005: 543, 668).

56 See Dorenko 2005: 19, 107–113. Irene Pietsch claims that Liudmila Putina tries to avoid alcohol because she was once diagnosed with hepatitis (see Pietsch 2001: 210).

57 The president's aid Lev Tishkov, featured in both *The President* and *Nord-Ost*, appears to be based on Yeltsin's first assistant, Lev Sukhanov (1935–98), whom Ol'bik helped to write his memoirs, *Three Years with Yeltsin* (*Tri goda s El'tsinym*, Riga: Vaga, 1992).

58 In yet another *roman à clef* (Mal'gin 2005: 148–154, 266–267), the president and a high-ranking member of his administration, Kuz'ma Kuz'mich Ivanov, nicknamed Couscous (presumably based on Viktor Petrovich Ivanov, then in charge of the Kremlin's human resources), discuss whether to keep or to dismiss the senile adviser Ignatii Prisiadkin (a caricature of the author Anatolii Pristavkin). Couscous argues that Prisiadkin cannot fulfill his duties any longer. For his part, the president insists that Prisiadkin is popular with human rights activists, and his dismissal will be interpreted as a sign of authoritarianism gathering strength in Russia.

59 This might not necessarily be a bad thing. As Bykov puts it in his fairy tale "The Splendours and Miseries of the Teletubbies" [*Blesk i nishcheta telepuzikov*], "No one knew for sure what the president was really like, but they loved him to bits – and the less they knew about him, the further their love for him grew" (Bykov 2005: 412).

60 It is also tempting to give some credence to the following statement: "Everyone knows that, to begin with, the president is a mistrustful individual who easily takes offence. Second, that he puts blind faith in his colleagues from security and intelligence agencies. And finally, that he often does something first and thinks about it later" (Mal'gin 2005: 111), but only because this is partially corroborated by an observation that, in Putin's view, as it seems at times, "the most efficient method [of achieving what you want] in modern politics is to muscle your way through with a total disregard for your opponents [*idti naprolom i lomat' cherez koleno*] (Kolesnikov 2005b: 278).

61 Literary critics are seldom helpful in determining whether a political novel has any literary significance beyond its political message. Thus, one critic said of *2008*: Dorenko "believes that if he combines a recognizable figure, caustic satire, and his interest in Taoism, he comes up with a novel. But these components do not gel" (Basinskii 2005). However, another critic opined on the same book that "this postmodernist mixture of trash, political thriller, anti-Utopia, mystical parody and Soviet-style *feuilleton* results in [. . .] a distinctive and original work" (Ivanova 2005).

62 The book was vindicated.

63 After several interrogations, it was decided not to open the case because no specific non-fictional employees have been named in the book.

64 It has also been reported that sometimes the Kremlin offers financial assistance to those authors who have managed to please it with their fictional interpretation of the president's self. Thus, at Vladislav Surkov's suggestion, Kononenko's site, vladimir.vladimirovich.ru, was bought for an undisclosed sum by an unknown oligarch (see Tsarik 2006).

65 The criminal case against Sorokin's *Blue Lard* caused a four-fold increase in the novel's sales (see Stepanov, undated).

66 To the best of my knowledge, none of the books discussed in the present article exceeded a print run of 60,000 copies.

67 At the World Congress of Information Agencies on September 24, 2004, Putin compared freedom of the press to a window: "If it's open, it's noisy, if it's closed, it's stuffy" (Kolesnikov 2005b: 240). More specifically, at the meeting with Columbia University students and staff on September 26, 2003, when asked what he thinks of those who accuse him of trampling free speech, Putin replied: "[Russia] has never had freedom of speech, so I don't even know what to trample!" (Kolesnikov 2005c: 110).

68 Although fictional portraits of Putin do not seem to emerge as frequently in the West, nothing can stop Western authors from expressing strong opinions of him when they wish to do so. In his recent spy thriller, Charles Cumming describes a Russian president called Sergei Platov – "a former KGB spy, [who] had green-lit the murder of Russian

civilians on foreign soil, held Eastern European countries to ransom over the supply of gas, and encouraged the murder of journalists and human rights activists brave enough to criticize his regime" (Cumming 2011: 11). In a critic's view, which is hard to dismiss, "Platov is very evidently Vladimir Putin, barely disguised by the alias" (Massie 2011). Cumming's novel reveals a dark secret from Platov's past: when stationed in Dresden in 1988, he attempted unsuccessfully to defect to Britain, and has tried ever since to eliminate anyone who knew about this attempt. Meanwhile, the Secret Intelligence Service (SIS) had been using the classified information about his defection "as leverage against him for years. Whenever Moscow became too heavy-handed, [SIS] would simply apply the thumbscrews of 1988" (Cumming 2011: 386). Whether or not this story can convince the reader, "I don't think the publishers would be well advised to send a complimentary copy to Mr Putin" (Massie 2011). (I am grateful to Donald Tait for drawing my attention to this book.)

69 An analysis of Putin's image in poetry (e.g., Vladimir Nesterov's panegyrics, cited in Kolesnikov 2005a: 24–27; Dmitrii Bykov's Pushkin-inspired satire about the so-called "Putin's Palace" in Gelendzhik, see Bykov 2011a), drama (see Teterin 2005), cinema (see Kishkovsky 2008 on the feature film *The Kiss Is off the Record* [*Potselui ne dlia pressy*], directed by Olga Zhulina), and popular music (such as "Someone Like Putin" [*Takogo, kak Putin*] by the Singing Together [*Poiushchie Vmeste*] girl band, "The Path of Light" [*Svetlyi put'*] by an indie band called the Russian Brothers, "He'd Smoke and Drink"[*Pil kuril*] by the Spleen [Splin] rock band, "Putin" by the Korean Pilots [*Koreiskie letchiki*] hip-hop band, "Gulliver" by the ex-punker Roman Neumoev and the ex-reggae musician Artur Strukov, and the techno track "Who Is Boris Berezovsky?" [*Boris Berezovsky – eto kto?*] by Aleksei Vishnia) falls beyond the scope of the present essay.

70 Non-fiction writers are not so lucky. Suffice it to mention Elena Tregubova, a former *Kommersant* journalist and Kolesnikov's predecessor in the Kremlin pool, who survived an attempt on her life in February 2004 and had to ask for asylum in the United Kingdom in April 2007 after the publication of her tell-all book, *The Tales of a Kremlin Digger* (Baiki kremlevskogo diggera, 2003), decidedly uncomplimentary about Putin and many of his associates.

71 According to the data collected by the Levada Center, in May–July 2008, when he was no longer president, Putin's approval ratings continued to hover at 80 per cent and above – 10 per cent higher than President Medvedev's approval ratings for the same period [see http://www.angus-reid.com/polls/view/four_in_five_russians_approve_of_putin/ (accessed April 30, 2011)]. Even in April 2011, when Putin's and Medvedev's ratings were at their lowest for the past 3–5 years, Medvedev was still trailing behind his prime minister, with 46 per cent against Putin's 53 per cent (see Clover 2011; the figures have been provided by the Public Opinion Foundation). Curiously, Medvedev does not seem to fascinate authors as a potential fictional character to the same extent as Putin does, possibly because the former is perceived as too dull and/or insufficiently independent. In urban folklore, he typically appears either together or in connection with Putin, who dominates ("Why does a new vodka called Medvedevka have only 39.5 per cent alcohol in it? Because it can't be stronger than Putinka, which has 40 per cent"). According to such popular jokes, Medvedev's prospects for another presidential term look doubtful: "Medvedev asks Putin whether both of them are going to stand for presidential re-election. Putin replies: 'Didn't you get prizes for the best Russian blog and the best Russian twitter?' 'I did.' 'Isn't that enough? One shouldn't get ideas above one's station [*naglet'-to ne nado*]." (I am

deeply grateful to Aleksandr Sushkov for sharing these jokes with me.) Bykov's poem "Dvuglavoe" (see Bykov 2011c), written on Putin's behalf and banned by the Dozhd' TV station even in its toned-down version (see Bykov 2011b), also expresses deep skepticism about Medvedev's chances for re-election in 2012.

Bibliography

Aksenov, V. (1983) *Bumazhnyi peizazh*. Ann Arbor, MI: Ardis.

Arbitman, R. (2007) "Operatsiia 'Mimo kassy,'" *Saratovskaia oblastnaia gazeta*, July 25.

Astakhov, P. (2007) *Reider*. Moscow: EKSMO.

Basinskii, P. (2005) "Mezhdu daivingom i vannoi," *Rossiiskaia gazeta*, November 3.

Blotskii, O. (2002) *Vladimir Putin: Doroga k vlasti*. Moscow: OSMOS Press.

Bogomolov, Iu. (2004) *Khronika pikiruiushchego televideniia*. Moscow: MIK.

Bykov, D. (2005) *Kak Putin stal prezidentom SShA: (Novye russkie skazki)*. St. Petersburg: RedFish.

Bykov, D. (2011a) "Skazka o rybake i rybke," *Kommersant-Vlast'*, March 7.

Bykov, D. (2011b) "Tandem v Rossii bol'she, chem tandem," *Kommersant-Vlast'* March 28.

Bykov, D. (2011c) "Dvuglavoe," *Novaia gazeta*, April 1.

Chantsev, A. (2007) "Fabrika antiutopii: Distopicheskii diskurs v rossiiskoi literature serediny 2000-kh," *Novoe literaturnoe obozrenie*, 86: 269–301.

Clover, C. (2011) "Medvedev and Putin Losing Ground in Polls," *The Financial Times*, April 23.

Cumming, C. (2011) *The Trinity Six*. London: Harper Collins.

Danilkin, L. (2007) *Chelovek s iaitsom: Zhizn' i mneniia Aleksandra Prokhanova*. Moscow: Ad Marginem.

Dorenko, S. (2005) *2008*. Moscow: Ad Marginem.

Dunlop, J.B. (2006) *The 2002 Dubrovka and 2004 Beslan Hostage Crisis: A Critique of Russian Counter-Terrorism*. Stuttgart: Ibidem.

Edel'shtein, M. (2011) "Molodogvardeiskaia rifma," *Lekhaim (Moscow)*, 1. Available at: http://www.lechaim.ru/ARHIV/225/edelshteyn_n.htm (accessed on April 30, 2011).

El'kina, T. (Undated). "Putin v literature." Available at: http://www.apn-n.ru/diskurs_s/767.html (accessed April 30, 2011).

Felshtinsky, Y. and A. Litvinenko, (2002) *Blowing Up Russia: Terror from Within*. New York: S.P.I. Books.

Friedberg, M. (1977) "Solzhenitsyn's and Other Literacy Lenins," *Canadian Slavonic Papers*, XIX.2: 123–137.

Gamazkova, I. and S. Sedov. (2004) *Skazki pro nashego prezidenta*. Moscow: Russkaia sem'ia.

Gasiorowska, X. (1979) *The Image of Peter the Great in Russian Fiction*. Madison, WI: University of Wisconsin Press.

Gevorkian N., A. Kolesnikov, and N. Timakova. (2000) *Ot pervogo litsa: Razgovory s Vladimirom Putinym*. Moscow: Vagrius.

Grigor'eva, E. (2002) "Novye knigi o Glavnom," *Izvestiia*, August 3.

Gurevich V. (2004) *Vladimir Putin: Roditeli, druz'ia, uchitelia*. St. Petersburg: Izdatel'stvo Iuridicheskogo Instituta.

Gurskii, L. (2009) *Roman Arbitman: Biografiia vtorogo prezidenta Rossii*, Volgograd: PrinTerra.

Hamilton, A. (2003) "Putin's Late Show Makes Queen a Lady in Waiting," *The Times*, June 24.

Howe, I. (1961) *Politics and the Novel*. London: Stevens & Sons Ltd.

Ivanova, M. (2005) "Oruell otdykhaet," *Kul'tura*, November 8.

Kharington, R. (2004) *Zolotaia kost', ili Prikliucheniia ianki v strane novykh russkikh*. Moscow: Novoe literaturnoe obozrenie,.

Kharms, D. (1999) *Tsirk Shardam*. St. Petersburg: Kristall.

Kishkovsky, S. (2008) "A Love Letter to Putin (But It's Not Addressed to Him)," *The New York Times*, February 6.

Kolesnikov A. (2005a) *Ia Putina videl!* Moscow: EKSMO.

Kolesnikov, A. (2005b) *Uvidet' Putina i umeret'*. Moscow: EKSMO.

Kolesnikov, A. (2005c) *Menia Putin videl!* Moscow: EKSMO.

Kononenko, M. (2005) *Vladimir Vladimirovich TM*. Moscow: Kolibri.

Kurkov, A. (2004) *Posledniaia liubov' prezidenta*. Khar'kov: Folio.

Kuznetsov, A. (2005) "Bestsvetnaia revoliutsiia," *Novaia Sibir'*, November 11.

Limonov, E. (1998) *316, punkt 'V.'* Moscow: Vagrius.

Loshak, V. (2006) "Oligarkh s perom," *Ogonek*, 10: 63.

Mal'gin, A. (2005) *Sovetnik prezidenta*. Tver': Kolonna Publications.

Margolin, E. (2007) "*Portret zhanra v zhanre tekhnologicheskogo portreta*." Available at: http://www.compuart.ru/Archive/CA/2007/11/7/ (accessed April 30, 2011).

Marsh, R. (1989) *Images of Dictatorship: Stalin in Literature*. London and New York: Routledge.

Massie, A. (2011) "*The Trinity Six* by Charles Cumming," *The Scotsman*, January 29.

Medvedev, R. (2007) *Vladimir Putin*. Moscow: Molodaia gvardiia.

Nazarov, O. (2006) "S detektivom za demokratiiu," *Literaturnaia Rossiia*, March 17.

Nesterov, A. (2007) "Sabadash vlasti," *Parlamentskaia gazeta*, April 27.

Ol'bik, A. (2002) *Prezident*. Donetsk: Stalker.

Ol'bik, A. and A. Indorbaev. (2005) *Nord-Ost*. Riga: MAPP.

Paton Walsh, N. (2002) "Putin Turns 007 in New Thriller Novel," *The Observer*, July 14.

Pietsch, I. (2001). *Heikle Freundschaften: Mit dem Putins Russland erleben*. Vienna: Molden.

Pribylovskii, V. (2003) "Putinoslavie: Khronika proslavlenii Putina Vladimira Vladimirovicha," in A.M. Verkhovskii, E.V. Mikhailovskaia, and V.V. Pribylovskii, *Rossiia Putina: Pristrastnyi vzgliad*. Moscow: Tsentr "Panorama." 193–204.

Pribylovskii, V. and Iu, Fel'shtinskii. (2004) "Operatsiia 'Naslednik': Shtrikhi k politicheskomu portretu V.V. Putina," *Nota Bene (Jerusalem)*, 1: 152–171; 2: 111–127; 4: 232–252; 6: 204–224.

Prokhanov, A. (2002) *Gospodin Geksogen*. Moscow: Ad Marginem.

Putley, J. (2006) "Russia's Colluders," *Prospect*, July 22. Available at: http://www.prospectmagazine.co.uk/2006/07/russiascolluders/ (accessed July 14, 2011).

Rancour-Laferriere, D. (ed.) (1989). *Russian Literature and Psychoanalysis*. Amsterdam: J. Benjamins.

Rybakov, A. (1987) *Deti Arbata*. Moscow: Sovetskii pisatel'.

Samarina, A. and A. Kornia. (2005) "Operatsiia 'Monarkh' startovala," *Nezavisimaia gazeta*, February 9.

Sedakova, O. (2007) "Put' Putina," *The New Times (Moscow)*, 46: 22–24.

Sedov, L. (1999) "Na dal'nikh podstupakh k vyboram," *Monitoring obshchestvennogo mneniia*, 1: 12–18.

Shenderovich, V. (2002) *Zdes' bylo NTV i drugie istorii*. Moscow: Zakharov.

Shestopal, E.B. (ed.) (2004) *Obrazy vlasti v postsovetskoi Rossii: Politiko-psikhologicheskii analiz*. Moscow: Aleteia.

Shestopal, E.B. (ed.) (2008) *Obrazy rossiiskoi vlasti ot El'tsina do Putina*. Moscow: ROSSPEN.

Shnaider, M. (1983) *Veselyi kukuruznik*. S. l.: Segal.

Smolenskii, A. and E. Krasnianskii. (2006) *Zalozhnik: Operatsiia "Memorandum."* Moscow: Vagrius.

Sokolov, M. (2004) "Prezident i personazh." January 27. Available at: http://archive.svoboda.org/programs/pr/2004/pr.012704.asp (accessed April 30, 2011).

Solov'ev, V. (2007a) *Evangelie ot Solov'eva*. Moscow: EKSMO.

Solov'ev, V. (2007b) *Apokalipsis ot Vladimira*. Moscow: EKSMO.

Solzhenitsyn, A. (1975) *Lenin v Tsiurikhe*. Paris: YMCA-Press.

Stepanov, E. (Undated) "*PR v sovremennoi russkoi literature*." Available at: http://futurum-art.ru/svezhij/pr.htm (accessed April 30, 2011).

Tarasov, A. (2002) "Gospoda Geksogen, Ivanov, Sorokin, na vykhod!: Pochemu 'Idushchie vmeste' naekhali na Sorokina," *Novaia gazeta*, July 4.

Teterin, V. (2005) "Putin.doc: Realisticheskaia p'esa v odnom deistvii s elementami absurda." In *Putin.doc: Deviat' revoliutsionnykh p'es*. Ed. D. Bochenkov. Tver': Kolonna Pub.: 9–36.

Topol', E. (1992) *Zavtra v Rossii*. Moscow: Informkul'tura.

Troitskii, N. and N. Melikova. (2005) "Vymysel, perevorot i Mitrofanov: Duma provela politicheskuiu ekspertizu knigi Sergeia Dorenko," *Nezavisimaia gazeta*, November 11.

Tsarik, V. (2006) "Prezident v pereplete," *Nasha versiia (Moscow)*, February 27.

Usol'tsev, V. (2004) *Sosluzhivets*. Moscow: EKSMO.

Uspenskii, B.A. (1998) *Tsar' i patriarkh: Kharizma vlasti v Rossii (vizantiiskaia model' i ee russkoe pereosmyslenie)*. Moscow: Iazyki russkoi kul'tury.

Vasil'ev A. (2005) "Pravda ob Andree Kolesnikove," in A. Kolesnikov, *Ia Putina videl!* Moscow: EKSMO: 5–7.

Volchek, D. (2005) "*Sergei Dorenko napisal roman o Putine*." October 22. Available at: http://archive.svoboda.org/ll/cult/1005/ll.102205-1.asp (accessed April 30, 2011).

Voronov, V. (Undated) "'Podvig razvedchika': Putin velikii, moguchii, uzhasnyi i ... mificheskii." Available at: http://www.library.cjes.ru/online/?a=con&;b_id=607&c_id=7264 (accessed April 30, 2011).

Warren, M. (2002) "Ambitious Putin Falls Out of Favour with Moscow's Old Guard," *The Daily Telegraph*, April 20.

Zheglov, A. (2007) "Prestupnyi vymysel: Pavlu Astakhovu grozit ugolovnoe delo za khudozhestvennuiu klevetu," *Kommersant*, August 14.

7 Post-Soviet self-fashioning and the politics of representation

Brian James Baer

> The power to impose a shape upon oneself is an aspect of the more general power to control identity – *that of others at least as often as one's own.*[1]
>
> (Stephen Greenblatt 1980: 1)[2]

Introduction

The fall of the Soviet Union in 1991 and the subsequent dismantling of its centralized economy and social institutions inaugurated a period of unprecedented freedom and social (as well as geographic) mobility in the newly independent Russian state under the presidency of Boris Yelstin. That freedom, which soon devolved into social and economic chaos, left many Russians searching for a way to define themselves in the absence of an ideological master narrative. It appeared initially that Russian Orthodoxy might fill the ideological gap, but while religious affiliation spiked in early post-Soviet Russia, the Church has failed to attract large numbers of regular worshippers. Research data from the mid-to-late 1990s reveal that while a majority of Russians self-identified as Orthodox, only 7 percent of those attended church once a month or more; over 60 percent did not attend worship services at all, showing what Zoe Knox's refers to as "a gulf between Orthodox self-identification and active worship" (2005: 6).

Without a structuring narrative, individuals in post-Soviet Russia were left to fashion new identities for themselves through the practice of *bricolage*, or the *ad hoc* construction of a persona from an especially "heterogeneous reservoir" of cultural scripts and signifiers (Lévi-Strauss 1968: 17). As Sheila Fitzpatrick notes in her book *Tear off the Masks: Identity and Imposture in Twentieth-century Russia*,

> Successful revolutions tear off masks: that is, they invalidate the conventions of self-presentation and social interaction that obtained in pre-revolutionary society. This happened in Russia after the October 1917 revolution which laid the foundations for the Soviet state. It happened again in 1991, when that state collapsed in such upheavals, people have to reinvent themselves,

> to create or find within themselves personae that fit the new postrevolutionary society. The process of reinvention is at once a process of reconfiguration (a new arrangement of data about oneself) and one of discovery (a new interpretation of their significance). It always involves strategic decisions (how should I present myself in this new world) and may also prompt ontological reflection (who am I really?).
>
> (2005: 3)

This chapter will examine two of the most influential and popular figures in contemporary post-Soviet society – President Vladimir Putin and the fictional detective Erast Fandorin, invented by the novelist Boris Akunin (the pseudonym of Grigorii Chkhartashili) – as paragons of a post-Soviet "process of reinvention" of the self, which, following Stephen Greenblatt, I call "self-fashioning." Although these men hold rather divergent political views, I argue that they employ similar strategies to fashion a new identity for themselves that, while borrowing freely from Soviet and prerevolutionary signifiers and practices, is distinctly post-Soviet.

Self-fashioning

Self-fashioning is a term coined by the literary scholar Stephen Greenblatt (1980) to describe how middle-class individuals in Renaissance England constructed and presented their selfhood through the manipulation of social standards, norms, and products. His analysis is based on the premise that "there is in the early modern period a change in the intellectual, social, psychological, and aesthetic structures that govern the generation of identities" (1980: 1). According to Greenblatt, this change, in turn, produced "an increased self-consciousness about the fashioning of human identity as a manipulable, artful process" (1980: 2). In his study of Renaissance self-fashioning, Greenblatt employs a methodology that includes both literary works and the "real" lives of selected Renaissance cultural and political figures, arguing that

> social actions are themselves always embedded in systems of public signification, always grasped, even by their makers, in acts of interpretation, while the words that constitute the works of literature that we discuss here are by their very nature the manifest assurance of a similar embeddedness.
>
> (1980: 5)

I refer to this justification in presenting my analysis of a political figure and a literary character. Moreover, Greenblatt notes, "great art is an extraordinarily sensitive register of the complex struggles and harmonies of culture and in part because, by inclination and training, whatever interpretive powers I possess are released by the resonances of literature" (1980: 5). By interpreting the interplay of the symbolic structures of literary texts "with those perceivable in the careers of their authors and in the larger social world as constituting a single, complex process of self-fashioning," Greenblatt argues, one can outline a poetics of culture (1980: 6).

The application of Greenblatt's notion of Renaissance self-fashioning to contemporary post-Soviet Russian culture may appear at first glance surprising. Both cultures, however, are characterized by unprecedented social mobility brought about by political and economic changes that displaced large numbers of individuals "in significant ways from a stable, inherited social world" (1980: 8). As Leon Aron puts it,

> In perhaps the world's largest *in vivo* existentialist experiment, the old rules have been swept away, opposition to the regime no longer serves as the sole moral compass, and millions of Russian men and women are attempting to devise and adhere to their own moral codes.
>
> (2002: online)

Svetlana Boym offers a similar assessment:

> With the end of the Soviet Union, there was a mass perception of the loss of some kind of Soviet communality and of a unified Soviet cultural text, a Soviet master narrative that had produced a distinct kind of conformism as well as a distinct form of dissidence.
>
> (1995: 150)

The absence of old rules, accompanied by a profound nostalgia for master narratives, has produced the conditions for a unique manifestation of self-fashioning that has the potential to offer unique insights into the poetics of post-Soviet culture.

Putin and Fandorin: friends or foes?

Georgi Chkhartashvili is a respected translator of Japanese literature and the former editor of the prestigious literary magazine *Inostrannaia literatura* [Foreign Literature]. In the mid-1990s, then in his mid-1940s, he began to write detective novels under the pseudonym B. Akunin – a double play on words, alluding to the famous Russian anarchist Mikhail Bakunin and to the Japanese word *akunin*, meaning "evildoer." Chkhartashvili's first novel, *Azazel'* [in English, *The Winter Queen*], was published in 1998, the same year Putin, out of the blue, was appointed prime minister by then president Boris Yeltsin. *Azazel'* introduced Russia to Erast Petrovich Fandorin, a dashing, preternaturally lucky young detective, who would become wildly popular during Putin's presidency – a bona fide celebrity.

While at first glance it might seem that Fandorin and Putin have little in common – Fandorin, after all, "lived" in the late nineteenth century – it was not long before both Russian and foreign commentators began to draw parallels between the two men. Both worked in intelligence, spoke foreign languages fluently, were accomplished practitioners of Asian martial arts, and were characterized by a certain "un-Russian" reserve in their demeanor. As one commentator noted, Fandorin is

> a bright, hardworking young man who is afraid of no one; Fandorin is also a fitness enthusiast who practices Japanese martial arts, which saves him on several occasions. The fact that this trait *mirrors the image* of the popular president of Russia, Vladimir Putin, does not hurt book sales
>
> (Bernbaum 2011; emphasis added)

Some critics have also suggested more general parallels between Fandorin's world – the final decades of the nineteenth century – and post-Soviet Russia under Putin. According to Aron,

> If today's Russia can be found in a 'distant mirror' (that is, following Barbara Tuchman, a moment in history that in some key respects is remarkably similar to the way a country lives now), such a mirror is almost certainly located in the last three decades of the 19th century.
>
> (2007: 141)

Aron insists that "the parallels with today's Russia, wearily enjoying a fragile economic and political stabilization after almost a decade of revolutionary turmoil, are obvious" (2002: online). Russian writer Andrey Kurkov expresses a similar view in regard to Akunin's novel *The Turkish Gambit* [*Turetskii gambit* 1998]. The ideas expressed in the novel, Kurkov asserts, "seem to correspond very closely with the situation in present-day Russia" (Kurkov 2005). A journalist for the Russian weekly *Afisha* noted the parallel drawn by critics between Fandorin and Putin "as bearers of an idea of government that can bring order to the Russian chaos" (Chkhartashvili 2011). Akunin himself, it seems, was very conscious of these historical parallels:

> "Society was making choices which are pretty much similar to the ones we're having to choose from now," Akunin said, comparing the assassinated Czar Alexander II to Mikhail Gorbachev and Boris Yeltsin, and the czar's successor, Alexander III, to Vladimir Putin, who succeeded Yeltsin. "Reactionary, authoritarian, anti-liberal," he elaborates, sporting the round glasses and graying beard of the universal dissident.
>
> (Chkhartashvili 2006a)

In fact, Akunin actively encourages his readers to draw parallels between Fandorin's time and the Russian present by playing with historical facts and making allusions to contemporary politics and politicians – a nostalgic invocation of a once politically charged Aesopian language.[3]

While many critics have noted similarities between Fandorin and Putin, and their respective eras, opinions diverge wildly as to the interpretation of those similarities. Are the parallels drawn by Akunin meant to praise Putin or to bury him? Joan Smith in *The Sunday Times* notes that "Boris Akunin's widely praised novels about an enigmatic 19th century Russian detective, Erast Fandorin, have been interpreted as allegories in praise of the current Russian president, Vladimir Putin" (Smith 2007). Kurkov also suggests that the Fandorin novels can be read as an apologia of sorts for Putin's exercise of state power: "Sometimes, while reading about Fandorin, I found myself thinking that the aim of these stories is to vindicate the secret service and the tough, pragmatic patriotism of today's Russian politics" (Kurkov 2005). The British journalist Omer Ali points out that Fandorin "espouses completely different views to the pro-democratic ones generally accepted in the West" (Chkhartashvili 2006b), aligning him politically with the Russian president. Aron asserts that Fandorin and Putin model a new "private" identity for Russians. For Aron, Fandorin represents the "quintessential pre-1917 *intelligent*" (2002: online), a "champion for the bourgeoisie" (2004: online), and a "private hero for a privatized country" (2007: 139). Aron suggests a similar focus on the independent (middle class) individual in Putin's support for bold entrepreneurs (although not too bold, given what happened to Mikhail Khodorovsky and possibly to Platon Prokhorov) (2007: 154).

The blogger Edward Lucas, however, cautions against reductive interpretations of the resemblances between Fandorin and Putin: "Much nostalgia for the Tsarist era remains – and the popularity of Boris Akunin's stories about the detective Erast Fandorin is a prime example. But under Mr. Putin, the clock has started to tick backwards in a more sinister way" (Lucas 2010). The nostalgia for prerevolutionary Russia expressed in Akunin's novels, Lucas suggests, should not be confused with the Soviet-era nostalgia of Putin and his government. The British journalist Luke Harding also rejects the interpretation of Fandorin as an apologist for Putin's policies, suggesting that the parallels embedded in Akunin's novels serve to expose the behavior of the regime rather than defend it:

> In Akunin's fourth Fandorin mystery, *The Death of Achilles* [Smert' Akhilessa 1998], Fandorin's old friend General Sobolev is murdered with the juices of a rare Amazonian fern – a sort of nineteenth-century version of the radioactive polonium used to kill the Russian dissident Alexander Litvinenko last year.
>
> (Chkhartashvili 2007)[4]

Chkhartashvili (2011) himself also has adamantly denied that any parallels between Fandorin and Putin imply support for the latter:

> In my estimation, Putin has the mindset of an adolescent, with all the attributes of that difficult age: flashy machismo and a bunch of complexes. In the 2000s, this corresponded to the stage of development of the greater part of the population. But the population has been maturing gradually, while Putin has stayed the same. He kisses tigers, rides horses, flexes his biceps,

and lifts weights. Please don't compare him with my Fandorin. From novel to novel Erast Petrovich has become a more mature person.

Rather than demonstrate whether Fandorin is indeed pro or anti Putin, I shall examine the "self-fashioning" of these two men as a contribution to the conceptual mapping of a post-Soviet poetics of culture.

Self-fashioning and the body

A key characteristic of Renaissance self-fashioning was a focus on the individual body, both as the new organizing center of the arts – the Italian architect Palladio, for example, based his buildings on the proportions of the human body – and as a microcosmic metaphor for good government. Ken Albala argues in *Eating Right in the Renaissance* that this was a time when there was "an explicit connection between the intensification of government at the political level and the growth of manners and self-government on a personal level" (2002: 218). "As one of many forms of [Renaissance] self-government," Albala contends,

> [t]he dietary regimens and their attempts to control and rationalize eating behavior also, logically, flourished in the sixteen and seventeenth centuries. [. . .] That the authors of these works considered the government of the body as analogous to that of states is quite clear. It is no coincidence that the words regime and regimen share a common root in the Latin *regere*, to rule, and are still sometimes used interchangeably for ruling both the body and the state.
>
> (Ibid.)

The self-conscious presentation of the body as a social fact and a political metaphor is one aspect of self-fashioning that Putin and Fandorin share. Neither Putin nor Fandorin has any qualms about showing off his physique. Putin was famously photographed shirtless astride a horse in Siberia, which had one blogger declare the president to be "a hot piece of muscle meat" (Steph 2007). A blog post on the *Foreign Policy* website appeared in 2009 with the tongue-in-cheek title, "Russia's in Trouble. Time for Putin to Take His Shirt off" (Downie 2009). Cassiday and Johnson note that "Putin's prowess in the judo ring, his boldness on alpine ski slopes and his unequivocably masculine physique recur constantly in representations of the Russian president" (2010: 686).

Fandorin, too, is a fitness fanatic, an early adherent of the modern fitness movement, which arose in the late nineteenth century. In the novel *Coronation* [*Koronatsiia*], for example, Fandorin is observed shirtless doing his exercises. The conservative butler who narrates the novel, Afanasii Ziukin, gazes at Fandorin as he exercises, naked from the waist up, exclaiming, "I couldn't tear my eyes away from his lean, muscular body" (2000: 151; translation mine). Fandorin's bodybuilding is presented here as a phenomenon somewhere "between fitness and performance, and between health and erotic display" (Flood 2003: 59).

On a metaphorical level, his lean body represents a new kind of Russian, and it is something the conservative butler finds both disturbing and exciting. It will lead him to rethink and ultimately to reject his traditional role – Ziukin comes from a family of domestic servants – as an unreflective subordinate who merely follows orders.

With the advent of free enterprise and the lifting of censorship restrictions following the fall of the Soviet Union, the male body, one could say, was released from the ideological constraints of Soviet ideology and was made available as an object of post-Soviet desire. While there were many public displays of physical fitness in the Soviet era, the emphasis was on the contribution of the physically fit individual to the collective – consider the mass exercise displays in May day parades on Red Square.[5] Moreover, the perfectly fit and proportioned bodies featured in Soviet representational arts were abstract representations, idealizations of the might of the Soviet people. Lilya Kaganovsky's work on the many physically maimed and mutilated heroes of Soviet literature and film suggests the degree to which those "individual" bodies were tagged as the property of the state (Kaganovsky 2008). Soviet leaders, on the other hand, rarely appeared in public without a suit, tie, and fedora – let alone without a shirt! And none of the Soviet leaders could be considered "fit." On a more general level, Soviet advertisements did not make use of semi-clad models, which by the 1960 has become the stock in trade of American advertising.

That all changed in the post-Soviet era, and, as Helena Goscilo points out, "The post-perestroika body in general has acquired formidable symbolic status in Russia" (Goscilo 2000b:45n). Cassiday and Johnson insist that the symbolic significance of a shirtless Putin should not be underestimated. "Comparable images," they note, "are extremely rare" (2010: 687). For both Putin and Fandorin, the display of their toned bodies is not only central to their individual self-fashioning, it also serves as a metaphor for good government, a point made by Goscilo in this volume. To the extent that the physically fit body is an outward symbol of the individual's control over mind and body, it can be seen, not unlike in the Renaissance, to justify the exercise of political power. The authors of *Risk Rules* note,

> Though perhaps vulgar for those with more refined tastes, Putin's shirtless forays into the wilderness are seen by many Russians as the picture of vitality – a sharp contrast to the state of the country and that of its drunken president of the 1990s.
>
> (Zonis *et al.* 2011: 72)

In the late nineteenth century, bodybuilding, with its focus on the "hard" body, transformed well-muscled men into symbols of "control, discipline and sexual power" (Flood 2003: 59). As Karen P. Flood points out, "Bodybuilders have transformed their bodies into very particular cultural products that have reflected both the anxieties of their cultural moment and the potential they see for individual achievement and mastery over the self" (2001: 60). Scholars in the field of Cultural Studies see bodybuilding as an irrefutable assertion of masculinity on the body itself, a reaction to middle-class (white) male anxiety over masculine identity, which was perceived to be threatened by white collar jobs that required no demonstration of physical power. The focus on bodybuilding in the self-presentation of Putin and Fandorin can also be seen, together with "the emergence of several magazines patently intended to boost men's morale" (Goscilo 2000b: 27), both as a reflection of post-Soviet anxiety over a perceived crisis of masculinity and as a means to overcome that anxiety through the disciplined transformation of the body.

The idea of discipline, in fact, is crucial here in that it protects these bodily displays from the charge of sensuality and decadence, and from any association with Western consumerism and attendant notions of sexual pleasure. Both Putin and Fandorin perform their physical pursuits with great seriousness, rarely smiling, never meeting the admiring gaze of those who observe them. The theme of discipline is elaborated through references to Asian martial arts (as opposed to American bodybuilding).[6] Putin, who holds a black belt in judo, takes his role as a judo master quite seriously. He has written, with Vasily Shestakov and Alexey Levitsky, a judo primer of sorts, *Judo: History, Theory, and Practice* (2004), and has issued a 90-min film, *Let's Learn Judo with Vladimir Putin* (2008) (for more on Putin and judo, see Chapters 1 and 8 by Goscilo and Chapter 2 by Cassiday *et al.*).

Martial arts are distinguished from Western body building by, among other things, their spirituality. In Putin's book, judo is described as an "incredible, mysterious and open world" (2004: 287), and when on a visit to China in 2006, Putin made only one special request: to visit the famous Shaolin Temple, "China's most famous school for martial arts" (Chai and Chai 2007: 169). As May-Lee Chai and Winberg Chai point out in their book *China A–Z*,

> Far from being viewed as simply a sport or a means of fighting, in China *wu shu* is considered an art form, a philosophy, and a means to cultivate unity of the body, soul, and the universe. The true goal of *wu shu* is not to beat up somebody, but to attain spiritual enlightenment for oneself through the strict mental and spiritual discipline that *wu shu* requires.
>
> (2007: 169)

Incidentally, the Shaolin Temple that Putin visited teaches Zen Buddhism, "which emphasizes long periods of meditation to purify the mind" (2007: 169).

Mister Aono, the only Japanese character in Akunin's novel *Murder on the Leviathan* [*Leviafan* 1998], also stresses the spiritual component of Asian martial arts. Mr. Aono symbolizes Japan's forced program of westernization during the Meiji period, when, according to Putin, Shestakov, and Levitsky, "the ancient martial arts, carried on by representatives of samurai clans, were threatened" (Putin *et al.* 2004: 3). Moreover, the forced westernization of Meiji Japan has many parallels with Russia's own forced westernization under Peter the Great, who is Putin's hero. In any case, this novel presents events crucial to Fandorin's eastward turn; the detective-diplomat is on his way from Constantinople to Calcutta, whence he will travel to Japan to take up a post in the Russian embassy. There Fandorin will develop an abiding love of Asian cultures and become the literary embodiment of Russia's perceived role as a bridge between East and West.

While Aono has much to learn about western customs, he mentors Fandorin in his observations about the eastern philosophy behind the practice of martial arts:

> Fandorin-san and I discussed the relative importance of Japanese and English gymnastics. I found myself in a position to be condescending, since in this sphere the superiority of the East over the West is self-evident. The difference, of course, is that for them, physical exercise is sport, a game, but for us it is the path for spiritual improvement. It is spiritual improvement that's important – physical perfection is of no importance, it is automatically dragged behind, as carriages follow a steam locomotive. I should mention that the Russian is very interested in sport and has heard something of the martial-arts schools of Japan and China. This morning I was meditating on the boat deck earlier than usual and I saw Fandorin-san there. We merely bowed to each another and did not enter conversation, because each of us was involved in his own business. I was bathing my soul in the light of the new day, while he, dressed in gymnast's tights, was performing squats and push-ups with each arm in turn and lifting weights that appeared to be very heavy. Our common interest in gymnastics rendered our evening conversation unforced, and I felt more relaxed than usual. I told the Russian about jiujitsu. He listened with unflagging interest.
>
> (Putin *et al.* 2004: 83–84)

Here the Russian is portrayed as the ideal pupil of the Japanese expert, and Fandorin will soon master the Asian martial arts.

The spiritual dimension that distinguishes Asian martial arts from Western exercise or bodybuilding speaks to Fandorin's Russianness insofar as spirituality was long considered a defining trait of Russians, distinguishing them in opposition to a cold, rational West. Aono explains the spiritual affinity of Russian and the East in more general terms:

> If Fandorin-san is capable of illumination, he owes it to the semi-Asiatic character of his homeland. In many ways Russia is like Japan: the same reaching out of the East for the West. [. . .] To emphasize one's individual "I" or to dissolve it in the might of the collective "we" – therein lies the antithesis between Europe and Asia. I believe the chances are good that Russia will turn off the first road on to the second.
>
> (Akunin 2004: 90)

If the spiritual dimension of martial arts distinguishes Putin and Fandorin from their soulless Western counterparts, epitomized for Aono by the bodybuilder, then the physical or athletic dimension of martial arts distinguishes them from their Russian Orthodox forebears. Clearly, the toned bodies of Putin and Fandorin bear little resemblance to the gaunt figure of the Christian ascetic. Moreover, while traditional Russian spirituality encourages a mystical transcendence, martial arts insist on the inseparability of spiritual awareness and action in the world. And because martial arts are an individual – as opposed to a team – sport and require no equipment or special gear, they not only distinguish the practitioner from the Soviet athlete submerged in group formations, but they also *naturalize* the athletic body. And so, these representations must be seen as complex cultural products that construct the Russian martial artist as both eastern (spiritual) and Western (fitness-conscious and self-reliant). In this way, the Russian martial artist avoids both paths sketched out by Aono: through spiritual discipline, the martial artist resists flaunting his individual "I," on the one hand, and dissolving into a collective "we," on the other.

Boym has remarked, "Unfortunately, in the mid-1990s, the mythical opposition between Russia and the West has acquired new currency, and now it predominates over economic, social, or historical differentiations, over the distinction between Soviet and post-Soviet, capitalist and socialist" (1995: 159). We see this phenomenon in the "eastern turn," which says as much about Russia's admiration for Asian cultures as it does about Russia's need to define itself against the West. As embodied by the Russian president and Fandorin, the martial artist represents a unique solution to the post-Soviet crisis of identity in that it purges the qualities of self-sufficiency and personal discipline, deemed necessary in a free market economy, from their traditional association with the West – something the New Russians failed to do – by linking them to eastern notions of spirituality that combine spiritual transcendence with physical powers. In other words, this spirituality is not your grandmother's *smirenie* (humility).

The importance of the martial artist as trope in Putin-era Russia should not be underestimated. It represents a uniquely Russian construction of the self-reliant professional, the roots of which Greenblatt traces to the self-fashioning of the Western Renaissance, which, of course, largely had bypassed Russia. The figure of the independent entrepreneur was tainted throughout the Yeltsin years by association with Western values, as evidenced in the portrayal of New Russians and Post-Soviet oligarchs. In fact, Akunin has stated openly that his detective novels represent a reconceptualization of the role of the writer, from a tortured prophet to a *professional* man of letters: "In Russia, you're supposed to write not with your brain but with the blood of your heart. I want to be a good professional" (Chkhartashvili 2006a). And he has made Fandorin, too, a modern professional, something which, Akunin admits, has very shallow roots in Russian soil: "Fandorin has a highly developed sense of dignity, which Russians lack. He is not given to overstatement like most Russians. He is reflective, not very sure of himself" (2006a). Putin's professionalism is underscored by terms such as "manager" (see Chapter 8 by Goscilo) and "technocrat" (Ryazanova-Clarke 2008: 306).

Self-fashioning and *bricolage*

Another prominent feature of self-fashioning in a postrevolutionary society is the self-conscious and often profligate manipulation of cultural codes and practices from other times and places, which I refer to as *bricolage*. The term, which was derived from the French verb *bricoler*, meaning "to tinker" or "to fiddle," was used by Lévi-Strauss to describe mythical thought, which makes

> crafty [. . . use of] a heterogeneous repertoire which, even if extensive, is nevertheless limited. It has to use this repertoire, however, whatever the task in hand because it has nothing else at its disposal. Mythical thought is therefore a kind of intellectual "bricolage" – which explains the relation which can be perceived between the two.
>
> (Lévi-Strauss 1968: 17)

While recognizing the validity of Jacques Derrida's observation that "if one calls bricolage the necessity of borrowing one's concept from the text of a heritage which is more or less coherent or ruined, it must be said that every discourse is *bricoleur*" (Derrida 1966: 285), I nonetheless maintain that some discourses are more *bricoleur* than others. The self-fashioning of Putin and Fandorin is characterized by a very high degree of *bricolage* indeed – a reflection of the postrevolutionary foment and semiotic chaos of post-Soviet society, described so vividly by Cassiday and Johnson. Moreover, to the extent that *bricolage* involves the use of inherited objects, it is perhaps inevitably characterized by stylization, something that, Goscilo points out, was "rampant in the 1990s, betraying the desire to disclaim an identifiable self in a slippage or retreat into culture's readymade" (Goscilo 2000a: 12).

Putin's first inauguration ceremony in 2000 is an excellent example of post-Soviet *bricolage*. Insofar as there were no Russian precedents for representing the peaceful transition of power through democratic means, post-Soviet inauguration ceremonies relied heavily on what Eric Hobsbawn and Terence Ranger (1983) referred to as "the invention of tradition". The traditions organizing presidential inaugurals in post-Soviet Russia were invented from a heterogeneous reservoir of historical motifs and practices, an example of post-Soviet *bricolage*. A comparison of Yeltsin's second inauguration in 1996 with Putin's first inauguration in 2000 underscores the invention and reinvention of traditions in post-Soviet culture. Yeltsin's second inauguration was held in a hall in the Kremlin palace, with a large curtained stage and comfortable, padded seating. Guests sat in chairs facing the stage, upon which the new president stood alongside representatives of the Russian Orthodox Church, the Russian judiciary, and legislative branch, surrounded by symbols of state power. A copy of the Russian constitution occupied a central place on the stage. Overall, the inauguration had the look of an awards ceremony.

Putin's first inauguration in 2000, on the other hand, represented a radical rethinking of the inauguration as an example of self-fashioning, but was no less an example of *bricolage* and invented tradition. Putin moved the inauguration to the "gilded grandeur of St. Andrew's Hall in the Grand Kremlin Palace, where Russia's last tsars once sat on the throne" (Myers 2004), and which, in its medieval grandeur, harks back to the Byzantine and Mongol roots of the Muscovite state. The medieval setting contrasted with the uniforms of the honor guard, which were patterned after uniforms worn during the time of Alexander I and Russia's wars with Napoleon. Putin himself was dressed in a dark business suit.[7] The staging of presidential power was also altered in Putin's inauguration. Given the relative small size of the hall, most guests were in adjoining rooms, where they were unable to see the president take the oath of office. The association of democracy with visibility and transparency, encouraged in Yeltsin's inauguration (the people as spectators), was, if not lost, at least attenuated. There were no chairs, and so guests stood throughout the ceremony, as in Russian Orthodox church services; when the ceremony was over, Putin walked *alone* through hall after hall to the applause of the guests standing on either side. The ceremony, which clearly downplayed the role of the legislature, as well as that of the presidential wife, focusing all attention on the individual leader, represented a major shift away from western-style inaugurations toward a more eastern, or byzantine, "scenario of power" (Wortman 1995). At the same time, this aesthetic *bricolage* can be said to reflect Putin's vision of government, which has been described as a "hybrid regime," to the extent that it "allows quasi-oppositional parties and movements to exist but at the same time limits their ability to alter the status quo through a variety of repressive measures" (Cassiday and Johnson 2010: 684).

The Putin administration's *bricolage* has its parallel in the style of Akunin's Fandorin novels, which are characterized by an eclectic play with Russia's political and literary history. Akunin's aesthetic reservoir is heterogeneous indeed, based as it is on very self-conscious acts of borrowing and imitation. The author evokes late nineteenth-century prose with his elaborate and restrained style, while on the level of plot he weaves a dense web of historical and intertextual references that are by no means restricted to Russian culture. In fact, many of the Fandorin novels are modeled on contemporary works of Western literature. *Coronation*, for example, has clear ties to Kuzuo Ishiguro's novel *Remains of the Day*. Moreover, while Akunin's stylized prose would seem to suggest an attitude of reverence toward his literary forebears, some of his acts of "borrowing" are quite radical. For example, the final novel of the Fandorin series, *The Diamond Chariot* [*Almaznaia kolesnitsa* 2003], opens with an entire paragraph lifted, without attribution, from the short story "Shtabs-kapitan Rybnikov" (1905) by Aleksandr Kuprin (1870–1938), about a Japanese secret agent who masquerades as a Russian war veteran. The story, in which the spy gives himself away by speaking Russian that is a little too good, suggests how radically Akunin plays with notions of originality and authenticity.

It is in the novel *Coronation*, however, that Akunin reveals most clearly a philosophy behind his *bricolage*; or, rather, he presents *bricolage* as a kind of existential philosophy. In the story of Fandorin's benevolent mentoring of a butler from subservience to independence, Akunin suggests a metaphoric reading of self-fashioning that links his aesthetics to his philosophy of life. Fandorin explains to Afanasii Stepanovich:

> Do you know, Afanasiy Stepanovich, what your mistake is? You believe that the world rests on some rules, that it contains meaning and or-order. And I have long understood: Life is nothing more than chaos. It has no order at all, and no rules. [. . .] Yes, I do have rules. But those are my r-rules, which I made for myself, and not for the world. So let the world be on its own, and I will be on my own. To the extent that I can. Personal rules, Afanasiy Stepanovich, are not a desire to rearrange the universe, but an attempt to organize, the best one can, the space d-directly closest to you. Not beyond that.
>
> (Trans. by Aron 2007: 147, with slight modifications; Akunin 2000: 248–249)

The butler Freiby, Ziukin's British counterpart, imparts a similar message, albeit with less fluency:

> "Then Freiby gently turned toward me, opened one eye and said: "Live your own life." He took out his dictionary and translated: "To live . . . one's . . . own . . . life." With that, he turned away, satisfied, as if he considered the topic exhausted, and once again closed his eyes. His strange words were pronounced in a tone typical of well-intentioned advice. I began to ponder what it could mean: To live one's own life. "Live your own life"? In what sense?"
>
> (2000: 153)

The political sense of Freiby's words are perhaps embedded in his very name: Be free!

The politics of self-fashioning

In his 2007 essay "A Private Hero for a Privatized Nation," Aron suggests that Putin and Fandorin share a new political vision for Russia, the foundation of which is the modern notion of the autonomous individual and the attendant concepts of privacy and private life – concepts that Boym, among many others, argues are utterly alien to traditional Russian culture (Boym 1995). For Aron, Fandorin represents an independent individual with a strong sense of personal dignity and responsibility who has successfully rid himself of the "inner slavery" of the Russian soul. Such self-fashioning, Aron implies, is a prerequisite for the emergence of a truly democratic, nonauthoritarian society. Aron then attributes a similar advocacy of private life to Putin, citing his 2002 State of Russia address:

> The most important thing today is to create conditions for the citizens of Russia to earn money . . . To earn and invest in the economy of their own country with profit to themselves. We must make Russia a flourishing and rich country [in which people are] comfortable and secure, [where they are] free to work and make money for themselves and their children without limitations and fear.
>
> (Aron 2007:154)

In order to link Fandorin's self-fashioning to Putin's, however, Aron must elide the distinction between democracy and capitalism, which he proceeds to do in his description of the aspirations of the Russian middle class. Economic and political autonomy, Aron seems to suggest, are the same thing.

The tendency to associate self-fashioning and individualism with democracy is a critique that has been leveled at Greenblatt's analysis of Renaissance self-fashioning. Self-fashioning, Greenblatt argues, is a reflection of a growing sense of individual autonomy, revealed, for example, in the Protestant notion that "the authority of God's word is assured by the inner experience of God's word; the true interpretation of Scripture is made possible by the feeling faith of the believer" (1980: 99). The progressive, republican implications of self-fashioning, however, should be made with great caution in order to avoid projecting a modern idea of autonomous individualism onto the English Renaissance. As the literary historian David Haley writes, "the theory of individualism has a very limited application to Shakespeare's society. [. . .] The theory draws on deep republican premises and is consequently strange. [. . .] Self-fashioning could not mean the same thing in Shakespeare's England that it does in a modern, republican society" (Haley 1993: 31).

Moreover, it is important to recognize that notions of self-fashioning were circulating in Renaissance Europe not only among members of the rising middle class but also in writings addressed to monarchs. Consider, for example, Machiavelli's *Prince* or the various *Mirrors for Princes* of the early modern period, which advocate that monarchs carefully manipulate their image in order to solidify their authority and to mask the exercise of coercive power, for, as Machiavelli writes,

> the vulgar are always taken by what a thing seems to be and by what comes of it; and in the world there are only the vulgar, for the few find a place there only when the many have no ground to rest on (2002) (for more on Putin and Machiavelli, see Chapter 8 by Goscilo)

If the self-fashioning of members of the middle class in Renaissance England projected a greater sense of personal autonomy, the mirrors for princes present such autonomy as the unique privilege of the leader.

The tension between aspirations for individual empowerment and justifications of autocratic rule run deep in Russian culture. That tension is at the heart of the

Soviet anecdote about a Chukcha, or Inuit, who is sent to Moscow to study at the university. When he returns home, his friends and family ask him what he saw in the Soviet capital. Chukcha takes a puff on his pipe and responds, "In our country, we have the slogan 'All for the Good of Man' (vse dlia blaga cheloveka), and in Moscow, I saw that man!" One senses a tongue-in-cheek allusion to this anecdote in the title of the journalist and Putin-watcher Andrei Kolesnikov's first book on the Russian president, *I Saw Putin!* [*Ia videl Putina!* 2004]. Centralized authoritarian rule by a few was masked in official Soviet culture by a lofty humanist rhetoric of individual empowerment through education, work, etc. Fandorin and Putin, I would contend, represent two different interpretations of the politics of self-fashioning.

While Fandorin teaches others how to emancipate themselves from a tradition-bound, hierarchical system by example, Putin's self-fashioning is difficult to separate from his authoritarianism. It is an assertion of individual autonomy, but for him alone. This was brought home at the inauguration of his hand-picked successor, Dmitrii Medvedev, which was described in the following way in an article in the *Economist* titled "A Strange Kremlin Wedding":

> They arrived separately but walked out together. Like a bridegroom in church, Vladimir Putin arrived for the ceremony first. In front of 2,400 guests, he entered through the Kremlin's oldest and grandest banqueting hall. Only after he had taken his place at the podium, with the patriarch of the Russian Orthodox Church in sight, did the television cameras show the "bridal" motorcade arriving. The new president, Dmitry Medvedev, walked in through an ordinary entrance and stood next to Mr. Putin. If there was any doubt about seniority in this tandem, Mr. Putin then spoke first, about "passing the symbol of state power to Dmitry Medvedev."
>
> (*Economist* May 8, 2008)

Compare this scenario with Fandorin's empowering mentorship of the butler Ziukin.

There is clearly no single or simple interpretation of the politics of self-fashioning. In Akunin's hands, self-fashioning appears to be tied to the rise of a Russian middle class with aspirations for more representative, republican forms of government. Putin's self-fashioning, on the other hand, suggests his unique individuality, an autonomy that sanctions his authoritarianism. Two Russian films – Sergei Bodrov's (2007) *Mongol: The Rise of Genghis Khan* [*Mongol*] and Andrei Borissov's (2009) *By the Will of Genghis Khan* [*Po vole Chingiskhana*] – offer revisionist portrayals of the Mongol overlord Genghis Khan's that can be read as narratives of self-fashioning that ultimately serve as apologias for authoritarian rule. Both films present Genghis Khan's biography from childhood to maturity as a process of self-fashioning, against great odds, which leads to the perfection of his self-government through sheer force of will. But this is not a model for the average Mongol; it is the unique attribute of the successful leader. As Greenblatt himself notes, "The power to impose a shape upon oneself is an aspect of the more general power to control identity – *that of others at least as often as one's own*" (1980: 1; emphasis added).

Cassiday and Johnson's work on Putin mania in contemporary Russia, however, suggests how difficult it is to attribute a single, monolithic interpretation to the complex phenomenon of self-fashioning, even as it relates to a politician with increasingly authoritarian aspirations. "Putin mania," they argue,

> defies any clear distinction between official and unofficial speech, bringing these realms together in a sometimes baffling amalgam. Styles of discourse that remained largely segregated from each other until the very end of the Soviet period have merged to give rise to a single conversation that is invariably hard to read
>
> (2010: 696)

Far from shutting down interpretation, this semiotic amalgam has endowed the Russian reader with a new "creative agency," or interpretive license, especially "in forums over which the Russian state exerts less perfect control, such as the Internet, the capitalist marketplace and the public square" (2010: 685). The real self-fashioning, Cassiday and Johnson suggest, is happening not in the Kremlin but in the interpretive practices of the post-Soviet public.

Even the story of self-fashioning recounted in Akunin's novel *Coronation* cannot, in the end, be read simply and exclusively as documenting the successful implantation of individual autonomy and private life in Russia. In typical Russian fashion, Akunin denies his readers a happy ending. Depressed when the charismatic Fandorin leaves his life, the butler Ziukin abandons his career as a professional domestic to join the no less hierarchical and regimented world of the Russian navy, choosing once again to valorize, in the Russian tradition, "heroic sacrifice over both private life and practical accomplishment" (Boym 1995: 133). Moreover, Ziukin feels little excitement over the adventure ahead; rather, he is overwhelmed by a sense of loss: "I felt a strange sensation. Fate and royal favor [. . .] raised me to heights of which I'd never dreamt, but the feeling was as if I'd lost everything I'd possessed, and lost it forever" (2000: 348).

This tragic ending echoes the conclusion of the first book in the Fandorin series, *Azazel'*, which ends with the brutal murder of Fandorin's wife on their wedding day. Fandorin is so traumatized by the event that he will never marry again, denying himself the private life he previously had pursued so ardently. The tragedy prematurely ages Fandorin, turning him into a kind of emotional cipher, lending him an air of inscrutability – another trait he shares with Putin and one that makes both men into a "*tabula rasa* on which politicians, journalists and citizens alike could inscribe the qualities deemed lacking" in Russia's past (Cassiday and Johnson 2010: 686). Moreover, by naming Fandorin's wife Liza, Akunin invokes the ill-fated couple from Nikolai Karamzin's sentimental classic "Bednaia Liza" [Poor Liza], making the tragic end of Fandorin's romance appear almost inevitable. In other words, Akunin consciously inscribes his hero within a Russian literary tradition that has rarely celebrated the joys of private life.[8] Rather than the architect of his own destiny, Fandorin turns out to be in the grip of a very Russian notion of fate, *sud'ba*, which implies, according to the cultural linguist Anna Wierzbicka, that "what happens is largely independent of human will" (Wierzbicka 1992: 74). And so, if in the figure of his dashing detective hero Fandorin Akunin is advocating a new Russia of private citizens, as Aron claims, these unhappy endings remind us that the struggle to fashion an autonomous and protected private realm in a society with a profoundly ambivalent relationship to the very concept of individualism promises to be long and hard.

Notes

1 Emphasis added.
2 For more on Fandorin as a post-Soviet celebrity, see Baer and Korchagina 2010.
3 Akunin practiced more obvious political satire in the collection of short stories *Skazki dlia idiotov* [Fairy Tales for Idiots], St. Petersburg: Neva, 2001.
4 Many believe that Putin ordered Litvinenko's murder.
5 For more on the symbolics of the Soviet body, see Goscilo 2006.
6 In order to understand the importance of the eastern turn in the post-Soviet cultural imagination, it is important to recognize that Putin and Fandorin, while arguably the most influential representatives of the trend, are by no means the only examples. In 1998, the same year that Putin and Fandorin appeared on the post-Soviet cultural scene, Ernst Rifgatovich Muldashev, a respected Russian eye surgeon and director of the All-Russian Eye and Plastic Surgery Center in Ufa, Bashkortostan, published the first in a series of books on his journeys to Tibet and Nepal to discover the origins of man and to uncover the secrets of human civilization. That book, titled *From Whom Did We Come?* [*Ot kogo my proizoshli?*], quickly become a bestseller. Like Putin and Fandorin, Muldashev is an extremely energetic man, an amateur athlete, who is a master in the competitive sport of orienteering. His statement, "Laziness is the most horrible thing on earth. People don't understand that it is an evil thing" (Muldashev 2010), describes the modern professional and could have been uttered no less credibly by the Russian president or Akunin's detective. A journalist for the Russian daily *Komsomol'skaia pravda*, Sergei Andreev, describes the energetic doctor as a kind of superman:

> By profession, he is an opthalmologist and a surgeon. He performs unique operations on eyes. In his free time he across the globe in search of Shambala and the Cities of the Gods, about which he has written several books. In Murmansk, the indefatigable doctor managed in a single day to meet with his colleagues from the local hospital and then with fans of his research. At both meetings, the rooms were packed.
>
> (Muldashev 2010)

But what makes him quintessentially post-Soviet – that is, freed from the taint of Soviet bureaucrats, on the one hand, and heartless Western businessmen, on the other – is the way he combines his professionalism with (eastern) spirituality. Muldashev notes, "I was a bellicose communist atheist during the Soviet era. I started to believe in shamans when in 1995 one of them saved me from a heart attack" (Muldashev 2010). Although described in one blog post as "Russia's number one contribution to looney land," Muldashev's books are widely discussed on Russian blogs and in the Russian press (*Estragon*, August 19, 2003. Available online at: http://www.abovetopsecret.com/forum/thread15322/pg (accessed October 5, 2011)).

7 Dress was a problem in these new democratic ceremonies. General Lebedev, for example, wore a tuxedo at his 1998 inauguration as Governor of Krasnoyarsk Krai.

8 In a feature article in the October 1, 2008, issue of *Vanity Fair* titled "Dead Soul," Masha Gessen (2008) describes the failed private life of Vladimir Putin:

> The man in the car leads a shielded and perhaps lonely existence. His older daughter, Maria, 23, is rumored to be living in Germany; her 22-year-old sister, Katerina, is a student at St. Petersburg University, though it is unclear whether she actually attends classes. Putin shares the dacha with his wife, Lyudmila, from whom he is said to be increasingly estranged. Another resident is a black Labrador named Koni. A night owl, Putin rarely takes his meals in company, and does not usually return home from work until late, often past midnight. His hobbies are those of a loner: downhill skiing and horseback riding. As he speeds through the city, alone, he listens to audiobooks, often popular histories of Russia, which he came to rule almost by accident nearly 10 years ago.
>
> (Online)

For Putin's relations with his family and especially his wife, see the chapters by Mikhailova, Rogatchevski, and Goscilo in this volume.

Bibliography

Akunin, B. (1998) *Azazel'* [*The Winter Queen*], Moscow: Zakharov.

Akunin, B. (2000) *Koronatsiia, ili poslednii iz romanov* [*Coronation, or the Last of the Novels*], Moscow: Zakharov.

Akunin, B. (2004) *Leviafan* [*Murder on the Leviathan*], Moscow: Zakharov.

Albala, K. (2002) *Eating Right in the Renaissance*, Berkeley, CA: University of California Press.

Aron, L. (2002) "A Private Hero for a Privatized Country." *AEI Outlook Series*. AEI Online. Available online at: http://www.aei.org/article/society-and-culture/a-private-hero-for-a-privatized-country/ (accessed November 21, 2011).

Aron, L. (2004) "A Champion for the Bourgeoisie: Reinventing Virtue and Citizenship in Boris Akunin's Novels," *The National Interest*, March 22. Available online at: http://nationalinterest.org/bookreview/a-champion-for-the-bourgeoisie-774 (accessed August 20, 2011).

Aron, L. (2007) "A Private Hero for a Privatized Country," *Russia's Revolution. Essays 1989–2006*, Washington, DC: The AEI Press. 139–156.

Baer, B.J. (2005) "Engendering Suspicion: Homosexual Panic in the Post-Soviet *Detektiv*," *Slavic Review* 64(1) (Spring): 24–42.

Baer, B.J. and N. Korchagina (2010) "Akunin's Secret and Fandorin's Luck: Postmodern Celebrity in Post-Soviet Russia," *Celebrity and Glamour in Contemporary Russia. Shocking Chic*, Helena Goscilo and Vlad Strukov (eds.), London and New York: Routledge. 75–89.

Bernbaum, J.A. (Undated) "Russia's Leading Popular Crime Writer," Official Website of Russian-American Institute (RAI). Available online at: http://www.racu.org/index.php?option=com_content&;task=view&id=51&Itemid=32 (accessed August 20, 2011).

Bodrov, S. (2007) *Mongol: The Rise of Genghis Khan* [*Mongol*], Moscow: Kinostudiia STV.

Borissov, A. (2009) *By the Will of Genghis Khan* [*Po vole Chingiskhana*], Epic Pictures.

Boym, S. (1995) "From the Russian Soul to Post-Communist Nostalgia," *Representations* 49(Winter): 133–166.

Cassiday, J.A. and E.D. Johnson. (2010) "Putin, Putiniana and the Question of a Post-Soviet Cult of Personality," *Slavonic and East European Review*, 88(4): 681–707.

Chai, M. and W. Chai. (2007) *Everything You Need To Know To Understand Chinese Customs and Cutlure*, New York: Plume.

Chkhartashvili, G. (2006a) "A Case of Crime and Reward: Mystery Writer a Star in Russia," *The Washington Post*, April 23. [Interview with Peter Finn.] Available online at: http://www.washingtonpost.com/wp-dyn/content/article/2006/04/22/AR2006042201064.html (accessed August 20, 2011).

Chkhartashvili, G. (2006b) "Interview – Boris Akunin," *Time out London*, May 15. [Interview with Omer Ali.] Available online at: http://www.timeout.com/london/books/features/322/Boris_Akunin-Interview.html (accessed August 20, 2011).

Chkhartashvili, G. (2007) "Move over Tolstoy. Detective Tales of Tsarist Era Take Russia by Storm," *The Guardian*, September 19. [Interview with Luke Harding.] Available online at: http://www.guardian.co.uk/world/2007/sep/19/russia.books (accessed August 20, 2011).

Chkhartashvili, G. (2011) "Itogi u levykh. Grigorii Chkhartashvili (Boris Akunin), pisatel', 54 goda," *Afisha*, January 4. [Interview.] Available online at: http://www.afisha.ru/article/8315/ (accessed August 20, 2011).

Derrida, J. (1966) "Structure, Sign, and Play in the Discourse of the Human Sciences," *Writing and Difference,* trans. Alan Bass, London: Routledge. 278–294.

Downie, J. (2009) "Russia's in Trouble. Time for Putin to Take His Shirt off," *Blog post, Foreign Policy*, August 5. Available online at: http://blog.foreignpolicy.com/posts/2009/08/05/vladimir_putins_muscly_vacation (accessed October 5, 2011).

Dracula, V. (Undated) "Retsenziia na fil'm "Mongol. Chast' pervaia" [Review of the film Mongol. Part I]. Available online at: http://www.vlg.kinoafisha.info/reviews/3213138/ (accessed August 20, 2011).

Fitzpatrick, S. (2005) *Tear off the Masks: Identity and Imposture in Twentieth-Century Russia*, Princeton, NJ: Princeton University Press.

Flood, K.P. (2003) "Bodybuilding," *American Masculinities. An Historial Encyclopedia*, B.E. Carroll (ed.), New York: Sage. 59–60.

Gessen, M. (2008) "Dead Soul," *Vanity Fair*, October 1. Available online at: http://www.vanityfair.com/magazine/toc/contents-200810 (accessed October 5, 2011).

Goscilo, H. (2000a) "Introduction: Centrifuge and Fragmentation," *Studies in Twentieth Century Literature* 24(1) (winter): 7–14.

Goscilo, H. (2000b) "Style and S(t)imulation: Popular Magazines, or the Aestheticization of Postsoviet Russia," *Studies in Twentieth Century Literature* 24(1) (Winter): 15–50.

Goscilo, H. (2006) "Post-ing the Soviet Body as Tabula Phrasa and Spectacle," *Lotman and Cultural Studies: Explorations and Extensions*, A. Schonle (ed.), Madison, WI: University of Wisconsin Press. 248–298.

Greenblatt, S. (1980) *Renaissance Self-Fashioning. From More to Shakespeare*, Chicago, IL: University of Chicago Press.

Haley, D. (1993) *Shakespeare's Courtly Mirror*, Cranbury, NJ: Associate Press of America.

Hobsbawn, E. and T. Ranger (eds.). (1983) *The Invention of Tradition*, Cambridge: Cambridge University Press.

Kaganovsky, L. (2008) *How the Soviet Man Was Unmade: Cultural Fantasy and Male Subjectivity under Stalin*, Pittsburgh, PA: University of Pittsburgh Press.

Knox, Z. (2003) *Russian Society and the Orthodox Church: Religion in Russia after Communis*, Oxon and New York: RoutledgeCurzon.

Kurkov, A. (2005) "The Tsar's Man." [Review of *Turkish Gambit* by Boris Akunin], *The Guardian*, January 29. Available online at: http://www.guardian.co.uk/books/2005/jan/29/featuresreviews.guardianreview17 (accessed August 20, 2011).

Lévi-Strauss, C. (1968) *The Savage Mind*, Chicago, IL: Chicago University Press.

Lucas, E. (2010) "Long Piece on Power and History. Report No. 30: Putin, Power and History, or Does the Past Still Matter?" May 3. Available online at: http://edwardlucas.blogspot.com/2010/05/long-piece-on-power-and-history.html (accessed August 21, 2011).

Machiavelli, N. (1908) *The Prince*, trans. T.K. Marriott. Available online at: http://www.gutenberg.org/files/1232/1232-h/1232-h.htm (accessed October 5, 2011).

Muldashev, E.R. (2009) *Ot kogo my proizoshli? Sensationnye resul'taty nauchnoi gimalaiskoi ekspeditsii* [*From Whom Have We Descended? The Sensational Results of a Scientific Expedition to the Himalayas*], Moscow: Olma Media Gruup.

Myers, S.L. (2004) "Putin Takes Oath for Second Term," *The New York Times*, May 8. Available online at: http://www.sfgate.com/cgi-bin/article.cgi?f=/c/a/2004/05/08/MNG4H6IBG71.DTL (accessed April 3, 2012).

Putin, V., V. Shestakov, and A. Levitsky. (2004) *Judo: History, Theory, Practice*, Berkeley, CA: North Atlantic Books.

Ryazanova-Clarke, L. (2008) "Putin's Nation: Discursive Construction of National Identity in Direct Line with the President," *Slavic Helsingiensia* 34: 311–331.

Smith, J. (2007) "The Spies Who Never Left Us," *The Sunday Times*, July 22. Available online at: http://entertainment.timesonline.co.uk/tol/arts_and_entertainment /books/article2099444.ece (accessed August 20, 2011).

Steph. (2007) "Vladimir Putin Goes Topless for Gay Tolerance?" [Blog posting] August 23. Available online at: www.celebritymound.com/?cat=1514 (accessed January 2, 2010).

Thornhill, J. (2009) "Grime and Punishment," *Financial Times*, October 30. Available online at: http://www.ft.com/cms/s/2/a025dd92-c4e3-11de-8d54-00144feab49a.html#axzz1VZiqkKJG (accessed August 20, 2011).

Wierzbicka, A. (1992) *Semantics, Culture, and Cognition: Universal Human Concepts in Culture-Specific Configurations*, Oxford: Oxford University Press.

Wortman, R. (1995) *Scenarios of Power: Myth and Ceremony in Russian Monarchy*, Vol. 1, Princeton, NJ: Princeton University Press.

Zonis, M., D. Lefkovits, S. Wilkin, and J. Yackley (2011) *Risk Rules: How Politics Threaten the Global Economy*. Evanston, IL: Agate B2 Publishing.

8 Putin's performance of masculinity

The action hero and macho sex-object

Helena Goscilo

Before PR lessons and pinup-manship

As Russia's fêted political idol, premier media personality, and current media-personality premier, Vladimir Putin during his presidency inspired verses, novels, plays, an opera, songs, portraits, sculptures, fan clubs, amorous declarations, genuflection by bloggers, and a battery of products imprinted with his image, from T-shirts and bed linens to confectionery.[1] Admirers and sycophants celebrated his birthday with priceless, if idiosyncratic, gifts (a mountain, a crown, a tiger), abandoning all restraint and common sense in their eagerness to express ardent devotion to the superstar leader. Enthusiasts lacking a mountain or a tiger found creative – indeed, outlandish – means of compensation, such as a pensioner in St. Petersburg who reportedly trained his dog to bark "Vova!" (a diminutive of Putin's first name) in honor of VVP (Blomfield, 2007a). Though Putin's endorsement of the reinvasion of Chechnya undoubtedly boosted his popularity even before the presidential election of March 2000, his subsequent elevation to the rank of a national treasure was less precipitous and increasingly media-orchestrated.

A cautious but meticulous "manager" who inherited a country in profound disarray, during the initial phase of his presidency Putin demonstrated his trademark efficiency and an intention to institute reforms,[2] but maintained an impassive profile and betrayed ignorance of PR and its incalculable power. No incident revealed Putin's inexperience in his new role more eloquently than his reaction to the *Kursk* disaster of August 12, 2000, which occurred in the midst of his public promise to restore Russia's "glory" as a military power by rebuilding its conventional forces (Applebaum 2000). Engaged in naval exercises in the Barents Sea, the submarine *Kursk* sank after two explosions destroyed the vessel, ultimately taking the lives of its entire 118-man crew. On vacation in Sochi at the time, Putin incurred indignant opprobrium in Russia and the West for temporizing and poor judgment: initially declining offers of rescue attempts from Britain, Norway, and the United States, he returned home 5 days after the tragedy, having placed national pride ahead of human life.[3] Moreover, he compounded his apparent callous indifference in a memorable moment during his interview on the Larry King show, when in answer to King's portentously earnest question, "Tell me, what happened with the submarine?" he blithely replied, with a smirk, "It sank" (Larry King Live, 2000).[4]

Reactions to his inadequate management of the catastrophe taught Putin a lesson that thereafter would determine his handling of public relations. His responses to the multiple crises that followed were swift, self-assured, and widely covered by both domestic and foreign media. In general, Putin quickly learned the benefits of appearing in the media limelight, particularly when he initiated policies and made decisions likely to appeal to the Russian population, such as increases in pensions, the disempowerment of the oligarchs, institutionalization of new holidays (e.g., People's Unity Day on November 4[5]), and financial support of culture, notably of the ailing film industry. According to public opinion surveys, by June 2007 Putin's approval rating had reached 81 percent – the highest of any leader in the world. And throughout the first decade of the new millennium his popularity never fell below 65 percent. Observers attribute Russians' approbation of Putin to the country's semblance of stabilization, its self-reassertion on the international scene, and the measurable improvements in living standards that transpired under his leadership. Undeniably, his economic reforms, in tandem with his implacable campaign against the despised nineties' oligarchs, as well as the government's seizure of control over natural resources – companies that make formidable profits, such as Gazprom and Rosneft – curtailed Russia's anarchic decade of Klondike capitalism.

Like his much-admired Peter the Great,[6] Putin focused on practical issues. While routinely proselytizing adherence to the constitution as the foundation of Russia's governance and political rectitude, he sidelined or turned a blind eye to the parlous state of Russia's ecology and human rights, as well as epidemic-scale corruption[7] and the Federal Security Service of the Russian Federation's (FSB) harassment, raids, and confiscations of records belonging to organizations not supportive of the Kremlin and arbitrarily charged with violation of one law or another – an exercise of force that seemed to be motivated solely by the Kremlin's self-serving interests. Little wonder, then, that the creation of Russia's Public Chamber in 2005 notwithstanding, a broad spectrum of commentators familiar with Putin's policies and statements as president saw (and continue to see) small likelihood of a genuine civil society eventually developing in post-Soviet Russia[8] (Figure 8.1). Yet, despite considerable unease and fluctuations in the West's attitudes toward Putin as authoritarian ruler, the consensus abroad is that he was (and remains) a world-renowned political star. Indeed, in 2007, by which time Putin had unequivocally established his priorities and *modus operandi*, *TIME* magazine featured him as Person of the Year – an "honor" accorded Hitler and Stalin in 1938 and 1939, respectively, and in 1982 . . . the computer.[9]

On home terrain, Russians in thrall to Putin across the social and geographical spectrum iterate the same summative formula: "[He's] a real man!" [*Nastoiashchii muzhik!*] For some Westerners, his status as a macho cult figure defies comprehension, merely seeming to confirm Russians' notorious unpredictability, immortalized in Winston Churchill's famous gloss on Russia as a riddle wrapped in a

Figure 8.1 Sergei Elkin's witty reflection on the frequently adduced parallel between Putin's Russia and the period of Stagnation (*zastoi*) under Brezhnev.

Source: Courtesy of Sergei Elkin.

mystery inside an enigma. Yet, in many significant ways, Putin's carefully calibrated public image slots quite neatly into traditional, fantasy-fueled paradigms of ideal masculinity. While Russians such as film director Nikita Mikhalkov bemoan the absence of a genuine hero – a paragon of charismatic manhood – on domestic screens, sundry polls and rhapsodic encomia indicate that for many Russians, their former president turned prime minister embodies precisely such an exemplar. "The Putin phenomenon" begs the question: How has a stolid bureaucrat metamorphosed into an international macho icon? That is the question this chapter addresses.

An icon of machismo or the modern Pericles

George Mosse opens his study of the forces and historical circumstances that created modern masculinity with a passage that could hardly speak more directly to Putin's macho public persona:

> Distinct images of masculinity – the way men assert what they believe to be their manhood – have been all pervasive in Western culture. The ideal of masculinity was invoked on all sides as a symbol of personal and

> national regeneration, but also as basic to the self-definition of modern society. Manliness was supposed to safeguard the existing order against the perils of modernity, but it was also regarded as an indispensable attribute of those who wanted change.
>
> (1996: 3)[10]

Indeed, it would be difficult to contest the symbolic value of "Putin" for Russia's regeneration and his stratagem of simultaneously preserving yet transforming the order that he governed as head of state and is now presumed to oversee in more mediated fashion (on Putin's function as that of restorer, see Chapter 4 by Gorham).

Historically, three cultural paradigms codified heroic masculinity – a cultural construct and social practice shaped by the ethos of a given society, albeit traditionally posited in essentialist terms: those of (1) the warrior (e.g., Alexander the Great), (2) the philosopher (e.g., Socrates), and (3) the ruler, who optimally synthesizes the other two (e.g., Pericles).[11] For self-evident reasons, in modern times, the outmoded concept of the *warrior* has vanished, though in our current hyperbolic age of devalued language, anyone risking his life for the nation or battling a potentially fatal disease is proclaimed a hero. Yet few would deny that "[t]he nexus linking war, militarism, and masculinities has remained an enduring and consistent feature of societies and their cultures across time" (Higate and Hopton 2005: 432). Though Putin has little in common with military heroes, the huge gallery of his PR photographs leaves no doubts that he appreciates the psychological significance of the next best thing – the spectacle of a leader wearing camouflage, owning a military-style Lada jeep, clutching weapons, and visiting army bases. Despite the frequent confusion nowadays between philosophy and ideology, contemporary intellectuals and particularly literary and cultural theorists qualify as reduced analogues to the ancient *philosophers*.[12] Though hardly a philosopher, Putin has an excellent command of rhetoric, and his speech strategies, especially his frequent "reminder" that he has thought or already spoken about a given problem implies his relentless engagement with ideas, however earthbound those ideas may be (see Chapters 4 and 5 by Gorham and Ryazanova-Clarke, respectively). *Rulers* possessing both military skills and outstanding intelligence or aesthetic vision exist only on the silver screen, their compensatory appeal predicated largely on their remoteness from real-life counterparts. A case in point is the American president in Wolfgang Peterson's bombastic *Air Force One* (1997), with Harrison Ford as the fictive national leader of physical courage, endless resourcefulness, and impeccable morality – at a time when Bill Clinton as president demonstrated physical skills of a decidedly non-military nature and imbued not "true-blue" uniforms, but blue dresses with a new, moist significance that led to impeachment hearings.

Anomalously, sundry cultural processes and products during the 2000s limned Putin's image along the lines of the ideal masculine paradigm (as Lilia Shevtsova puts it, he "*was the right man, in the right place, at the right time*" (2007: 38); emphasis in the original). While fantasy and desire inevitably fuel breath-stopping narratives of a national leader's exceptional endowments and achievements, several aspects of Putin's persona actually facilitated his construction as a masculine icon incarnating the wise ruler who seamlessly unites the warrior and the thinker. Fundamental to the citizenry's admiration for Putin was his contrast to Boris Yeltsin, from whom he quickly distanced himself. Mentally alert and physically fit, Putin was hailed as the masterful, self-confident alpha male, apparently in full control of both himself and the nation. Once past the *Kursk* catastrophe, he projected an image of reasonableness, lucidity, and steadfast commitment to the nation he was steering in the competitive and combustible climate of today's world. Unlike the erratic Yeltsin, who seemed driven above all by impulse and alcohol, Putin created the impression of thoughtful, well-informed competence – a competence that gradually became amplified into infallible judgment in the eyes of many, and thus a part of his "star quality."

Secondly, Putin's sporting skills parallel the warrior's in their challenging physicality: whereas Yeltsin played the court-circumscribed game of tennis, his successor swims, rides, mountain-skis, works out daily with weights, and boasts a black belt in judo – a skill advertised by widely circulated images of Putin in judo positions and apparel, and imprecisely associated with lucrative martial arts action films starring Jean-Claude Van Damme and Bruce Lee (Figures 8.2 and 8.3). His instructional 2008 DVD, *Let's Learn Judo with Vladimir Putin*, confirmed Putin's reputation as a "fighting man," already inferred in part from his combative stance on Chechnya and his outspoken criticism of both the United States and the United Kingdom during his second term. And photographs on the Internet of Putin riding a Harley-Davidson motorcycle, co-piloting a fighter jet, operating a train (Duke 2007), visiting dangerous zones and sites of disaster, and – outfitted in camouflage and combat boots – purportedly rescuing a TV crew from a tigress cemented this image of intrepid action (Figure 8.4).

Putin's masculinity is grounded in the body and what that body can withstand – a material guarantor that, as Putin learned, reassures the public. It therefore is unsurprising that the main attraction in Moscow's newly opened Tochka G (G Spot) – Russia's first sex museum, founded and curated by Aleksandr Donskoi – is reputedly a painting by Vera Donskaia-Khilko titled *Wrestling* (2011), which depicts Putin and Obama preparing to do battle with their enormous phalluses.[13] The explanatory text alongside the work clarifies the realized visual metaphor: "Putin has two members [one red, one green, presumably traffic-light signals for 'stop' and 'go,'], as a symbol of hyperpotency, a symbol of the gray cardinal" (Elder 2011). Certainly, no other world leader boasts comparable physical vigor, with the possible exception of the scandal-ridden Italian Prime Minister, Silvio Berlusconi (b. 1936), who, like his friend Putin, frequently appears in the media limelight, but whose widely reported bodily exertions are largely confined to the bedroom (Figure 8.5). By contrast, while media-generated images of Putin have stimulated erotic desire among the female population and some gays, the Kremlin has throttled romantic rumors and speculations about Putin's sexual interest in much younger women. It has done so, I contend, to preserve his public persona as stimulating but not manifesting sexual desire. His energies are presumably invested in more serious endeavors than extra-marital frolics, and though he

Figure 8.2 The consummate Russian embodiment of macho discipline conducting a master class in judo with World and Olympic champion, Japanese judo artist Yasuhiro Yamasita, December 25, 2005.

Source: Courtesy of the Presidential Press and Information Office, www.kremlin.ru, on Wikimedia Commons.

Figure 8.3 The Judo-Putin toy.

Source: Courtesy of Alexander Plyushchev on Wikimedia Commons.

Figure 8.4 Fostering heroic associations by posing in a strategic bomber TU-160 before the beginning of military exercises by the long-range aircraft of the Air Forces and Northern Fleet, Chkalov Airfield, Moscow Region, August 16, 2005.

Source: Courtesy of the Presidential Press Service, www.kremlin.ru, on Wikimedia Commons.

unquestionably has become a sexual object, his demeanor and status as national icon militate against attributing a sexual subjectivity to him. His public kisses are reserved for children and animals (see Chapter 3 by Mikhailova). Consequently, whereas Berlusconi's antics are generally deemed symptomatic of widespread corruption in the Italian government, in the Russian public's collective unconscious Putin's energy and physical prowess symbolize a resurgent, dynamic Russia eager to take its place in the sun.

Putin's warrior identity is articulated not only in "body talk," though that body has been inordinately loquacious recently, but also in increasingly "tough talk" with regional leaders and foreign dignitaries, particularly if the latter appear critical of Russia's internal affairs, as in the case of American Vice President Joseph Biden, Jr. Moreover, Putin's periodic resort to salty language heard above all in men's locker rooms certifies his credentials as a Man's Man (see Chapter 4 by Gorham).[14] These features, together with his low-key, self-assured manner, partly explain why Russians credit Putin with impregnable will and undeviating purpose. In the current global context, his reputation as a political leader to be reckoned with – one prepared to make internationally unpopular decisions for the sake of Russia's best interests – places Russia on the map of key world players.

Aided by the Kremlin, Putin's ability to create a public persona of unshakable probity modeled on Hollywood's action heroes resulted in bloggers' hosannas as early as 2001 and 2002. His ubiquity conveyed boundless vitality and his trustworthiness as a safekeeper of Russia's well-being on all fronts. And his continuing

Figure 8.5 Putin presenting *The Silvio Berlusconi Effect*, a volume about the Italian Prime Minister's political career, to his happy friend, in Sochi, April 2, 2002.

Source: Courtesy of the Presidential Press and Information office, www.kremlin.ru, on Wikimedia Commons.

annual ritual since 2001 of a 3-hour exchange by telephone with Russian citizens (*Priamaia liniia s Prezidentom* [Direct Line with the President]), broadcast on TV and radio, only solidified the beguiling impression of a dedicated, responsive, and effectual leader (see Ryazanova-Clarke 2008).[15] Detractors justifiably called the performance in 2009 "the usual combination of politics and conspicuous munificence" (Balmforth 2009), with Putin (no longer president) reassuring participants with promises of continued improvements while simultaneously highlighting his record of achievements. This carefully choreographed show, as Ryazanova-Clarke has noted, helped to construct "three salient Presidential roles: a military commander, a competent technocrat and a superman" (2008: 326) (Figure 8.6).

The Hollywood superman

Touted as a decisive man of action, Putin to a much greater degree than such Hollywood prototypes as Arnold Schwarzenegger, Sylvester Stallone, and Bruce Willis projects an aura of self-restraint that only enhances his reputation as a Real Man. As Yvonne Tasker's study of action cinema, *Spectacular Bodies*, maintains,

> In contrast to the images of anarchic violence that have critically accompanied muscular movies, it is, in fact, the values of self-control rather than chaos, and the practices of training and discipline which are extolled as central terms in the definition of bodybuilding and in the image of the

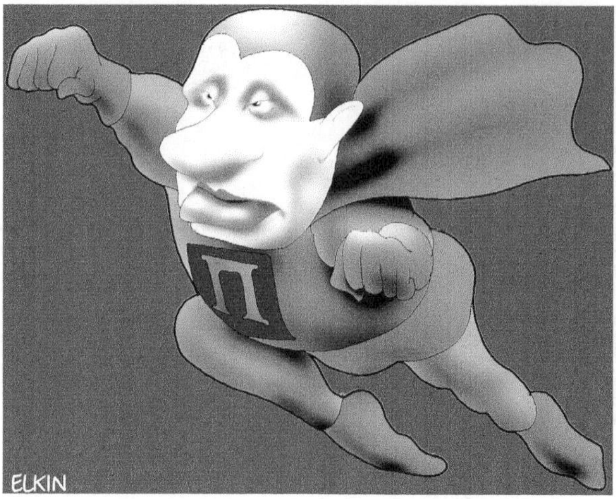

Figure 8.6 Superman Putin, faster than a speeding bullet, in Sergei Elkin's realization of metaphor.

Source: Courtesy of Sergei Elkin.

> muscleman hero of 1980s [American] cinema. The visual spectacle of the male body that is central to muscular movies puts into play the two contradictory terms of *restraint* and *excess*.

Tasker (1993: 9) goes on to point out that despite possessing excessive physical strength, "the hero is [. . .] defined by his restraint in putting his strength to the test." Though restraint has never been regarded as Russians' salient trait, in the new millennium, the Russian president's image was molded precisely according to this Hollywood blueprint. In fact, whether consciously or not, through his posture, facial expressions, and occasionally clenched fists Putin regularly manages to convey the disciplinary process of achieving self-control when confronted with stupidity, incompetence, or simply a view counter to his own (on the impression of verbal self-restraint, see Chapter 4 by Gorham).[16] His attained external impassivity evokes the "tough guys" in Hollywood film and therefore is legible as super-masculinist. The recent facelift and botox treatment that have removed some of Putin's wrinkles certainly ally him with Hollywood image-preservation in the battle against physical evidence of age (Stewart and Eccles 2011) (Figure 8.7).

The role of cinema, and especially action movies, in popular images of Putin emerges most colorfully, perhaps, in the first episode ("Hidden Threat") of 25-year-old freelance political commentator Sergei Kalenik's tongue-in-cheek comic strip, posted in May 2011 on the pointedly named site http://www.superputin.ru/episode1.html; and boasting 7 million hits by mid-July (Weir 2011).[17] Titled *Chelovek kak vse* [A Man like Everyone Else], the comic teems with intertexts

Figure 8.7 Putin: "Hey, fellow! Another Botox for me!" Bartender: "You've already had enough!" Reference to Putin's recent excessive Botox treatment.

Source: Courtesy of Sergei Elkin.

and political allusions in a narrative featuring the martial arts expert Putin, his aid Medvedev, and Deputy Prime Minister Igor' Sechin as members of the Super League of Heroes. "A year before the end of the world" (projected as 2012 – the year of the presidential elections), they confront a series of enemies including not only terrorists, but also citizen-zombies complaining about real-life developments during Putin's presidency: elimination of NTV and gubernatorial elections, the Khodorkovsky case, abuse of official sirens to bypass Moscow's congested traffic, etc. Putin is unquestionably the superman in command, helped by Medvedev, here cast as a technology-loving "gnome" who can metamorphose into a bear (*medved'*). Garbed in the white kimono (*gi*) he usually sports during his judo sessions, Putin casually destroys an al-Qaeda cell (Figure 8.8), saves a busload of citizens threatened by a bomb (see Keanu Reeves in Jan de Bont's *Speed* 1994), and enters The Gloom (see Timur Bekmambetov's *Night Watch* 2004), which is inhabited by zombies (see *The Walking Dead*).[18] At the cliff-hanger conclusion inherent in the genre and calculated to arouse impatience for the next installment, Putin prepares to fight the preternaturally gigantic Japanese Fat Troll, a sumo wrestler who rules over the zombies (Figure 8.9). Tellingly, not only does Medvedev play second fiddle to Putin, but the current president's dossier singles out humor as his signature trait, whereas Putin's cites his "Nordic temperament"[19] and his acceptance by everybody as "one of them" (*svoi*) – referencing the multiple interpretive perspectives on Putin's enigmatic persona that generate the diverse, often contrary, Putin images inundating the country and the Internet.

Figure 8.8 Putin as savior in the Superputin comic strip by Sergei Kalenik.

Source: Courtesy of Sergei Kalenik on Wikimedia Commons.

Figure 8.9 The confrontation between Putin and the Japanese Fat Troll in Sergei Kalenik's Superputin comic strip.

Source: Courtesy of Sergei Kalenik.

The recently posted second episode, called "Attack of the Clones" (echoing the fourth *Star Wars* film by George Lucas), emphasizes media and their construction of a pseudo-reality that is today's Russia. It does so through references to Ostankino and figures from television and film, including Disney's Donald Duck and the director Nikita Mikhalkov. With Medvedev as his bear-assistant, Putin battles enemies of love and humanity in a scenario that, once again, teems with political barbs and ironically spotlights sundry aspects of his public persona. Revealingly, one of the last tongue-in-cheek illustrations shows a panoramic screen comprising an incoherent mélange of visuals drawn from various media – the entire composite spectacle labeled *Reality* [*Real'nost'*]. Kalenik's satirical view of contemporary Russian life is congruent with Guy Debord's notion of spectacle substituting for lived life.

Variety notwithstanding, it could hardly be more obvious that a potent masculinity resides at the core of Putin's public persona, most recently illustrated in a new computer game called *Voinushka* [translated as Shoot 'em up], available on the social networking sites VKontakte and Odnoklassniki since its launch in April 2011. The game stars a youthful, khaki-clad, gun-toting Putin and his button-poppingly busty, red-haired aide in a Soviet army fur hat, cum rifle, in whom some perceive an unintended resemblance to Anna Chapman, the self-promoting member of the Russian spy ring flushed out in the United States last summer (2010) (Figure 8.10). Predictably, in the game Putin issues orders and "is the constant right hand of the player," for, according to the relevant company's chief marketing officer, Varvara Zolotova, "He is the leader, just as in life he is for the young people. [. . .] Putin is a popular hero, young people really like him both as a political figure and as a person." The fast-moving, bullet-rich scenario, as well as Putin's gun-gripping stance in the opening page of the game, recalls ads for the James Bond films ("Anna Chapman 'helps Putin in computer game'" 2011). Particularly in light of Putin's career in the security services, the suggestive kinship with Bond – dubbed the "cyborg-aristocrat" by one critic on account of his superiority, sexual irresistibility, and the prosthetic gadgets and technologies that are an extension of his honed body – is unmistakable (O'Donnell 2005). That parallel was more directly drawn in the posters that suddenly appeared on Moscow's bus stops in mid-July 2011, which depicted Putin as the stylishly garbed super-agent by superimposing his face on Daniel Craig's body, accompanied by the words "VV prikroet" [VV will protect (Russia?)][20] (Figure 8.11). Tellingly, in 2000, Putin's PR team planned to cast Putin as a modern Stirlitz, the Russian secret agent protagonist of Tat'iana Lioznova's uniquely successful TV series, *17 mgnovenii vesny* [17 Moments of Spring 1973], based on Iuliian Semenov's spy novel (1969) with the same title. In an interview that year the Kremlin political consultant Gleb Pavlovskii acknowledged that his team

> secretly polled [people] to find out what kind of person the Russian people considered heroic [. . .only to realize]that in Putin they had a Stirlitz, the dashing fictional KGB [*sic*] officer who is the hero of a popular old film, an undercover agent in the SS in Germany in World War II, who embodies Russian ideals. They immediately launched a campaign to turn Vladimir Putin into another Stirlitz.
>
> (Orth 2000)[21]

Figure 8.10 The computer game *Voinushka*, with Putin as top agent and his female aide as top-lush agent. Posted on the site VKontakte (vk.com).

Figure 8.11 The Bond connection. Daniel Craig's body, Vladimir Putin's head. Anonymous poster briefly appearing at Moscow bus stops in summer 2011.

In other words, *Voinushka* overtly reinforces features that from the outset helped to mold Putin's public image. Accordingly, though Putin's spokesman, press attaché Dmitrii Peskov, bristled at the oversight of Moscow's Progrestar Inc., which never requested permission to cast Putin as the game's leading actor, *Voinushka* has not been removed from the sites. After all, a year before the next round of presidential elections, the role of a fearless "cool leader" can hardly damage Putin's reputation of top macho candidate for the post he earlier occupied for 8 years.

The legacy of Stalin and Machiavelli

Of all Soviet rulers, only Stalin inspired a kindred adoration among the populace.[22] Likewise renowned for his virile image, Stalin resorted to questionable stratagems to maintain power, adopted military garb during peacetime, and posed as an expert on all modes of cultural production. Sundry scholars and journalists have analogized the two men as objects of personality cults, not always taking into account the differences in the historical context, specific circumstances, and nature of those cults (see Chapter 2 by Cassiday *et al.*).

The administrative styles of both leaders, I contend, partly derived from Niccolo Machiavelli's controversial handbook for rulers, titled *The Prince* (wr. 1513, pd. 1532), a copy of which Stalin reportedly kept on his nightstand. While Putin's familiarity with the tract is uncertain, his reign conformed to its major precepts. Guided above all by pragmatism, Machiavelli sanctions dubious means for desired ends, declares sound laws and a strong military force prerequisites for maintaining a state, and advocates discipline as well as shrewdness in a leader. An effective ruler, he insists, should be "a great pretender and dissembler," who shows "greatness, courage, gravity, and fortitude" (*The Prince*, Chapter 19), paying more attention to his reputation than to his conscience. Clearly, conduct that results in the ascription of traits rather than genuine possession of them is primary in Machiavelli's scheme of things. The masses, he argues, should deem the ruler's judgments irrevocable, and he should keep them happy and entertained with "festivals and spectacles at convenient seasons of the year," while also appearing as "a patron of ability [. . .] honor[ing] the proficient in every art" (Chapter 21). The relevance of these "rules of reign" for Putin's years in office is self-evident, for the pragmatic, shrewd, disciplined Putin assumed the incontrovertibility of his pronouncements, appeared at an endless array of festivals and openings, distributed prizes to authors, painters, musicians, performers, actors and actresses, and monitored public perception of his standing among the populace on a daily basis. While emphasizing the primacy of law (e.g., iterating that a third consecutive presidential term would violate the Russian constitution),[23] as an intelligent man Putin understood the distinction between formal and genuine adherence to it. Therefore, while outwardly preserving legality, he devised a practical solution for the role he would play after the expiration of his second term. The appointment of his protégé Medvedev as replacement ensured that Putin would retain far-ranging administrative power as Russia's prime minister – one, moreover, with broadly publicized respect for the constitution.

Though Machiavelli frequently has been dubbed a cynic, what he counseled was essentially a policy adopted by most politicians today: cultivation of a public image and effective PR as means of preserving control over the state so as to oversee its affairs with maximal effectiveness. Putin embraces those principles in a kindred spirit of utilitarianism. It is no coincidence that in an interview he briefly commended Anatolii Chubais (decidedly not a favorite of Putin's) for his pragmatism: "I thought that he largely lived in a world of illusions. But he proved to be a pragmatist and capable of perceiving the realities of life instead of being ruled by some ephemeral ideas."[24] When speaking of Ludwig Erhard (1897–1977), West Germany's Chancellor (1963–66) and Minister of Economics after 1949, he similarly declared, "I also like Erhard. He's a very pragmatic person" [*I eshche mne nravitsia Erkhard. Ochen' pragmatichnyi chelovek*] (*Ot pervogo litsa* 2000: 175). Generally considered the mastermind behind the rebirth of the German post-war economy, Erhard probably impresses Putin as his parallel in restoring economic health to a nation mired in chaos. These two judgments about administrators confirm practical efficacy as Putin's mantra, which also serves as the decisive measure in his opinion of others and forms the cornerstone of Machiavelli's philosophy of rule.[25]

Eroticized power and female desire

During the second half of the 2000s, the orchestration of Putin's image took a decidedly sexualized turn along cynosural lines. In an explicitly pin-up mode, indefatigably reproduced photographs of his bare-chested self, riding and fishing on vacation in Siberia in 2007 and 2009 reportedly caused a sensation, and not just in Russia (Figure 8.12). The mass-market newspaper *Komsomol'skaia pravda* [Komsomol Truth] printed a huge color photo of the presidential pecs under the headline "Be like Putin," together with an illustrated guide to the requisite exercises for building up a torso like his. Apparently, Russian gay chatrooms and blogs hummed with excitement, while women posting comments on the newspaper's web site claimed to be "screaming with delight and showering him with compliments" ("Gay Russians claim bare-chested Putin as one of their own" 2007). While reportedly plunging both men and women into a frenzy of desire, Putin, like Greta Garbo, seemingly "wanted to be alone" (the photo-op scenarios show "a man and his rod," "a man and his horse," etc.) – an inaccessible and self-sufficient anchorite who just happened to be photographed repeatedly while engaged in gender-coded pursuits.

Similarly, the topless Putin on a free poster accompanying a special 2008 issue of the celebrity gossip magazine *Sekrety zvezd* [Secrets of the Stars] devoted to the president capitalized on the success of its earlier circulation-breaking issue featuring the bare-chested Putin on the cover, which had sold over 400,000 copies (Blomfield 2008). In short, the most exposed presidential pecs in the world ensured Putin's identity as a sex symbol – a status he has reinforced as prime minister by additional torso exposure during his 2009 holiday in Siberia as he

Figure 8.12 A case of overexposure.

Source: Courtesy of Sergei Elkin.

swam, white-water rafted, climbed a tree, and hand-fed his horse (Halpin 2009). A historically attested site of physical hardship and stoic survival, Siberia seems Putin's setting of choice for coy self-exposure – a place where he can shed his shirt and the constraints of urban propriety, cultivate his rugged side, and be a Real Man.[26]

An inspirational if unattainable model for Russian men (as urged in the marketing directive "Be like Putin"), Putin manifestly constitutes an object of impassioned desire for women. According to the extravagant claims in the Putin issue of *Secrets of the Stars*, "There's not a single woman who would not dream of embracing and kissing Vladimir Vladimirovich and hearing his declaration of love" (Blomfield 2008). Though publicly Putin displays more interest in dogs and dolphins than in women, the media have worked unremittingly on his eroticization as an elusive love object – never subject. That process has been facilitated by the nature of Putin's public appearances. Unlike Mikhail Gorbachev, who preferred to attend events with his beloved Raisa, Putin travels solo, rarely accompanied by his spouse, and reserves his avowals of affection not for her, but for Russia and his dogs – particularly the famous Koni, who, unlike Liudmila Putina, played a visual role in his 2004 presidential campaign (Figure 8.13). Furthermore, published interviews with both Putin and his wife suggest a total absence of intimacy between the two. As a consequence, despite Putin's frosty and aloof air, fantasies percolate around his spurious "availability," fanned by the media's speculation and misinformation about his relationships with beautiful women less than half his age.

Sex and sect

Accordingly, last year a group of female fans enrolled in the Journalism Department at Moscow State University joined the ranks of Putin's birthday well-wishers to demonstrate their love for the prime minister in uninhibited – indeed, naked – fashion. As a gift for his 58th birthday (October 7, 2010), under the guidance of 23-year-old journalism graduate Vladimir Tabak, they assembled a calendar featuring cheesecake photographs of themselves in skimpy lingerie and suggestive poses, with "come-on" invitations and heated reactions to his fabled macho identity: "They've extinguished the forest fires, but I'm still burning!"(*Lesa potushili, a ia vse eshche goriu!*; March), "You're my premier/first" (*Vy – moi prem'er*; October), "If only everyone had such a man" (*Vsem by takogo muzhchinu*; January), "Well, who if not you?' (*Nu, a kto, esli ne vy?*; August), and so forth (Figure 8.14). The young women's pouting mouths, facial expressions, and mammary exposure belong to the visual conventions of girlie magazines, with the December illustration (black panties and moist, parted lips) and "personal message" cum the young woman's telephone number faithfully reproducing sexual solicitations found in telephone booths, sex ads, and the like. Headlined "We Love You Vladimir Vladimirovich" and first posted on the blog of Nashi member Aleksandr Iarosh, the calendar attracted considerable attention on the Internet and reinforced Putin's image of alluring virility, even to women who could conceivably be his granddaughters.[27] Some of their fellow students in the Journalism Department countered by posting an alternate calendar of themselves in black outfits, with tape over their mouths, implicitly decrying Putin's *modus operandi* and alluding to the current censorship by reviving such long-forgotten questions as "Who killed Politkovskaia?" Unsurprisingly, the first calendar, which instantly flooded the Internet and also briefly went on sale in supermarkets in Moscow before being pulled, found an appreciative audience among Russians, particularly men, and reportedly sold 50,000 copies at $8.73 each (Weir 2011; Ustinova and Klim 2010). Quite grotesquely, it "spawned a Putin party at a Moscow nightclub, complete with topless dancers, on International Women's Day" (Ioffe 2011). And the young women's apparent yearning to "serv(ic)e" Putin doubtless kindled the desire of female readers and visitors to the relevant Internet site, for, as fanzines have taught us, publicly proclaimed fantasy-based desire tends to be contagious.

Apparently, students in Russia have too much free time at their disposal, as evidenced by the calendar and a recent video called *Armiia Putina* [Putin's Army], named after an organization of 1,200 female members posted on the main Russian networking site Vkontakte. The video, which looks professionally produced,[28] spotlights as protagonist yet another female student – one who urges young women to disrobe in support of the prime minister. In vertiginously high heels and a snug black jacket over a white, low-cut top, the blonde quickly negotiates Moscow's streets, her jaunty voiceover expressing boundless love for Putin as a "chic man" (*shikarnyi muzhchina*) and national icon:

Figure 8.13 Developing and honing muscles while a mesmerized Koni watches, June 14, 2002.

Source: Courtesy of the Presidential Press and Information Office, www.kremlin.ru, on Wikimedia Commons.

Figure 8.14 "You're the best!" Evidently, April is not the cruelest month, as illustrated in the calendar produced by female students in the Journalism Department of Moscow State University, 2010, under the guidance of Vladimir Tabak.

Source: Courtesy of Vladimir Tabak.

> Hi! My name's Diana. I'm a student. I'm crazy about the person who's changed the life of our country. He's a fine politician and a chic man. He's Vladimir Putin. Millions adore and trust him. But there are some who throw dirt at him. Maybe they're scared. Maybe they're just weak. Because they'll never be in his position.[29]

After this gushing encomium, as the camera zooms down on her cleavage, "Diana" joins two female friends, presumably also admirers of Putin, sunning at the Moscow River and happily sucking mixed drinks through straws. The smiling trio brings up the site of Putin's Army on a laptop, after which "Diana" scribbles in red lipstick on a white top, "I'll tear [up my top] for Putin" [*Ia porvu za Putina*], and proceeds to follow through on her intention.[30] Meanwhile, the voiceover invites all young women to participate in a contest by submitting a video showing what exactly they are willing to "tear [up]" for Putin, to do for their "president" [*sic*]. Described by journalists as "sexy" and "racy" (rather than naive and tacky), the video could lead one to conclude that a company specializing in technology underwrote the manufacture of the video, for product placements include "Diana's" iPhone and the Apple laptop used to access the Putin's Army site, while the announced prize for the best "tear [up]" is an iPad2. Thus Putin, impassioned young women, and the latest technology constitute a *ménage à trois* in yet another effort to package Putin as an object of desire.[31] According to one report, Tabak characterized the project as "just a personal reminder of how attractive the prime minister is to young women" (Roth 2011a) – a view predictably shared by Kristina Potupchik, press secretary of the Kremlin-indentured youth group Nashi (Weir 2011). According to several journalists, the video "has gone viral" since its posting on the blogging platform Live Journal by Kirill Shchitov, a young deputy in Moscow's Duma and a fervent Putin devotee (Weir 2011).[32]

Difficult as it would be to surpass the students' calendar and video in vulgarity, those items nevertheless pale beside the lunacy of another mode of gendered Putin worship – quite literally, worship. A village southeast of Moscow called Bol'shaia El'nia recently has witnessed the rise of an all-female sect that venerates Putin as the reincarnation of the Christian missionary Paul the Apostle, "on a special mission from God" (Osborn 2011) to fight the antichrists (Chaykovskaya 2011). Its members dress like nuns, subsist on a diet of turnips, carrots, peas, and buckwheat, and pray in front of Putin's portrait, mounted alongside Orthodox Russian icons on the iconostasis. The "upbeat patriotic Soviet songs" they substitute for hymns encompass such numbers as the children's favorite *Pust' vsegda budet solntse* [Let there always be sunshine] (Chaykovskaya 2011). Mother Fotina (née Svetlana Frolova), the founder of the sect, who formerly served a term in prison (Chaykovskaya 2011), points out that Paul the Apostle originally was a military commander who persecuted Christians, but underwent a conversion – hence the analogy with Putin:

> In his days in the KGB, Putin also did some rather unrighteous things. But once he became president, he was imbued with the Holy Spirit, and just

> like the apostle, he started wisely leading his flock. It is hard for him now but he is fulfilling his heroic [*sic*] deed as an apostle.
>
> (Osborn 2011)

The local village priest apparently dismisses Mother Fotina's "teachings" as "a nonsensical mixture of Orthodoxy, Catholicism, the occult, Buddhism and political information," but, astonishingly, does not suspect her of madness (Osborn 2011), despite her claim that she has known Putin since he was Vladimir I of Kiev, and she was his grandmother, Ol'ga (Chaykovskaya 2011). Though devoid of the calendar's and the video's frankly lubricious orientation, the female sect in its mere existence, not to mention its credo and practices, nevertheless shares with the university students a perception of Putin as a supernaturally endowed idol. In short, if Putin appears as the perfect macho icon for male emulation, for women he embodies the perfect Man by virtue of his sex appeal, reliability, and "heroic achievements."

Tough-guy tenderness or symbolic self-assertion?

Putin's is a salvific manly strength in solitary splendor, rendered all the more seductive by his ostensible capacity for kindness, even tenderness, highlighted in the numerous photographs documenting his touted love for animals (see Chapter 3 by Mikhailova). Those prepared to forget Putin's hunting and fishing (i.e., killing animals), as well as his indifference to Russia's catastrophic environmental problems, doubtless find his photo-op bonding with dogs, horses, dolphins, fish, goats, and cows disarming in a man whose public image fully embraces and exploits the conventions of machismo. At the same time, his affinity for animals subtly intimates his ability to bond with anyone and everyone, highlighted in Kalenik's *Chelovek kak vse*. That skill is part of his comprehensive "caring" for Russia and all that it comprehends.

Unlike several insightful colleagues (Cassiday, Johnson, Mikhailova), I do not believe that Putin's selective osculation is either a spontaneous or a calculated outlet for his "feminine side." As confirmed by the case of the artist Aleksandr Shednov (Shurik), whose 2009 "portrait" of Putin in a woman's low-cut dress led to his arrest and beating, explicitly "feminizing" Putin carries a heavy penalty. Traditional gender codes, of course, may incline one automatically to view images of Putin molding pots[33] and kissing a child or animal as implicit expressions of a "secondary," latent femininity, and the temptation to do so may have been particularly strong 20 years ago, before globalization and the spread of feminism throughout much of the Western world. In the case of Putin, however, such a perspective strikes me as misguided for several interrelated reasons. First, by the time Putin launched his kiss campaign, the hyper-masculinity of his public persona was too entrenched to be questioned or modified. After all, to what extent did the posthumous revelation that Ernest Hemingway had been dressed in girl's frocks as a child affect the image of big-game hunting machismo that he had assiduously cultivated for decades? As Bryce Traister in a commentary on Hemingway's "masculinist canonicity" points out, the writer created "a modernist heteromasculinity coterminous with the very meaning of twentieth-century manliness" (2000: 285). Second, since Putin's kisses target those who are powerless and incapable of reciprocity (as Mikhailova acknowledges), they sooner imply Putin's exercise of arbitrary power and symbolic possession – both 6-year-old boy and animals are simply part of *his* domain, and therefore, according to Putin mythology, come under his benevolent paternal guardianship. Third, such behavior is atypical of national leaders and therefore highlights Putin's uniqueness, attracting media coverage no less than do his flaunted physical skills and phenomenal popularity. I contend that the spectacle of Putin's kisses provides a *frisson* – an erotic emotional charge – for the viewer confronted with the unexpected, dramatic contrast between toughness (Putin's invincible image) and ostensible tenderness (the unexamined initial interpretation of the act). Cultural conventions dictating that men not cry render the sight of men's tears all the more effective and the same principle applies to perceived tenderness.[34] Putin's exploitative kiss-acts subscribe to the precepts of The Factory of the Eccentric Actor (FEKS), the avant-garde-indebted group founded in 1921 by film directors Grigorii Kozintsev (1905–1973) and Leonid Trauberg (1902–1990), which advocated cynosural devices as a means of eliciting strong reactions from audiences – the goal expressly achieved by Putin-smooches. And who can doubt that a man sufficiently self-confident to perform an act that binary gender coding traditionally labeled feminine merely offers additional corroboration of his masculinity, not the least because of his apparent indifference to whether others perceive that act as gender-transgressive.

The seductive combination of toughness and gentleness may be traced back to a paradox posed by the foremost strongman in the Bible: namely, Samson, who, among other feats, vanquished a lion with his bare hands. After seeing bees swarming around the lion's carcass, he formulated the famous conundrum "out of the strong came forth sweetness" (Judges 14:14). Adopted for marketing purposes in England, that paradox was embossed on all cans of Lyle's golden syrup (dating back to 1885), together with a visual of the dead lion cum bees. One exegete reads the paradox as "present[ing] the mystery of the Cross" (Pink 1938), which arguably could be paralleled to the ritualistically invoked enigma that is the macho Putin's public persona. That image relies in part on the conviction that something inaccessible and unique resides at the core of a charismatic, powerful individual. The question that may never be answered is whether Putin's manly strength and his photographed "sweetness" are solely the phantoms or products of others' presumptions and desires or symptomatic of Putin's readiness to assimilate and perform the rituals inseparable from that fantasy-fueled magnetic image.

Conventional concepts of masculinity favor action, judicious exercise of control, and the tough, hard body that presumably reflects strong will and discipline, while heroism implies superiority to the implicit norms of a given culture. The mythology elaborated to showcase Putin's public persona of singular heroic masculinity is so hyperbolic as to verge on parody. One of the most recent strategies involved a curiously misguided effort to fashion Putin as a restorer not only of Russia's status in the world, but also of the classical world heritage. While scuba

Figure 8.15 Coinciding with Guy Debord's critique of contemporary capitalist society, Sergei Kalenik's subversive comic strip (Superputin) exposes "Reality" as spectacle or a form of reality show.

Source: Courtesy of Sergei Kalenik.

diving in the Black Sea at the Fanagoria excavation site, Putin purportedly discovered two ancient Greek vases dating from the early sixth century AD, and, predictably, television cameras captured him brandishing the trophies. According to a researcher in the area, however, the vases were planted there in preparation for Putin's visit, just like the road to the site, which had been repaved to welcome him (Roth 2011b: 8). In short, the production of Putin as macho ideal enacts a process decried by the French Marxist Guy Debord in his 1967 volume, *Society as Spectacle*: "All of life presents itself as an immense accumulation of spectacles. Everything that was directly lived has moved away into representation" – which is why "Putin" has to be enclosed in quotation marks (Figure 8.15).

Some observers, such as Aleksandr Morozov, director of the Center for Media Research at the Institute of Cultural History, believe that Putin's PR stunts have palled and currently elicit irony among Russians (Roth 2011b: 8). Indeed, various items posted on the Internet, such as Elkin's caricatures, Rabfak's *Durdom* video, and the satirical *Citizen Poet* project, funded by the billionaire Mikhail Prokhorov and featuring poet Dmitrii Bykov, actor Mikhail Efremov, and producer Andrei Vasil'ev, testify to distress at Putin's anticipated "sure win" in the 2012 elections (see Barry 2011).[35] With his United Party's popularity now at an all-time low of 51 percent (Barry 2011) and the next presidential elections just months away, Putin clearly intends to stay in the spotlight through further "manly adventures." Few who have followed Putin's ascendancy doubt that he will reclaim the presidency in March 2012, and his recent Hollywoodesque Botox treatment suggests that he plans to market his manly self as a vigorous, wrinkle-and-frown-free leader. Though skeptics may wax critical or sardonic, in the eyes of his admirers,

Putin is, as rappers phrase it, "da man!" – something voters will not be allowed to forget as the campaign for the 2012 presidential election gains momentum.

Notes

1 On the Putin industry, see Julie A. Cassiday and Emily D. Johnson, "Putin, Putiniana and the Question of a Post-Soviet Cult of Personality," *Slavonic and East European Review*, 88, 4 (October 2010): 681–707; Helena Goscilo, "The Ultimate Celebrity: VVP as VIP *Objet d'art*," *Celebrity and Glamour in Contemporary Russia: Shocking Chic*. London: Routledge, 2011. 29–55; on the literature devoted to Putin, see Andrei Rogatchevski, "Putin in Russian Fiction," *Journal of Communist Studies and Transition Politics* 24, 4 (2008): 629–656.

2 For a cogent analysis of how Putin changed track after his first term, effecting a shift from oligarchic capitalism to bureaucratic capitalism, see Shevtsova (2007: especially 118–131).

3 Despite negative reactions to Putin's conduct, the expectation that his rating would plummet after the tragedy proved unfounded. For a concise summary of the event and speculation about its effect on Putin's public image, see Bryan Knowles, "Will the Drama of the *Kursk* Sink the Presidency of Vladimir Putin?" *SpeakOut*, June 15, 2000. Available at: http://speakout.com/activism/issue_briefs/1369b-1.html (accessed July 2, 2001).

4 On this performance, see Andrei Piontkovskii's brief piece titled "King and the President," in which he contends that the West is enchanted by Putin because there he adopts a different persona from the one he reveals at home, using vulgar language and indulging in hysterical outbursts. First published in the newspaper *Novaia gazeta* (September 14, 2000), the commentary was reprinted in a collection of items authored by the opposition, ironically titled *Nashe svetloe budushchee ili Putin navsegda* (2004: 75–77).

5 At the same time, Putin decreed the elimination of Constitution Day, which commemorated former President Boris Yeltsin's adoption of the Russian Constitution on December 12, 1993 – a peculiar move on the part of a president who tirelessly urged respect for the constitution.

6 Vladimir Churov, who worked with Putin during the latter's stint in the St. Petersburg mayor's administration, recalls that when Soviet leaders' portraits, which conventionally decorated the offices of official institutions, were removed from the walls, and each employee could choose a replacement, virtually everyone opted for a portrait of Yeltsin. Putin ordered a portrait of Peter the Great (*Ot pervogo litsa* 2000: 80–81).

7 According to Garry Kasparov's testimony before the US Congress on June 17, 2011, estimates by the leading Russian expert in corruption, Georgii Satarov, on the overall sum spent on bribes in the Russian economy skyrocketed from $33 billion to more than $400 billion per year during Putin's rule. See "Kasparov to US Congress: Medvedev Is Bait for a Trap," *La Russophobe* (June 23, 2011). Available at: http://larussophobe.wordpress.com/2011/06/23/kasparov-to-u-s-congress-medvedev-is-bait-for-a-trap/ (accessed July 2, 2011).

8 Others, such as Shevtsova, however, see a "civil society in the making" within Russia (Shevtsova 2007: 274). Since the creation of Russia's Public Chamber was the brainchild of Putin, who, moreover, selected the first 42 members, the institution hardly shines as a beacon of independent thinking and critical judgment. Furthermore, it exerts scant influence on events, for its powers are purely consultative.

9 Mikhail Gorbachev was named Person of the Year in both 1987 and 1989.

10 The upsurge of masculinity studies within the United States during approximately the last decade has bred a broad spectrum of notions about what constitutes heteronormative masculinity. For a useful survey of the scholarship, see Traister (2000).

11 According to an official history of Italian fascism, the fascist man, Mosse points out, "unites culture, knowledge, and action" – a resilient paradigm congruent with Putin's image (Mosse 1996: 162).

12 For instance, Louis Pierre Althusser (1918–1990), Jean Baudrillard (1929–2007), Jürgen Habermas (b. 1929), Paul Ricoeur (1913–2005), Richard Rorty (1931–2007).

13 Unlike the penis, which is merely a physical appendage, the phallus is the symbol of gendered authority and power – a distinction that some critics see implicit in Freud, elaborated in Lacan, and regularly cited in feminist texts.

14 This trait has been satirized in various visuals and in the 2010 New Year's Eve stage show broadcast on Channel One, with animated puppets of Medvedev and Putin "summarizing" their achievements of the preceding year. In the course of the show, the Putin puppet uses the euphemism "na tri bukvy" [a three-letter . . .] and is prevented from using the words "v zhope" [lit. in the ass] by the more circumspect and proper Medvedev. For an acidic commentary on the show as an exercise in PR, see the article by the scriptwriter for the genuinely controversial puppet show *Kukly*, Viktor Shenderovich, "Bezumstvu khrabrykh," *Ezhednevnyi zhurnal*, January 4, 2010. Available at: http://www.shender.ru/paper/text/?.file=305 (accessed April 1, 2010).

15 A surprising inconsistency in the polls during 2006, however, showed 76 percent of respondents supporting Putin, whereas only 17 percent deemed him a successful leader (Shevtsova 2007: 282). Such a discrepancy begs the question of why Russians would support a president whom they found wanting. Lilia Shevtsova's reasonable answer is – lack of better alternatives, a view with which I concur not only regarding 2006, but also 2012.

16 See Service (2007) for a rather exaggerated description of Putin's visible efforts at "containing" his "fury."

17 The strip, with excellent visuals by unidentified cartoonists, offers the option of being viewed in Russian, English, Polish, German, French, Finnish, and Dutch. It also asks the public to vote on who commissioned the strip: Putin, Medvedev, Sechin (who also plays a role in it), Volochkova, and other, even disarmingly sillier options.

18 A popular TV series that debuted in 2010, *The Walking Dead* is based on the American comic series by the same title (2003–), which was inspired by George Romero's cult classic *Night of the Living Dead* (1968) about the survivors of a "zombie apocalypse."

19 In the given context, Nordic alludes to Putin's laconic inscrutability, while simultaneously evoking the historical legend of Rurik, the ninth-century Varangian who founded the Riurik dynasty in medieval Rus', which ruled until the late sixteenth century. Not incidentally, Riurik is credited with establishing order among warring tribes – a protomodel for Putin's reign.

20 In a ritual statement disassociating both Putin and the Kremlin from public visuals portraying Putin in glamorous roles, Dmitrii Peskov indignantly called the poster illegal and disclaimed all knowledge of its provenance. See "Plakaty s prem'erom vyzvali voprosy," Interfaks [Interfax], July 15, 2011. Available at: http://www.edinaya-odessa.org/news/n_rus/31948-plakaty-s-premerom-vyzvali-voprosy.html (accessed July 18, 2011).

21 I am indebted to Robert Mulcahy for acquaintance with this source.

22 The journalist Andrei Piontkovskii in one of several anti-Putin items in *Novaia gazeta* (2003), reprinted in *Nashe svetloe budushchee ili Putin navsegda*, draws a specific

parallel between the delegates' ovation greeting Putin at the XIII congress of the Russian Union of Industrialists and Entrepreneurs (RSPP) and that extended to Stalin at the XVII Congress of the All-Union Communist Party (1934), which Piontkovskii uses as a starting point for analogizing the two leaders (see *Nashe svetloe budushchee ili Putin navsegda* 2004: 42). Like Stalin, Putin also ignites hatred, obvious to anyone conversant with this collection as well as the late journalist Anna Politkovskaia's publications. See especially the last chapte, titled "Akaky Akakievich Putin II," in Anna Politkovskaya, (2004) *Putin's Russia: Life in a Failing Democracy*, trans. Arch Tait, New York: Metropolitan Books, Henry Holt & Co., 230–244.

23 Politkovskaia points out that his decision to appoint regional governors on the pretext of strengthening national security after the Beslan tragedy, violated the constitution (254). That under Putin security is the major concern – one publicly proclaimed at every turn – is also the thesis of *Securitising Russia* (2006). See Edwin Bacon, Bettina Renz, and Julian Cooper, (2006) *Securitising Russia: the domestic politics of Putin.* Manchester and New York: Manchester UP.

24 Ia dumal, chto on v bol'shei stepeni zhivet v mire illiuzii. Okazalos', chto on vse-taki pragmatiki sposoben vospriniat' realii zhizni, a ne rukovodstvovat'sia kakimi-to efermernymi ideiami (*Ot pervogo litsa* 2000: 174).

25 Practicality motivates many actions by Putin, not the least his appointments of and reliance on the FSB. As Shevtsova (2007: 44) points out, "He chose his team, not on the basis of professional allegiances or ideological or political affiliation, but simply because these were the people he knew."

26 In his article "Real Men Go to the Bania," Ethan Pollock posits the bania as a locus of masculinity, but it is one utterly alien to the public image of Putin, for male camaraderie in the post-Soviet bania (typically luxurious, unlike its modest Soviet forerunners) inevitably involves drinking vodka, exposes men's flabby, overfed bodies, and is often associated with criminals, whose discussions of illegal ventures cannot be overheard there. See Ethan Pollock, "Real Men Go to the Bania," *Kritika: Exploration in Russian and Eurasian History* 11, 1 (Winter 2010): 47–76. For a vivid Western screen depiction of the bania and its usage by the criminal world, see David Cronenberg's *Eastern Promises* (2007).

27 Tabak reportedly followed up with a "reality series" called *ZhurFak*, taped inside the Journalism Department, to the displeasure of the University's administration (see Roth 2011a).

28 While some have no doubts about the professional nature of the video (Weir 2011), others, such as Tabak, believe that the product is an individual, amateur job (Roth 2011a).

29 Available at: http://www.youtube.com/watch?v=gG2XV2n9efc (accessed July 21, 2011).

30 Journalist Andrew Roth ungrammatically detects "full-scale cognitive dissonance when Diana begins to tear apart her tank top with a dainty cross hanging just above her cleavage," showing his ignorance of how borders between sex and money, sex and power, money and power, power and Church have been erased in today's Russia. Moreover, a cross strategically suspended above half-revealed breasts draws attention to them and may simply function as ornament, without any connection whatever to religious belief (Roth 2011a).

31 While tearing up the tank top is a sexually suggestive gesture, one would expect the Russian verb to be *sorvat'* (to tear off), but *porvat'* may be used here, as Julia Ioffe proposes, to imply the threat of tearing someone to pieces, according to criminal slang (Ioffe 2011). I find it more likely, however, that the video avoids *sorvat'* precisely because it explicitly denotes disrobing.

32 According to one journalist (whose "facts" are sometimes inaccurate), the video has attracted approximately a million views on YouTube (Roth 2011a).

33 A photograph of Putin with a rare smile concentrating on making a clay pot appeared, inter alia, on the cover of the September/October 2002 issue of the American magazine *Russian Life* (see visuals for Chapter 2 by Cassiday *et al.*).

34 A major attribute of masculinity, as Mosse remarks, is the will power demonstrated in self-restraint, summarized in the cliché "real men do not cry" (Mosse 1996: 4).

35 According to Barry, 12–14 million Russians follow the weekly videos of *Citizen Poet,* which at first appeared on the Internet television station Dozhd', but after the station's self-censoring decisions, transferred to direct postings on the Internet (Barry 2011).

35 According to Barry, 12–14 million Russians follow the weekly videos of *Citizen Poet.*

Bibliography

"Anna Chapman 'helps Putin in computer game.'" (2011) *DAWN.COM*. May 17. Available at: http://www.dawn.com/2011/05/17/anna-chapman-helps-putin-in-computer-game.html (accessed June 3, 2011).

Applebaum, A. (2000) "Putin's salvage operation." *Slate*. August 21. Available at: http://www.slate.com/id/88489/ (accessed August 27, 2001).

Balmforth, T. (2009) "A wish list for Santa Putin." *Russia Profile*. December 3. Available at: http://russiaprofile.org/politics/a1259869514.html (accessed December 3, 2009).

Barry. E. (2011) "Satirizing Putin with boldly poetic flair." *The New York Times*, November 18. Available at: http:www.nytimes.com/2011/11/19/world/Europe/mocking-Vladimir-putin-with-poetic-flair-in-russia.html?_r=1@emc=eta1 (accessed November 20, 2011).

Blomfield, A. (2007a) "Putin cast as hero in play for 55th birthday." *Telegraph*. October 5. Available at: http://www.telegraph.co.uk/news/worldnews1565247/Putin-cast-as-hero-in-play-for-55th-birthday.html (accessed April 18, 2008).

Blomfield, A. (2007b) "Vladimir Putin strips off for holiday snaps." *Telegraph*. August 16. Available at: http://www.telegraph.co.uk/news/worldnews/1560485/Vladimir-Putin-strips-off-for-holiday-snaps.html (accessed April 10, 2009).

Blomfield, A. (2008) "Vladimir Putin hailed as virile vampire." *Telegraph*. June 19. Available at: http://www.telegraph.co.uk/news/worldnews/europe/russia/2158556/Vladimir-Putin-hailed-as-virile-vampire.html (accessed November 30, 2009).

Cassiday, J.A. and E.D. Johnson. (2010) "Putin, Putiniana, and the question of a post-Soviet cult of personality." *Slavonic and East European Review*, 88, 4(October): 681–707.

Chaykovskaya, E. (2011) "Sect believes Putin is a modern day St. Paul." *The Moscow News*. May 12. Available at: http://themoscownews.com/politics/20110512/188660658.html (accessed May 14, 2011).

Davidoff, V. (2011) "How Putin pads numbers." *The Moscow Times*. June 20. Available at: http://www.themoscowtimes.com/opinion/article/how-putin-pads-numbers/439134.html (accessed June 28, 2011).

Debord, G. (1995). *The Society of Spectacle*. Trans. Donald Nicholson-Smith. New York: Zone Books.

Dobrenko, E. and E. Naiman. (eds.) (2003) *The Landscape of Stalinism. The Art and Ideology of Soviet Space*. Seattle, WA and London: University of Washington Press.

Duke, B. (2007) "Gay icon Putin is now revered as 'The Chosen One.'" *The Freethinker*. December 12. Available at: http://freethinker.co.uk/2007/12/12/gay-icon-putin-is-now-revered-as-';the-chosen-one'/ (accessed February 3, 2009).

Elder, M. (2011) "Moscow museum celebrates sex." *The Guardian*. July 12. Available at: http://www.guardian.co.uk/artanddesign/2011/jul/12/moscow-sex-museum-sparks-controversy?intcmp=239 (accessed July 13, 2011).

"Gay Russians claim bare-chested Putin as one of their own." (2007) *Mail Online*. August 23. Available at: http://www.dailymail.co.uk/news/article-477089/Gay-Russians-claim-bare-chested-Putin-own.html (accessed March 16, 2008).

Halpin, T. (2009) "Bare-chested Vladimir Putin strikes a macho pose." *The Times*. August 5. Available at: http://www.timesonlinc.co.uk/tol/news/world/Europe/article6738969.ece (accessed February 2, 2009).

Higate, P. and J. Hopton. (2005) "War, militarism, and masculinities," in M. Kimmel, J.R. Hearn and R.W. Connell, eds. *Handbook of Studies on Men and Masculinities*. Thousand Oaks, CA and London: Sage. 432–447.

Ioffe, J. (2011) "Taking it off for Putin." *The New Yorker*. July 21. Available at: http://www.newyorker.com/online/blogs/newsdesk/2011/07/putins-army.html. (accessed July 26, 2011).

Jeffords, 1994Jeffords, S. (1994) *Hard Bodies: Hollywood Masculinity in the Reagan Era*. New Brunswick: Rutgers University Press.

Kolesnikova, N. (2010) "Last action hero: Vladimir Putin's year of adventure." *Foreign Policy*. December 22. Available at: http://www.foreignpolicy.com/articles/2010/12/21/last_action_hero?page=0,1 (accessed January 16, 2011).

Koteyko, N. and L. Ryazanova-Clarke. (2009) "The path and building metaphors in the speeches of Vladimir Putin: back to the future?" *Slavonica* 15, 2(November): 112–127.

"Larry King Live." (2000) September 8. Available at http://www.youtube.com/watch?v=dqDqvKYDv9M (accessed March 6, 2011).

Mosse, G.L. (1996) *The Image of Man: The Creation of Modern Masculinity*. New York: Oxford University Press.

Nashe svetloe budushchee ili Putin navsegda. (2004) Moscow: Integral-Inform.

Neale, S. (1983) "Masculinity as spectacle: reflections on men and mainstream cinema," *Screen* 24 (6): 2–16.

O'Donnell, P. (2005) "James Bond, cyborg-aristocrat," in E.P. Comentale *et al*., eds. *Ian Fleming and James Bond: The Cultural Politics of 007*. Bloomington, IA: Indiana University Press. 55-68.

Orth, M. (2000) "Russia's dark master." *Vanityfair.com*. October 2000. Available at: http://www.vanityfair.com/politics/features/2000/10/putin200010 (accessed August 29, 2000).

Osborn, A. (2011) "All-female sect worships Vladimir Putin as Paul the Apostle," *Telegraph*, May 12. Available at: http://www.telegraph.co.uk/news/worldnews/eirp[e/russia/8509670/All-female-sect-worships-Vladimir-Putin-as-Paul-the-Apostle.html (accessed June 4, 2011).

Ot pervogo litsa: razgovory s Vladimirom Putinym. (2000) Moscow: Vagrius. [Interviews with N. Gevorkian, A. Kolesnikov, N. Timakova.]

Pink, A.W. "The riddle of Samson," September 1938. *Studies in the Scriptures. Believer's Web*. Available at: http://www.believersweb.org/view.cfm?ID=1111 (accessed July 1, 2011).

Rogatchevski, A. (2008) "Putin in Russian fiction." *Journal of Communist Studies and Transition Politics*, 24, 4(December): 629–656.

Roth, A. (2011a) "A Putin fetish," *Russia Profile*. July 20. Available at: http://russiaprofile.org/politics/41317.html (accessed July 20, 2011).

Roth, A. (2011b) "The guns of august," *Russia Profile*, August 18. Available at: http://russiaprofile.org/politics/43317.html (accessed August 26, 2011).

Ryazanova-Clarke, L. (2008) "Putin's nation: discursive construction of national identity in *Direct Line with the President*," *Slavica Helsingiensia* 34: 311–331.

Sakwa, R. (2004) *Putin: Russia's choice*. London and New York: Routledge.

Service, R. (2007) "President Vladimir Putin: should we be afraid of the ex-KGB man?" *The Independent*, September 9. Available at: http://www.independent.co.uk/news/people/profiles/president-vladimir-putin-should-we-be-afraid-of-the-exkgb-man-401563.html (accessed November 24, 2008).

Shevtsova, L. (2007) *Russia – Lost in Transition: The Yeltsin and Putin Legacies*. Washington, DC and Moscow: Carnegie Endowment for International Peace.

Stewart, W. and L. Eccles. (2011) "From Russia with botox: has Putin had a facelift … or just plenty of sleep? Mystery as bags under eyes vanish." *Daily Mail*, September 27. Available at: http://www.dailymail.co.uk/news/article-2041991/Vladimir-Putin-plastic-surgery-Facelift–;just-plenty-sleep.html (accessed October 1, 2011).

Tasker, Y. (1993) *Spectacular Bodies: Gender, Genre and the Action Film*. New York and London: Routledge.

Tkachenko, M. (2011) "'Putin's Army' supports PM with racy video," *CNN*, July 20. Available at: http://www.koat.com/politics/28593193/detail.html (accessed July 20, 2011).

Traister, B. (2000) "Academic Viagra: the rise of American masculinity studies," *American Quarterly*, 52, 2(June): 274–304.

Ustinova, A. and L. Klim. (2010)"'Smart girls' strip for calendar on Putin's 58th birthday to show support," *Bloomberg*, October 7. Available at: http://www.bloomberg.com/news/print/2010-10-07/-smart-girls-strip-for-calendar-on-putin-s-58th-birthday-to-show-support.html (accessed October 15, 2010).

V. Putin: Razgovor s Rossiei [Stenogramma "Priamoi linii s Prezidentom Rossiiskoi Federatsii V.V. Putinym"]. (2003) Moscow: Olma-Politizdat.

Weir, F. (2011) "'Putin's Army' tries sexy messaging ahead of 2012 elections," *Christian Science Monitor*. July 18. Available at: http://news.yahoo.com/putins-army-tries-sexy-messaging-ahead-2012-elections-175549699.html (accessed July 20, 2011).

Index

Note: page numbers in *italic* refer to illustrations.